TIMOTHY B

C++ for Java Programmers

ADDISON-WESLEY

An imprint of Addison Wesley Longman, Inc.

Reading, Massachusetts   Harlow, England   Menlo Park, California
Berkeley, California   Don Mills, Ontario   Sydney   Bonn
Amsterdam   Tokyo   Mexico City

Sponsoring Editor: Maite Suarez-Rivas
Senior Production Editor: Amy Rose
Assistant Editor: Molly Taylor
Production Coordinator: Brooke D. Albright
Composition/Art: Windfall Software
Copyeditor: Jerry Moore
Proofreader: Carmen Wheatcroft
Cover Design: Night & Day Design

Library of Congress Catalog Card Number: 99-072280
ISBN 0-201-61246-1

Access the latest information about Addison-Wesley titles from our World Wide Web site:
http://www.awl.com/cseng

The programs and applications presented in this book have been included for their instructional value. They have been tested with care but are not guaranteed for any purpose. The publisher does not offer any warranties or representations, nor does it accept any liabilities with respect to the programs or applications.

Many of the designations used by manufacturers and sellers to distinguish their products are claimed as trademarks. Where those designations appear in this book, and Addison-Wesley was aware of a trademark claim, the designations have been printed in initial caps or all caps.

This book was typeset in ZzTEX on a PC. The font families used were Berkeley, Rotis Sans Serif, and MathTime. It was printed on #50 Rolland, a recycled paper.

Reprinted with corrections, July 2000

2 3 4 5 6 7 8 9 10—MA—03020100

Preface

The reader that I envisioned when developing this book is a programmer with a year or more experience with Java, who has a good understanding of the language and Java libraries, and who wants to learn more about the programming language C++. Programs in Java and C++ bear a superficial resemblance to each other, but beneath the surface lie myriad practical and philosophical differences. The programmer who is not aware of these differences will encounter a host of problems in trying to move from one language to the other.

This book is not intended to be a complete and thorough introduction to the language C++. The length of the book alone should be enough to indicate this fact, since most recent introductions to the language C++ run to a thousand pages or more. Instead, I tried to organize the differences between C++ and Java into a coherent framework that facilitates the transition from one language to the other. When you desire more information on a specific topic, you should consult one of the recent descriptions or tutorials on the language C++.

Further Reading

There are literally hundreds of books on Java and/or C++. I have, of course, seen only a small fraction of them. The following list therefore comprises books that I have read and appreciated, reflecting more than a fair amount of whimsy and chance.

Excellent coverage of the language C++, including recent changes to the language, can be found in the books by Stroustrup (*The C++ Programming*

Language [Stroustrup 97]) or Lippman (*C++ Primer* [Lippman 98]). Slightly less thorough but in some ways more readable descriptions are presented by Eckel (*Using C++* [Eckel 89]) and by Horstmann (*Mastering Object-Oriented Design in C++* [Horstmann 95]).

Two other books authored or coauthored by Bjarne Stroustrup, the designer of C++, present much of the philosophy that lays behind the design of the language (*The Annotated C++ Reference Manual* [Ellis 90] and *The Design and Evolution of C++* [Stroustrup 94]). A collection of papers by others involved in the evolution of the language C++ is provided by Waldo (*The Evolution of C++* [Waldo 93]). Another book by Lippman (*Inside the C++ Object Model* [Lippman 96]) describes the internal C++ view of the world.

The Standard Template Library, a major recent addition to the language C++, is explained in an earlier book of my own [Budd 98a], as well as in books by Musser [Musser 96] and by Glass [Glass 96].

Various books describe good C++ programming style. Perhaps the best of them are the text by Cargill [Cargill 92] and the pair of books by Meyers [Meyers 98, Meyers 96].

A wealth of information in the question and answer style of a FAQ is available in the books that collect FAQ information on C [Summit 96] and C++ [Cline 95]. (A Java FAQ book [Kanerva 97] also has some discussion of C++).

Several books are almost the opposite of this book, that is, explanations of Java for programmers familiar with C++. One of the best is the book by Chew [Chew 98]. The more recent book by Wigglesworth and Lumby [Wigglesworth 99] covers more of the recent changes to Java. The book by Daconta and others [Daconta 98] is more complete, in that it covers both Java and JavaScript. Pappas [Pappas 96] presents material specific to the Borland C++ system. Boone [Boone 96] tends to dwell more on the programming environment and design differences and less on differences in the languages.

In an earlier book I tried to explain object-oriented programming in a language independent fashion, including examples from both Java and C++ [Budd 97].

A book by Coplien [Coplien 92] presents an interesting discussion of many of the more exotic features of C++ for the adventurous reader who desires to explore further than most programmers ever want to go.

Marginal Notes

I used four types of marginal notes in this book to highlight material of particular importance.

Definition

 Rule

 Warning

 Note

A Definition introduces a term that may be unfamiliar to you if your only background is in the language Java.

A Rule provides advice that you are strongly encouraged to follow. As with all rules, there may be times when the advice must be rejected, but rules generally reflect years of painful learning concerning the consequences of not performing some action.

A Warning highlights a potential danger that you should be aware of. Often Warnings reflect subtle issues easily overlooked or places where Java and C++ constructs have similar appearances but different meanings.

A Note simply provides an additional or important bit of information that you might otherwise easily overlook.

Acknowledgments

Several people provided useful advice and suggestions, both in the conception of this book and comments on the many early drafts of the manuscript. They include Joseph Bergin (Pace University), Alistair Campbell (SUNY at Buffalo), Timothy Chan (University of Miami), Sudarshan Dhall (University of Oklahoma), Yechiel Kimchi (The Technion, Israel), Joe Pfeiffer (New Mexico State University), Mike Westall (Clemson University), Salih Yurttas (Texas A&M), and students Nandhini GanapathiRaman, Thomas Godin, David Hackenyos, and Hari Narayanan, from Oregon State University.

It is a pleasure to acknowledge my editor at Addison-Wesley, Maite Suarez-Rivas, who from the first has shared my vision for the book, even if she could not remember her Alice-in-Wonderland stories.

Contents

Basic Philosophical Differences

GIVEN THEIR HISTORICAL ROOTS, it is not surprising that programs in Java and C++ have a similar appearance. However, because of the contrasting goals and objectives stated by the designers of the two languages, it is also not surprising that at a deeper level they are very different. Thus, to understand C++, you must first comprehend a bit of its history, philosophy, and background.

1.1   The Language C

To appreciate C++ you have to realize that it is a descendant of an earlier language, C. The language C was conceived and implemented at Bell Labs in the early 1970s by research scientist Dennis Ritchie. The primary objective for the language was to help Ritchie and fellow researcher Brian Kernighan create an operating system for a small computer they had sitting in their lab. This system, in turn, was mainly to help them develop programs for their own use. They called this operating system Unix, a name intended to contrast with Multics, an operating system running on the much larger machines of that period. Other researchers at Bell Labs soon became interested in Unix, and its use spread. In time Unix—and with it C—became popular in both the research and commercial worlds.

The fact that C and Unix developed in tandem is important because from the first, C was a language designed for systems programming. The language emphasized modern (for the time) control flow constructs and data structures, an economy of expression that would eventually draw equal parts praise and damnation, and a useful ability to access the underlying machine at both a very high level of abstraction and at a primitive and direct level.

C was designed so that even a relatively naive compiler could generate reasonably good assembly language code. Consider, for example, the following typical C idiom for copying one string value into another:

```
while (*p++ = *q++)
    ;
```

The statement is a while loop with no body, only a test for completion. The test portion itself seems not to include booleans (the = operator is an assignment, not a comparison test, a subtle but vital distinction easily overlooked by the novice programmer). Instead it relies on the fact that arithmetic values can be converted into booleans, an integer zero being interpreted as false and anything nonzero as true. The test also relies on an assignment being an expression, as well as a side-effect producing operation. An assignment will return the updated value of the left-hand side, and thus the loop will terminate once a zero value has been assigned. Both the expression from which the assignment draws values and the target expression are determined by pointers, the pointers being dereferenced in both cases to obtain the appropriate memory locations. Finally, the increment operators update the pointer values, advancing them to the next memory locations while at the same time they are yielding their current contents. The statement implicitly relies on the convention that strings (in C, arrays of character values) are terminated by a null character, a byte with zero value. Although great havoc will ensue if this condition is not satisfied, no run-time checks are performed to ensure its validity. (For example, there is no limit on how far into memory the pointer q can travel before it is determined that a null character will not be found.)

The increment and decrement operators, compound assignment operators, pointer arithmetic, and assignments as values, when combined all meant that even relatively complex statements, such as this one, could be realized by short sequences of assembly language instructions.

Features such as the explicit use of pointers, the variety of bit-level operations, and a simple memory model were ideally suited for getting close to the hardware and creating programs that ran quickly and required little memory. Compilers for C were soon developed for a variety of machines, and the language became a popular alternative to assembly language for systems programming. (Indeed, C is now commonly referred to as a "portable assembly language.")

This is not to say that the language was without controversy. From the first, objections have been raised that the language is too concise for human understanding, and the lack of run-time checks made programs more error-prone than necessary. Programmers in C were forced to accommodate themselves to the fact that the typical error message from a running C program often said little more than "there was an error while your program was in, or near, the computer."

1.2   The Development of C++

C++ grew out of an earlier language named C

The language C++ started out as a collection of macros and library routines for the C language.[1] Only after a period of use did it evolve into a new language of its own. Nevertheless, the newly renamed language C++ was explicitly intended to be more-or-less backward compatible with C. That is, any legal C program should still be a legal C++ program.[2]

This decision, to make C++ an extension of the earlier language rather than a totally new language, was cause for confusion during the early 1980s. While the consequence of this decision provided a valuable service to the industry by introducing object-oriented techniques to the large body of C programmers, many people wrongly assumed that it would be easy to retrain a C programmer to be a C++ programmer—perhaps almost as easy as adding two characters to the person's job title. What this presumption ignored was the fact that the way one goes about structuring the solution to a problem in object-oriented fashion is very different from the way one structures a program in the imperative style of C. Only with time and experience were these differences recognized.

Other ramifications of this decision remain. The C programming language brought with it a rich collection of libraries—for example, the standard I/O library. Since C programs were also C++ programs, C++ had to accommodate them as well, even though they were not particularly well matched to the new object-oriented features of the language. The result is that there are now *two* I/O libraries in common use, the older standard I/O library from the C world and the newer stream I/O system more adapted to C++ (see Chapter 10).

Efficiency is a primary goal in C

The underlying philosophy of C—concise representation, pointer arithmetic, omission of run-time checks, the simple memory model, correspondence of arrays and pointers, and the elevation of "uncompromising efficiency" as a virtue above almost all others—were carried over into C++. These characteristics made their impact on the language in many ways, both large and small. The designer

---

[1] *Classes: An Abstract Data Type Facility for the C Language*, Bjarne Stroustrup, *ACM Sigplan Notices*, 1982.

[2] This assertion is true in spirit but not exactly true in fact. The language C++ necessarily introduced a few new keywords, and the two languages have now diverged in a very small number of ways. However, the heritage of C++ from C cannot be questioned, and the impact of that heritage is the issue being addressed here.

of the language has stated that an explicit goal was that programmers should not have to pay (in space or execution time) for features that they do not use. For this reason, to cite one example, object-oriented polymorphic function dispatch is provided only if the user explicitly requests it (using the virtual keyword), and not otherwise. Similarly, the language goes to great lengths to store values on the activation record stack, rather than the heap, because stack-based values are almost always more quickly managed than heap-based values. But this efficiency in execution speed is purchased at the cost of complications in language semantics, a topic we address more fully in Chapter 4.

The attitude that programmers should not have to pay for features that they do not use permeates the language. Another example will further illustrate this influence. Imagine that an integer variable holding a negative number is right-shifted by one location. What bit value should be moved into the topmost position? If we look at the machine level, architectural designers are divided on this issue. On some machines, a right shift will move a zero into the most significant bit position, while on other machines the sign bit (which, in the case of a negative number, will be 1) is extended. Either case can be simulated by the other, using software, by means of a combination of tests and masks.

Given the lack of consensus regarding hardware systems, we can imagine the following argument being made, which would lead to the resolution we see in C++. "The situations where the two interpretations differ is not the common use; in fact it may be rather rare, as it only arises when negative values are shifted. If we adopt either convention as a language definition, then at least on some machines *all* right shifts will be impacted, as every right shift will need to test for the condition. However, it is unnecessarily costly to penalize all right shift operations because of a rare condition. We can get around this problem by asserting that the outcome in this situation is not specified by the language, and thus whatever result is produced by the underlying hardware is correct."

The result of some operations in C++ is purposely unspecified

In half a dozen or so similar cases in the language, the outcome of an operation is left purposely unspecified, largely so that whatever instruction is provided by the underlying machine can be used and still be said to satisfy the language specifications. For example, another common situation is the result of dividing or taking the remainder of a negative integer value—the result is either rounded toward zero or toward negative infinity, depending on the platform. Yet another example is the order of execution when a statement includes two autoincrements of the same variable, as in the following:

```
a[i++] = i++; // which increment is done first?
```

Java, however, provides a precise specification in all these cases, which means that Java must in some cases correct in software for hardware instructions that do not match the language definition.

C++ performs fewer run-time checks than Java

Finally, there is a difference in attitude toward run-time checks between Java and C++. Since the beginning of programming, countless debugging hours have been spent tracking down problems that were ultimately discovered to be caused by undefined pointer values or array subscripts out of range. These are features that Java (with a different philosophical outlook) would have detected by means of automatically generated run-time checks but that the C++ language does not generally uncover. Once more the attitude regarding C++ is that, if run-time checks are important, the programmer should explicitly write them; if not explicitly called for, the language should not impose their cost in situations where they may not be necessary.

The preceding explanation should not be construed to imply that Bjarne Stroustrup made wrong decisions in designing C++;[3] rather that it is important to understand the forces motivating those decisions in order to understand the language we have today.

1.3 The Legacy Problem

Legacy code is software written for earlier systems or libraries

Much of the difficulty in dealing with C++ programs comes from the problem of dealing with *legacy code*. Even when new code is being developed, it will often incorporate features from earlier or current libraries or systems that can be thought of as legacies. The problem of legacy code is particularly troublesome in the case of C++ because the language has changed over time, not only evolving from C but also having new features added over a period of many years.

The following list describes some of the more common aspects of the problem of legacy code:

- The use of libraries, such as the Standard I/O library, that predate the development of C++.

- The use of the preprocessor to create symbolic defined constants, rather than const variables. Tricky use of preprocessor macros to save execution time, rather than inline function invocations. (The original language C had neither constant variables nor function inlining.)

- The use of simple string functions that manipulate arrays of character values, rather than using the newer string data type.

---

[3] Although some have argued so. Typical is the following quote from Andrew Appel: "Life is too short to spend time chasing down irreproducible bugs, and money is too valuable to waste on the purchase of flaky software. . . . One might say, by way of excuse, 'but the language in which I program has the kind of address arithmetic that makes it impossible to know the bounds of an array.' Yes, and the man who shot his mother and father threw himself upon the mercy of the court because he was an orphan." [Appel 97]

- The use of various different names and implementation techniques for representing boolean values, which predate the addition of the bool data type.

- The overuse of global variables, which predates the understanding of classes as a better encapsulation technique.

- The use of various different container libraries, which predate the adoption of the Standard Template Library.

- The use of various techniques, such as void * pointers, to get around the type system interfering with general purpose containers in code that predates the introduction of templates.

Because of the legacy code problem, the C++ programmer must not only learn the current (and hopefully best) practices but must also be conversant with practices of the past.

1.4   The Language Java

Java was originally envisioned as a language for creating systems to be embedded in consumer products, such as VCRs. It was also developed at a time of increasing processor speeds and decreasing memory costs. In this context, efficiency and the ability to generate compact machine code took a backseat to issues of safety and robustness. James Gosling, the creator of Java, borrowed much of the basic syntax of the language C++, thereby ensuring that programmers with considerable experience with the old language would feel comfortable with the new. But instead of efficiency, the new bywords were simplicity and security.

Even Bjarne Stroustrup, the developer of C++, has stated: "Within C++, there is a much smaller and cleaner language struggling to get out."[4] Some would argue that this language is Java, wherein simplicity is achieved by eliminating many of the features of C++. Figure 12.1, which describes some of the features in C++ that have no correspondence in Java, is just one indication of this. In many cases simplicity is brought about by eliminating choices that the C++ programmer has to make; for example, all methods in Java are potentially polymorphic, instead of the programmer having to decide which are and which are not. This indeed incurs an overhead, but an acceptable one, and so the language comes down on the opposite side of C++ in the trade-off between simplicity of language and efficiency of execution.

Java eliminates all the situations that in C++ are explicitly left unspecified by the language definition. These include the meaning of shifts and divisions

---
[4] [Stroustrup 94, Section 9.4.4].

when negative numbers are manipulated, the size of primitive values, and several others. This is a conscious trade-off on the part of designers that preserves a consistent behavior on all platforms, potentially increasing the complexity of software to make up for differences in the underlying hardware.

Run-time checks are another trade-off, this time between efficiency of execution and safety. The C++ attitude is that, if safety (say, detecting the use of uninitialized values) is important, the programmer should explicitly code it, and if not the program should not pay (in execution time) for the feature. But experience has shown that far too few programmers will spend the effort to explicitly check for uninitialized values, verify that their array index values are in range, or that their pointers do point somewhere—and far too many programming errors result as consequence. Thus Java comes down on the opposite side of this divide and will always verify array index bounds, check for the use of undefined variables, and perform other run-time checkable tests.

Another area of philosophical difference is memory management. C++ leaves the management of dynamically allocated memory to programmers, few of whom will actually perform this task correctly. In contrast, Java provides a garbage collection system that will scurry about behind the scenes, taking care of memory management tasks for the programmer. This increases execution time but results in fewer programming errors.

Java also benefited from being developed later, after many years experience with C++. The problems involved in the explicit manipulation of pointer values were by then legendary. An appreciation of the importance of object-oriented features as an improvement over imperative software development was simply not possible when C++ was being designed, but was clear by the mid 1990s. And the designer of Java could draw on many years of experimentation with libraries and additions to C++, such as with threads packages or with the exception mechanism, both of which have precursors in C++.

A final example of the differences in philosophy between the two languages is the memory model (which is actually distinct from the issue of memory management discussed previously). The C++ memory model is very close to that of the underlying machine and therefore can be efficiently implemented. But some aspects of this model have unfortunate consequences for the object-oriented portions of the language, in particular an interaction between memory use and polymorphic method binding. Values that are truly polymorphic cannot be automatic, and values that are automatic cannot be truly polymorphic.[5] Since polymorphism may or may not be important for any particular problem, the language C++ allows both types of values. Java simplifies the language by having

---

[5] This distinction is explained in more detail in Chapter 4.

only one object format, but it is purchased at the expense of always using the more costly heap-based memory model.

Many people, both authors and users, have remarked that Java programs execute slowly.[6] There are many reasons for this, but the most important one is the philosophical differences that we have outlined. A Java program in execution is simply doing more work than is the equivalent C++ program. Garbage collection, multithread management, and run-time checks must use some execution time, regardless of how necessary they are. However, recent innovations in Java implementation (ideas such as Just-in-Time compilers) have improved performance dramatically. Whether this rate of improvement can be sustained is uncertain. On the one hand, there is the run-time cost necessitated by Java. On the other hand, the simpler language Java provides more opportunities for improvement by a good optimizing compiler than does C++. How these two forces will balance and whether Java runtimes can ever consistently come close to C++ performance are open questions.

1.5   The Better Language

It is not our intent to argue that one language is "better" in any sense than the other; indeed, such a question is almost meaningless because the objectives and intended purposes of the two languages are so dissimilar. Rather, each language should be appreciated on its own merits, for the way it goes about addressing the problems of particular concern. Java was intended to aid in developing programs that would work correctly and securely in systems with minimal interaction (such as embedded systems), even at the cost of execution time. C++ was designed to facilitate the creation of efficient and small executable files for applications such as systems programming. In the end, both languages can be appreciated on their merits as tools that address the problems they were intended to solve, without detracting from either.

1.6   Further Reading

Bjarne Stroustrup has discussed several times his motivation in designing C++, notably in two books [Ellis 90, Stroustrup 94] and in journal articles [Stroustrup 98].

---

[6] See [Tyma 98], for example.

James Gosling discussed the development of Java at the 1996 OOPSLA conference (James Gosling, *The Feel of Java*, unpublished talk) and in the book that currently represents the definitive description of the language [Arnold 98].

Test Your Understanding

1. True or False:

    (a) The language Java is based on an earlier language, J.

    (b) The language C was developed in tandem with the Unix operating system.

    (c) The value 7 can be used as a boolean in C++.

    (d) The language C++ was originally a set of macros called simply Classes.

    (e) Any legal C program is a legal C++ program.

    (f) In C++ efficiency is held as a virtual above all else.

    (g) The exact meaning of some integer division or remainder operations is left unspecified by the C++ language.

    (h) Java was designed as a language for writing controllers to be embedded in consumer products, such as VCRs.

2. Where was the language C original developed?

3. For what purpose was the language C originally developed?

4. What are some of the reasons that C became popular as a systems programming language?

5. What are some of the advantages that C++ derived from being an extension of C? What were some of the disadvantages?

6. Why is there an inherent conflict between uncompromising efficiency and portability?

7. Why is there an inherent conflict between uncompromising efficiency and run-time safety?

8. How many different interpretations are possible for the following sequence of statements:

```
i = 4;
a[i++] = i++;
```

9. What are some aspects of the legacy problem?

10. What was the original purpose for the language Java? Contrast this with the original purpose for C++. How are the two different purposes reflected in the languages?

11. For what types of programs is an emphasis on efficiency above all other concerns an appropriate decision? For what types of programs is it not appropriate?

2

Fundamental Data Types

WE BEGIN WITH A DISCUSSION OF THE FUNDAMENTAL DATA TYPES, including integers, characters, and floating point values. In neither Java nor C++ are these values considered to be objects, in the technical sense of the word. Thus they lack the glamour and allure currently associated with the buzzword "object-oriented," and can easily be thought of as ordinary and pedestrian. Nevertheless, they are the workhorse elements with which all real activity is eventually performed.

There are also a number of surprising differences in the way the two languages handle these basic data types.

2.1   Integers

Both the languages C++ and Java have the notion that integers can be both **short** and **long**, in addition to their natural representations. On the one hand, in Java a **short** integer is explicitly a 16-bit quantity, an integer is a 32-bit quantity, and a **long** is a 64-bit quantity. On the other hand, the C++ standard is mute concerning the number of bits assigned to each, except to note that an integer value must be at least as large as a short integer and that a long integer must be at least as large as a simple integer. Thus it would be perfectly legal for a compiler to, for example, use 32-bit quantities for all three. It is not uncommon for either a **short** or a **long** to be the same size as a simple integer.

 Long and/or short may have the same size as integer

In C++ the designations **long** and **short** are modifiers for the **integer** data type, instead of type names in their own right. Thus it is legal to declare a value as both

11

short and integer. However, it is also possible to use the modifiers by themselves, in which case the base type integer is understood:

```
short int x; // declare x as a small integer
long y; // declare y as long integer
```

The modifier long can also be applied to double precision values (see Section 2.2).

Another pair of modifiers that can be applied to integer are signed and unsigned. An *unsigned integer* can only hold quantities that are greater than or equal to zero. Typically, however, they can maintain numbers that are larger than those represented by a signed quantity that uses the same number of bits. For example, a 16-bit signed integer variable can hold values between −32768 and 32767, whereas an unsigned 16-bit integer can maintain values between 0 and 65535.

An unsigned integer can only hold nonnegative values

Assigning a negative value to an unsigned variable is confusing

The language permits a signed value to be assigned to an unsigned variable without casts or warnings. However, if the signed value is negative, the result will be an unexpectedly large number:

```
int i = -3;
unsigned int j = i;
cout << j << endl; // will print very large positive integer
```

Integer division involving negative numbers is platform dependent

There is little agreement among machine designers on the exact meaning of integer division when one or both arguments are negative. On some machines the integer division −23/4 will yield −5, the smallest integer greater than the algebraic quotient, while on other machines the same calculation will yield −6, the largest integer less than the algebraic quotient. For this reason the language C++ definition leaves the meaning in this situation undefined so that language implementors will be free to use the "natural" instruction provided by the underlying hardware. The language Java, however, explicitly states that integer division truncates toward zero so that −23/4 will yield −5.

The language C++ definition insists that the following equality must always be preserved:

```
a == (a/b)*b + a%b
```

Never use the remainder operator with negative values

Because division involving negative numbers is not completely defined, a similar situation holds with respect to the remainder operator %. In C++ the result of the calculation 21 % −5 is machine-dependent, and can either be 1 or −1, matching whatever interpretation is selected for division. In Java it is specified as −1.

Right shifts are also explicitly underdefined in the language. A right shift of an signed quantity can either fill the high-order bits with zero values or extend the sign bit. Both choices are permitted by the language definition, and on any particular machine the alternative selected probably will depend on the interpretation provided by the instruction on the underlying hardware. A right shift of an unsigned quantity must always fill with zero values and corresponds to the Java >>> operator, which is not part of the C++ language. The effect of either a right or a left shift where the right argument is negative, or where it is larger than the number of bits in the left argument, is undefined.

The modifiers signed and unsigned are orthogonal to long and short, thus permitting a large number of combinations:

```
unsigned long a; // can hold largest integer value
signed short int b;
```

Signed characters are often used to hold very small integer values

C++ does not recognize the Byte data type in Java. Instead the data type signed char is often used to represent byte-sized quantities.

2.1.1   Characters

A character value in C++ is typically only an 8-bit quantity, although again the language definition provides only a minimum length, and a compiler that devoted 16 bits to each character (as does Java) would in theory be legal. As in Java, it is legal to perform arithmetic on characters, which indeed is much more common in C++ programs than in Java programs.

The Java Unicode escape format (for example '\u0ABC') is not recognized by C++. However, arbitrary character literals can be represented by their octal values. The ASCII character 2, for example, is represented as '\062'. Hexadecimal constants can also be written by beginning with the text 0x, as in '\0xFF'.

Wide characters are a recent addition to the C++ language

As a type, characters can be signed or unsigned. An explicitly signed character is typically used more as a very short integer value than as a true character, as literal character values are represented in the same way whether they are signed or unsigned.

A relatively recent addition to the C++ language is the data type w_char, a "wide character" that is explicitly larger than a normal character.[1] Typically the name w_char is simply an alias for another integer data type, such as short.

---

[1] It would perhaps have been more logical to use the name long char to represent 16-bit characters. We can conjecture that this was not done because the type name is defined as an alias for a short integer by means of a typedef statement and therefore cannot be represented by a two-word name.

2.1.2   Booleans

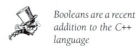

Booleans are a recent addition to the C++ language

The boolean data type is named **bool** in C++, instead of **boolean** as in Java. This is a relatively recent addition to the language C++, and is still infrequently used. Historically, integer values were used to represent boolean quantities. A nonzero arithmetic quantity was interpreted as true, and a zero value was false. It is still legal to use integers in this fashion, for example, to control a while loop:

```
int i = 10;
while (i) { // will loop until i is zero
   .
   .
   .
   i--;
}
```

Needless to say, although legal, this usage is somewhat more error prone than the explicit use of boolean values. For example, should the variable i somehow be negative when the **while** loop begins, it will create an infinite loop (or at least a very long one).

One place the integer-as-boolean interpretation is widely used is in the manipulation of string values. The string copy idiom described in Chapter 1 is a typical example:

```
while (*p++ = *q++) ;
```

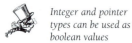

Integer and pointer types can be used as boolean values

Here the program will terminate when a character (that is, an integer) zero value is copied by the assignment. All nonzero values will be interpreted as true, whereas the zero value is interpreted as false.

The **bool** data type reveals its heritage by the fact that it is still considered to be an explicit integer data type, although it cannot be signed or unsigned. For example, arithmetic operations can be applied to **bool** values, which result in the **bool** value being converted into an integer (0 for false, 1 for true). Similarly, integer results can be assigned to **bool** variables, in which case a nonzero value is converted to 1:

```
bool test = true;
int i = 2 + test; // i is now 3
test = test - 1; // test is now 0, or false
```

Even pointer values can be used as booleans, with the interpretation that the value is considered false if it is null, and true otherwise. Thus it is not uncommon to see pointer variables being tested by an if statement in the following manner:

```
aClass * aPtr; // declare a pointer variable
   .
   .
   .
if (aPtr) // will be true if aPtr is not null
      .
      .
      .
```

Note that the test to determine whether a pointer is non-null is different from a test to determine whether the object the pointer references is nonzero, as we showed in the string copy example.

Legacy code can contain different boolean abstractions

Perhaps more than other features, the boolean data abstraction is an area where the programmer can expect to encounter problems with legacy code (see Section 1.3). Because the bool data type is a relatively recent addition to the language, but one that nevertheless has obvious application, there were various competing alternative designs for implementing this data type in the days prior to the C++ standard. For example, some schemes implemented boolean values as simple integers, while other techniques used an enumerated data type. These alternatives differed not only in their implementation but also in their naming conventions.

To cite just one example, users developing code with the Microsoft Foundation Classes (MFC) on Windows systems will encounter methods that require or return a value of type BOOL. This type is distinct from the bool data type, and care must be taken in mixing the two. Many other schemes are still commonly found in different situations.

2.1.3   Bit Fields

A seldom used feature of C++ allows the programmer to specify explicitly the number of bits to be used in the representation of an integer value. This is often used to pack several different binary values into small structure, such as an 8-bit byte:

```
struct infoByte {
    int on:1; // 1-bit value, 0 or 1
    int :4; // 4-bit padding, not named
    int type: 3; // 3-bit value, 0 to 7
};
```

Don't use bit fields

The exact layout of the bits is implementation-dependent. As a practical matter the use of bit fields often saves neither time nor space, since in the generated assembly language more complex code is needed to extract or set such fields.

2.2   Floating Point Values

Floating point quantities are represented in three ranges of magnitude—float, double, and long double. The type double is the most commonly used type; for example, floating point literals are implicitly defined as double precision. Similarly, all mathematical routines in the standard library use double instead of float.

 Never use float; use double instead

In fact, there is almost no reason for any value ever to be declared as float.

C++ is much more flexible with conversions than is Java. For example, assigning a floating point value to an integer variable is illegal in Java without a cast but is perfectly acceptable in C++:

```
int i;
double d = 3.14;
i = d; // may generate a warning
```

Better compilers may generate a warning on this statement, but nothing more. When constructors are used as conversion operators, or when explicit conversion operators are present (see Section 7.15), the programmer should take great care as these operations can be invoked implicitly without any indication being given in the program.

 Math routines will not throw an exception on error

The standard mathematical library routines (see Section A.6 in Appendix A) will never throw an exception and will seldom halt execution unless the underlying hardware throws a hardware fault. An integer division by zero will often cause the latter behavior. Instead of halting execution, the standard routines will set a global variable named errno. It is the responsibility of the programmer to check this value after each invocation:

 Always check errno

```
double d = sqrt(-1); // should generate error
if (errno == EDOM)
    .
    .        // but only caught if checked
    .
```

Java supports three floating point values that are not numbers: Nan, NEGATIVE_INFINITY, and POSITIVE_INFINITY. Such facilities are permitted in a platform-dependent fashion in C++, but they are not required.

2.3   Enumerated Values

Despite the similar name, an enumerated value has nothing in common with the Enumeration class in Java. An enum declaration in C++ creates a distinct integer type with named constants:

```
enum color {red, orange, yellow};
```

The values red, orange, and yellow become named constants after the point of this declaration. A value declared as color can hold only values of this type.

The names of enumerated constants must be distinct. The following could generate an error:

```
enum fruit {apple, pear, orange}; // error: orange redefined
```

Enumerated constants can be converted into integers and can even have their own internal integer values explicitly specified:

```
enum shape {circle=12, square=3, triangle};
```

The only operation defined for enumerated data types is assignment. An enumerated constant can be assigned to an integer and incremented, but the resulting value must then be cast back into the enumerated data type before it can be assigned to a variable. The validity of the cast is not checked:

```
fruit aFruit = pear;
int i = aFruit;    // legal conversion
i++; // legal increment
aFruit = fruit(i); // fruit is probably now orange
i++;
aFruit = fruit(i); // fruit value is now undefined
```

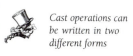

Cast operations can be written in two different forms

Cast operations can be written by using either the form type(value) or the older (type)value syntax, which is common to both C++ and Java. Nowadays, the latter form is generally discouraged, although there are situations in which it is still applicable. It is not legal to change a pointer type, for example, by writing

```
int * i;
char * c;

c = char *(i); // error: not legal syntax
```

However, in this situation a static_cast (Section 6.3) would be even better.

2.4   The void Type

As in Java, the data type **void** is used to represent a method or function that does not yield a result. In C++ the type can also be used as a pointer type to describe a "universal" pointer that can hold a pointer to any type of value. We discuss this use in more detail in Chapter 3, when we discuss pointers.

2.5   Arrays

An array need not be allocated by using new

An array in C++ can be created by simply declaring the type and the number of elements. It does not need to be allocated by using the **new** directive, as in Java. When declared in this form, the number of elements must be a value determined at compile time:

```
int data[100]; // create an array of 100 elements
```

The number of elements can often be omitted. This is true, for example, if the array has an explicit initialization clause:

```
char text[ ] = "an array of characters";
int limits[ ] = {10, 12, 14, 17, 0};
```

Note that the square brackets follow the name. It is not legal to place the square brackets after the type, as in Java:

```
double[ ] limits = {10, 12, 14, 17, 0}; // legal Java, not C++
```

The limits can also be omitted when arrays are passed as arguments to a function:

```
// compute average of an array of data values
double average (int n, double data[ ] )
{
   double sum = 0;
   for (int i = 0; i < n; i++) {
      sum += data[i];
   }
   return sum / n;
}
```

In C++, arrays do not know how many elements they contain

Unlike in Java, arrays are not objects and do not possess any methods. They do not "know" their extent. The only operation that is normally performed on an array is the subscript.

There is a close association in C++ between arrays and pointers. We explore it in Section 3.6.

2.6   Structures and Unions

Before the advent of object-oriented languages, many programming languages included the concept of a *structure*. A structure is like a class definition that includes only data fields, in which all access is public, and that does not use inheritance. In other words, a structure is simply a way of packaging a collection of data fields as a unit.

The C++ struct data type is heir to this tradition in languages (in particular, it is upward compatible with the earlier language C), but it moves slightly in the direction of the more complete class facility. In fact, the major difference in C++ between a struct and a class is that the access to members in structures is by default public, rather than private, as in classes:

```
// holds an int, a double, AND a pointer
struct myStruct {
    int i;
    double d;
    anObject * p;
};
```

A union is similar to a structure, but the different data fields all share the same location in memory. They can be thought of as being laid one on top of another. Obviously, only one field can therefore be used at any one time. Unions were commonly used in pre–object-oriented days to create a general purpose data area that could hold many different types of values. Thus

```
// can hold an int, a double, OR a pointer
union myUnion {
    int i;
    double d;
    anObject * p;
};
```

For the most part, object-oriented languages have made unions unnecessary by introducing polymorphic variables. That is, rather than creating a structure that will hold three different types of values, a programmer can create a polymorphic variable that can hold values from three different types of subclasses.

2.7   Object Values

Much of the material in the following chapters is devoted to differences in the interpretation of classes and objects in Java and C++. However, we begin this discussion with some simple observations. The first is that Java uses *reference semantics* for assignments. This means that a variable assigned from another variable will actually share the same value. We can demonstrate this by creating a class that is nothing more than a simple box:

```java
class box { // Java box
    public int value;
}

box a = new box();
box b;

a.value = 7;    // set variable a
b = a;          // assign b from a
a.value = 12;   // change variable a
System.out.println("a value " + a.value);
System.out.println("b value " + b.value);
```

The result will verify that by changing **a** we have in fact altered the value of **b**, since they refer to the same object value.

Java and C++ use different semantics for assignment

The language C++, however, normally uses *copy semantics* for assignment. The equivalent program is superficially the same but gives different results:

```cpp
class box { // C++ box
public:
    int value;
};

box a; // note, explicit allocation not required
box b;

a.value = 7;
b = a;
a.value = 12;
cout << "a value " << a.value << endl;
cout << "b value " << b.value << endl;
```

The output will show that a was assigned the value 7 by the assignment statement and that this value was then copied into the variable b. Since a copy was made, this value was independent of the value being held by variable a. The variable a has subsequently been updated and now holds the value 12, but unlike Java this change has not modified the value held by the variable b.

The language C++ does include the concept of a *reference variable*, which is a variable declared as a direct alias. We have more to say about reference variables in Chapter 3. However, the correspondence is not exact. A reference variable in C++, for example, can never be reassigned to a new value:

```
box a = new box(); // java reference assignment
box b = a;
b = new box(); // reassignment of reference

box a;    // C++ example
box & b = a; // reference assignment
box c;
b = c;   // error: not permitted to reassign reference
```

2.8   Functions

The language C++ permits the definition of functions that are not members of any class. Such functions are invoked simply by name, without requiring the specification of a receiver:

```
// define a function for the maximum
// of two integer values
int max (int i, int j)
{
   if (i < j) return j;
   return i;
}

int x = ...;
int y = ...;
int z = max(x, y);
```

A *prototype* declaration simply declares the name of a function and the argument types but does not include a function body:

```
// declare function max defined elsewhere
int max(int, int);
```

In C++ every function name must be known before it can be used

Prototypes are necessary in C++ as every function name with its associated parameter types must be known to the compiler before it can be used in an invocation.

2.8.1   Order of Argument Evaluation

Order of argument evaluation in C++ is undefined

A subtle difference between Java and C++ concerns the order of argument evaluation. The language Java explicitly states that arguments are evaluated left to right. Consider the following example program:

```
String s = "going, ";
printTest (s, s, s = "gone ");
    .
    .
    .
void printTest (String a, String b, String c)
{
    System.out.println(a + b + c);
}
```

The output will always be "going, going, gone" as the first two arguments will be evaluated before the assignment to the third is performed. But in C++ the order of argument evaluation is left implementation dependent. Many systems (but not all) will evaluate arguments right to left, not left to right. On these systems the output will be "gone gone gone."

2.8.2   The Function **main**

In C++ main is a function outside any class

As in Java, execution in C++ programs begins in a function named **main**. Unlike Java, this function is not part of any class. The function need not—in fact, should not—be declared as **static**. Earlier versions of the language C++ permitted the return type for **main** to be declared as **void**, and most compilers will still accept this form. However, the language C++ definition now requires that the return type be declared as **int**, with the integer value indicating the success or failure of the program. A return value of zero indicates successful execution, whereas a nonzero value is interpreted as unsuccessful. (What the operating system does with a nonzero return value is platform dependent and is not defined by the language.)

Always return zero on successful completion of the main program

The function can either be written with no arguments or with two. When written in the two-argument form, the first argument is an integer value and the second is an array of pointers to character values (that is, strings):

```
int main (int argc, char *argv[ ])
{
    cout << "executing program " << argv[0] << '\n';
    return 0; // execution successful
}
```

The integer argument is a count on the number of entries in the character array. We discuss the relationship between pointers and arrays shown in this example in Chapter 3. We discuss the manner in which strings are handled in C++ in Chapter 8.

The first command line argument in C++ is always the application name

The Java programmer will notice one difference in the command line array: In Java the array values consist entirely of the command line arguments, but in C++ the first (that is, zero indexed) element is the executable program name, and the first actual argument is found at index position 1.

2.8.3   Alternative **main** Entry Points

Note that **main** is the entry point for programs that is specified by the language, but individual libraries may provide their own version of **main** and then require a different entry point. For example, many Windows graphical systems come with their own **main** routine already written, which will perform certain initializations before invoking a different function (such as **WinMain**). The MFC library takes this one step further. It eliminates the main routine altogether and instead begins execution when an instance of the application class (a subclass built on top of a MFC-provided class) is created.

Test Your Understanding

1. In what ways are the data types **short** and **long** different in C++ and Java?

2. What is the difference between a **signed** and an **unsigned** integer value?

3. Why can integer division result in different answers on different machines?

4. How many bits does the C++ language specify for a **char** data type?

5. What value will be assigned to the variable i by the following program?

```
signed char a = '2' * 4;
int i = a;
```

6. How many times will the following program loop?

```
int i = 16;
while (i)
    if (! (i % 2)) i += 3;
    else i = i >> 1;
```

7. What will be the value of the variable i after the following code fragment is executed?

```
int i = 3;
bool j = i;
i = j;
```

8. What is the effect of the following program?

```
bool b = true;
for (int i = 0; i < 10; i++)
    if (b -= 1)
        cout << "yes";
    else
        cout << "no";
```

9. What are the three legal types of floating point values?

10. What are the two varieties of names that an enumerated type declaration creates?

11. What are the two different ways in which a cast operation can be written?

12. Write a declaration for an array of 100 double precision values.

13. Write a declaration for an array of 100 pointers to double precision values.

14. What are some ways that a C++ array is different from a Java array?

15. Explain why the procedure **average** in Section 2.5 requires two arguments, whereas a similar procedure in Java could be written with only one argument.

16. In what ways is a structure different from a class? In what ways is the C++ idea of a structure different from the historical concept of the type found in languages such as C?

17. What is the danger in the following program fragment?

```
union {
    int i;
    double d;
} dataFields;

dataFields.d = 3.14159;
dataFields.i = 7;
double x = 2 * dataFields.d;
```

18. What is the difference between an assignment performed with reference semantics and one that uses copy semantics?

19. What is a function prototype?

20. How is the function main in C++ different from the function main in Java?

21. Explain the relationship between the values printed by a signed negative integer, and the value printed when assigned to an unsigned variable.

22. Write a program that will empirically determine the maximum and minimum values for both the signed and unsigned versions of the integer data types char, short, int, and long.

23. Write a program to test the division and remainder operations with negative integers on a particular platform. Then write a rule that explains your observed results.

24. Empirically investigate the order of evaluation rules for several different platforms.

25. Write a procedure that takes as argument an array of double precision values and returns the median value in the array.

3

Pointers and References

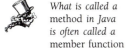

What is called a method in Java is often called a member function in C++

POWERFUL OBJECT-ORIENTED MECHANISMS, such as run-time selection of over-ridden methods, are in large part possible only because of the indirection provided through the use of pointer values. It is often said that the language Java has no pointers. This is true in a superficial sense, in that the Java programmer seldom thinks about explicit pointer values. But in actuality, just below the surface of the language, almost everything in Java is represented internally by pointer values. The language C++ in general hides much less from the programmer's view, and thus the use of pointers in C++ programs is explicit and direct. C++ provides a variety of different mechanisms for manipulating pointer values, and an explanation of these mechanisms is the topic of this chapter. We explain the use of pointers and object-oriented programming in Chapters 4 and 5.

3.1   Java Pointers

We begin by explaining the assertion that pointer values really do lurk just below the surface of the language Java. Recall the **box** class definition described in Section 2.7:

```
class box { // Java box
    public int value;
}

box a = new box();
a.value = 7;   // set variable a
```

The declaration of a variable, such as the variable a, results in space being set aside and labeled a. This space is just large enough to hold a pointer value. The value that we normally think of as being the quantity held by a is not allocated until the new operation is performed. This situation can be pictured as follows:

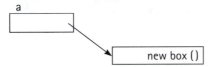

A second variable can be declared and assigned the value held by a:

```
box b;
b = a;
```

Internally, the locations a and b are distinct, but the memory values they reference are the same. This can be pictured as follows:

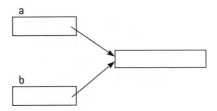

Because internally they reference the same value, changes to either a or b will be reflected in the other variable.

Rather than being implicitly hidden from the programmer, pointers in C++ are explicit and must be directly manipulated in code.

3.2   Pointers on Pointers

A *pointer* is simply a variable that maintains as a value the address of another location in memory. Because memory addresses have a fixed limit, the amount of storage necessary to hold a pointer can be determined at compile time, even if the size or extent of the object to which it will point is not known.

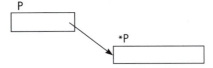

Avoid confusing the pointer itself and the object the pointer references

The pointer itself will usually reside in a local variable, and the value the pointer refers to will often be a dynamically allocated heap value. However, neither condition is guaranteed. We discuss the distinction between heap and stack values in more detail in Chapter 4. Pointer values are used whenever there is a need for one or more levels of indirection at run time. Among the reasons for using pointer values are the following:

- A single pointer variable must reference a variety of different values over the course of execution, or

- A pointer will reference only a single value, but the particular value it will reference cannot be known at compile time, or

- The amount of memory necessary to hold a value cannot be determined at compile time and must be allocated a run time.

A null pointer is analogous to an uninitialized variable in Java

A *null pointer* is a value that does not reference any other memory location and should not be considered to point to any valid object. A pointer variable can always be assigned the numeric value zero in order to make it null, although the actual internal value used to represent the null pointer can differ from one platform to another. A pointer can also be tested for equality to the value zero to determine whether it represents a null pointer. A pointer that is not equivalent to a null pointer on such a test is said to be non-null.

Four principal mechanisms are used to access values denoted by a pointer. The mechanism used will depend in part on the type of value the pointer references:

- A pointer can be explicitly *dereferenced* by using the unary * operator. If p is a variable holding a pointer to a value of some type, then *p is the value addressed by the pointer. We discuss pointers to simple values in Section 3.4.

- A pointer to a structure, or class, can combine pointer dereferencing and member field extraction by using the pointer operator. If p is a pointer to a value of a class type that contains a member field x, then p->x is the same as (*p).x. We discuss the use of pointers and structures in Section 3.5.

- A pointer variable can be subscripted. This is useful only if the pointer addresses an array of objects. The subscript index is used to determine the element accessed by the expression. We discuss the connection between pointers and arrays in Section 3.6.

- An integer value can be added to or subtracted from a pointer in order to yield a new pointer. It is assumed (but not verified) that the pointer references an array of values. We explore this assumption when we discuss pointers and arrays in Section 3.6.

A pointer can be distinguished from a *reference*, which is an internal pointer. We discuss references in Section 3.7.

The manipulation of pointers can be tricky, and is one of the most common sources of programming errors. For this reason it is important to fully understand the use and manipulation of pointers.

3.3   The address-of Operator

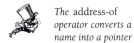

The address-of *operator converts a name into a pointer*

Pointers can be used to reference either newly allocated memory, created using the **new** operator, or to reference other memory values. In the latter case the ampersand is used as the *address-of* operator. It determines the address in memory for a variable argument. This address can then be assigned to a pointer variable. The following code fragment illustrates the use of this function with the routine **scanf**, which reads text from the standard input and then parses the text and converts it into a variety of different values.[1] For real and integer conversions the **scanf** function requires a pointer to the location where the value will be stored.

```
int i; // location for final value
int *p; // pointer variable
p = & i; // set p to point to i

scanf("%d", p); // scan number into i
```

Often the address-of operator is applied directly in the argument, which avoids the need to explicitly declare a pointer variable. The preceding example could be written more directly as follows:

```
int i; // location for final value

scanf("%d", &i); // scan number into i
```

Like all operators in C++, the address-of operator can be overloaded to provide a new meaning when used with an object value. We consider this issue in detail in Chapter 7.

---

[1] Although **scanf** is an excellent illustration of the use of pointers as arguments, the use of the function itself is now discouraged. The function is part of the legacy inherited from the earlier language C, and the functionality it provided is now available in a more robust form by the stream input library, described in Chapter 10.

3.4   Pointers to Simple Values

When a pointer is referencing a primitive data type, such as an integer or a real, only two major operations can be applied to the pointer value. The first is to compare the pointer value to another pointer. The second is to dereference the pointer value. The dereference results in a memory location, which can then be used as the target for an assignment:

```
int i = 7;
int j = 11;
int *p = & i; // set p to point to i

*p = *p + 3; // i now has the value 10
```

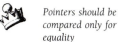

Pointers should be compared only for equality

Pointers should be compared only for equality, to test whether two pointers refer to the same memory value. Ordering tests are legal, but they generally are not what the programmer intends. One pointer is considered less than another if the value it references is found in memory at a smaller address. Since exact memory locations are inherently platform specific, such a test has limited utility.

There is a difference between modifying a pointer value and modifying the value that a pointer refers to. The preceding example changes the value that p references, namely, the variable i. The following changes p itself so that it will point to the variable j:

```
p = & j; // change p to point to j
```

Nothing prevents a pointer from referencing a deleted value

With all pointer values it is important to remember that the pointer itself and the value it references are separate and may be managed independently of each other. In particular, the programmer should be careful to ensure that, whenever a pointer is used, the value it references will still exist. Executing the function Set followed by the function Use in the next example is an almost certain recipe for disaster, as the value the pointer refers to will have been overwritten by the time it is used:

```
int * p; // global pointer variable

void Set ()
{
    int i; // local variable
    i = 7; // give i a value
    p = & i; // set p to point to it
}
```

```
void Use ()
{
   double d;
   d = 3.0;
   d += *p; // use the value that p points to
}
```

3.4.1   Pointers to Pointer

A pointer to a value that is itself a pointer is declared using multiple levels of star symbols. A common example is the declaration of the argument values supplied to the main procedure under Unix and some other operating systems. The main procedure is provided with two arguments. The first is an integer value that contains the number of elements in the second argument. The second argument is an array of string values. Given the close relationship between arrays and pointers (see Section 3.6) and the fact that primitive strings are represented as pointers to character (see Chapter 8), this second argument is often declared as a pointer to a pointer to a character:[2]

```
int main (int argc, char ** argv)
{
   .
   .
   .
   cout << "name of program " << **argv << '\n';
   return 0;
}
```

The first character in the name of the program can be printed, as shown, by finding the value of the pointer that argv references and then finding the value of the first character this element points to.

3.4.2   Pointers and const

A constant pointer is different from a pointer to const

The placement of the modifier const indicates whether it is the pointer itself or the value it points to that is constant:

---

[2] It is just as often declared as an array of pointers to character values. An example in this form was shown in Section 2.8. We explore the relationship between pointers and arrays in Section 3.6.

```
int i = 7;

const int * p  = &i; // pointer to a constant
int * const q  = &i; // constant pointer

*p = 8; // not allowed, p points to a const
*q = 8; // allowed, q is pointing to non const
p = q;  // allowed, p itself is not constant
q = p; // not allowed q is constant
```

To create a pointer that cannot be changed—and that references a value that itself cannot be changed—two **const** modifiers must be used:

```
const int * const r = & i;
```

3.4.3   void * Pointers

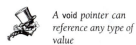

A void *pointer can reference any type of value*

The data type **void** * (called either *pointer to void* or *void-star pointer*) is a special declaration type in C++ that can be used to hold any type of pointer value. It is used in much the same manner as the data type **Object** in Java. That is, a pointer to void is a universal type, a type that can reference anything. Any pointer type can be converted into a void pointer:

```
double d;
double * dp = & d;

void * p = dp;
```

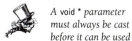

A void * *parameter must always be cast before it can be used*

As with **Object** values in Java, converting from a void-star pointer back into the original pointer type requires a cast:

```
double * dp2;

dp2 = (double *) p; // convert p back into pointer to double
```

If the security of the conversion cannot be easily verified, the safer **dynamic_cast** operator should be used (see Section 6.3). (Note that conversions of pointers is one situation in which the **type(value)** syntax cannot be used for casts.)

3.4.4   Pointers to Functions

It is possible to form a pointer whose value is a function. The syntax used for describing such a value, however, is rather unintuitive. The following code fragment declares a function that takes two integer values as an argument and returns a floating point result. This is followed by the declaration of a global variable that illustrates the form used to declare function pointers:

```
double fdiv (int i, int j) { return i / (double) j; }


double (*fptr) (int, int); // declare variable fptr
fptr = & fdiv; // assign value
```

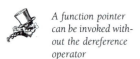

A function pointer can be invoked without the dereference operator

The declaration of **fptr** asserts that it is a pointer to a function that requires two integer arguments and returns a floating point value. The variable is then set by the assignment statement to point to the function **fdiv**. To call such a value the pointer dereference need not be written, although no harm results from being precise:

```
double x = fptr(7, 14); // call ftpr directly
double x = (*fptr) (7, 14); // dereference ftpr and call
```

One common use for function pointers is in conjunction with the system library routine **qsort**. The function in this case is a comparison function, which must take exactly two arguments that are declared as void star pointers and return an integer result. (Since **qsort** was created before the introduction of the boolean datatype to the C++ language, it uses the older convention that nonzero integer values are true and that integer zero represents false.) Let's assume, for example, that we have an array of 100 double precision values. They could be sorted as follows:

```
double values[100];

int comp (void * a, void * b)
{
    double * d1 = (double *) a;
    double * d2 = (double *) b;
    return (*d1) < (*d2);
}

qsort (values, 100, sizeof(double), &comp);
```

The built-in function **sizeof**, used in this example, takes as an argument a type description and yields the size requirements (in byte units) for the type.

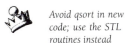

Avoid qsort in new code; use the STL routines instead

The **qsort** facility predates the Standard Template Library (STL), and for newer code it is preferable to use the **sort** generic library routine from the STL (see Chapter 9).

It is also possible to form pointers to member functions. However, both the syntax and the interpretation are even more obscure than pointers to functions, and as the need for this facility is rather rare, we do not discuss it here.

3.5   Pointers to Structures

The arrow operator is a combination of dereference and field access

When pointers refer to classes or structures, a special syntax can be used to combine pointer dereferencing and member or data field access. The arrow operator, formed as a two-character combination of – and >, has the same effect as dereferencing a pointer and using the field access operator on the result:

```
struct link {
    int value;
    link * next; // pointer to next link in chain
};

link finalElement; // declare a single default element
link * firstLink = & finalElement; // set pointer to initially
                                    // refer to this

(*firstLink).value = 7; // these two statements
firstLink->value = 7; // have the same effect
```

Let's assume that we have a series of link values combined into a linked list structure. The following code fragment prints out the values of the list and illustrates the use of pointer operations:

```
for (link * p = aList; p != &finalElement; p = p->next)
    cout << *p << " ";
```

3.6   Pointers to Arrays

In C++ there is a close association between a pointer and an array. In fact, we could argue that the language C++ assumption that all pointers always reference arrays. This is because a number of operations can be used with pointers that make sense only if the pointer references an array. However, as we shortly demonstrate, a danger is that there is no run-time test to ensure that these expectations are satisfied.

Pointers can be subscripted just like arrays

An expression of type `'array of ...'`, when used by itself as a value, is converted into a pointer type. An array of integers, for example, is converted into a pointer to integer. The base type for the pointer is the element type, not the array type:

```
int values[100];
```

```
int * p = values; // legal, as values is converted into a pointer
```

As with arrays, pointer values can be subscripted:

```
p[4] = 7; // references same value as values[4]
```

Neither pointer nor array index values are checked to ensure they are in range

No attempt is made to ensure that the index value is in range for the underlying array, or even that the pointer does indeed reference an array. Accessing or modifying a value that is out of range is a common, and subtle, source of programming errors:

```
p[310] = 7; // index value too large
p[-4] = 12; // index value too small
```

Rarely is there a legitimate reason for out-of-bound index values. More often they are simply a programming error. Occasionally, they are a sign of malicious intent. The famous Internet worm in 1988 operated by indexing a string array with out-of-range values, writing new assembly instructions to the known positions, and then executing the new instructions.

It is legal to perform arithmetic on pointers

It is also possible to perform arithmetic on pointer values. Adding or subtracting an integer from a pointer changes the pointer to reference the next or previous elements in sequence. That is, adding 1 to a pointer advances it to the next element, adding 2 skips an element, and so on. Again, no attempt is made to ensure the legitimacy of these operations.

A common use of pointer arithmetic is in loops. For example, strings in C++ are simply pointers to character arrays, terminated by a character with value zero. (We discuss strings in more detail in Chapter 8.) The following code fragment finds and prints all the vowels in a text string:

```
char * text = " ... some text ";

// p++ advances pointer to next location
for (char * p = text; *p != '\0'; p++)
   if (isVowel(*p))
      cout << "vowel value is " << *p << "\n";
```

Although it is legal, it is rare for pointers to be incremented or decremented by quantities other than 1. However, adding integer values to a pointer to yield another pointer is relatively common.

3.7   References

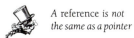

A reference is not the same as a pointer

A *reference* in C++ is an alias, an alternative way to name an existing object. Although most often references are implemented internally as pointers, this need not always be the case (the compiler can optimize away the underlying pointer in some circumstances). References and pointers differ in three important regards:

- A reference can never be null; it must always refer to a legitimate object.
- Once established, a reference can never be changed to make it point to a different object.
- A reference does not require any explicit mechanism to dereference the memory address and access the actual data value.

A reference is declared by using the ampersand, as in the following code fragment:

```
int i = 7;
int & j = i; // j is an alias for i
j++; // i is now 8
i += 3; // i is now 11, as is j
```

Operators do not operate on a reference per se; rather they operate on the value that the reference designates. For example, the increment operator in the preceding code fragment is not actually applied to j, but rather to the value that j refers to, namely, i.

A reference can be used as the target of an assignment. Some functions will return a reference as a result for precisely this reason. This is illustrated by the following somewhat contrived example:

```
int values[100];

int & index(int i) { return values[i + 2]; }

index(27) = 12; // changes values[29];
```

References are very similar to the way that Java interprets assignment of object values. Consider the following piece of Java code:

```
class box { // Java box
   public int value = 0;
}

box x = new box();
box y = x;
x.value = 7;
// changing x will change y
System.out.println("Value of y box " + y.value);
// reassigning x will not change y
x = new box();
System.out.println("Value of y box " + y.value);
```

Since x and y reference the same object, a change in x will result in a change in y. A difference between C++ and Java references can be seen in a subsequent assignment. Changing the variable x in Java would have no effect on y, which could continue to refer to the previous value, whereas such a change would alter both values in C++. This difference is perhaps more easily seen in the context of parameter values, which are just a form of assignment.

3.7.1   Pass by Reference Parameters

The most common use of references is in parameter passing

The most common use of references is as a pass by reference parameter. A reference parameter is an alias for the corresponding actual argument value. Modification of one can produce modification of the other. To illustrate, consider the following simple function:

```
void passTest (int & i)
{
   i++;
   i = 7;
}

int main ()
{
   int j = 5;
   passTest(j);
   cout << j << '\n';
   return 0;
}
```

If the argument to passTest is declared as pass by value, without the ampersand, then the modification of i within the procedure has no effect on j. But passed by reference, as shown, the value j is an alias for i. Thus changes in j result in a modification of i.

Primitive types in Java are passed by value, as in C++. We cannot use the wrapper class Integer in this example because an Integer value cannot be changed once it is created. However, it is useful to note that in general the parameter massing mechanism used by Java to pass object values is different from either of the possibilities permitted in C++. Consider a superficially similar function in Java:

```
static void passTest (box i)
{
   i.value++;
   i = new box(7);
}

public static void main (String [ ] args)
{
   box j = new box(5);
   passTest(j);
   System.out.println("J is " + j.value);
}
```

None of the parameter passing options in C++ matches the Java semantics

In Java, i is a reference to j, and thus the change in i will alter j. But reassigning i to a new value has no effect on j. (An accurate description is to say that a Java parameter is an object reference that is passed by value.) The following table of the final value for j illustrates that the Java parameter passing mechanism is different from both pass by value and pass by reference in C++.

	value of j
C++ pass by value, Java primitive	5
C++ pass by reference	7
Java objects	6

You should study this mechanism carefully to determine how the three different results are produced.

3.7.2   References as Results

References can also be used as a result type for a function. There are two reasons for doing so:

- A reference can be used as the target of an assignment. Therefore a function call that returns a reference can be used on the left side of an assignment.

- Returning a reference is more efficient than returning a value. Therefore large values can be returned by reference.

A good example of the first case is a subscript operator in a string or vector class. In Chapter 4 we present one such example. In that example the **string** class overlays a more primitive array of character values, and the subscript operator simply returns a reference to an individual character:

```
class string {
    .
    .
    .
    char & operator [ ] (unsigned int index)
        { return buffer[index]; }



    .
    .
    .
private:
    char * buffer;
};
```

The subscript operator returns a reference, so individual character positions can be changed by using an assignment:

```
string text = "name:";
text[0] = 'f'; // change name to fame
```

The second reason to use a reference as a result is that returning a reference is much more efficient than creating and returning a new value. However, care must be exercised in doing so. As we show in Chapter 4, a reference must always refer to an object that is known to exist. Returning a reference to a value that will soon be deleted, such as a local variable, leads to eventual disaster. The following example illustrates the hazard:

```
double & min (double data[ ], int n)
{
    double minVal = data[0];
    for (int i = 1; i < n; i++)
```

```
    if (data[i] < minVal)
        minVal = data;
    return minVal; // error, reference to local
}
```

Test Your Understanding

1. What is a pointer?

2. What are three reasons why pointers are useful in programs?

3. What is a null pointer?

4. What does it mean to dereference a pointer? How is this operation written in C++?

5. What is the relationship between addresses and pointers? How can the address of a variable be assigned to a different pointer variable?

6. What is the difference between modifying a pointer variable and modifying the value that the pointer references? Give an example to illustrate each type of modification.

7. What is the difference between a pointer to a constant and a constant pointer?

8. What is special about the void * pointer type?

9. What does the built-in function sizeof take as argument? What does it compute?

10. What is an equivalent synonym for the arrow operation p− >a?

11. What are some of the ways that pointers and arrays are similar?

12. What is the difference between a pointer and a reference?

13. How is pass by reference different from pass by value? How is each different from the Java parameter passing mechanism?

14. Given the function definition

```
void swap (int & x, int & y)
{
    int temp = x;
    x = y;
    y = temp;
}
```

describe the effect of the following statements:

```
int data[10];
data[3] = 7;
int i = 3;
swap (i, data[i]);
```

15. What are two reasons that a function might return a reference type as a result?

4

Memory Management

In Java the task of memory management is largely conducted in the background, just beyond the issues of concern to the typical programmer. This *can* be an advantage, as it eliminates a complex task, allowing the programmer to concentrate on more application-specific details. But it also means that the Java programmer has little control over memory management.

The C++ programmer must always be aware of how memory management is being performed

In C++, in contrast, memory management is explicitly under the direction of the programmer. If properly used, this can work to the programmers advantage, permitting much more efficient use of memory than is possible with Java. But if improperly used (or, more often, ignored), memory management issues can bloat a program at run time or make a program very inefficient. For this reason, writing effective C++ programs requires an understanding of how the memory management system operates.

Because the programmer is responsible for memory management in C++, a variety of errors are possible that are rare or unusual in Java. They include the following:

C++ does not perform dataflow analysis to detect potentially undefined local variables

- Using a value before it has been initialized. (The language Java requires a dataflow analysis that will detect many of these errors. The language C++ has no such requirement.)

- Allocating memory for a value and then not deleting it once it is no longer being used. (This will cause a long-running program to consume more and more memory, until it fails catastrophically.)

- Using a value after it has been freed. (Once returned to the memory management system, the contents of a freed location are typically overwritten in an unpredictable way. Thus the contents of a freed value will be unpredictable.)

We illustrate each of these potential errors with examples in the remainder of this chapter.

4.1 The Memory Model

To understand how memory management is performed in C++, you first need to appreciate the C++ memory model, which differs fundamentally from the Java memory model. In many ways, the C++ model is much closer to the actual machine representation than is the Java memory model. This closeness permits efficient implementation, but at the expense of increased diligence on the part of the programmer.

Stack-resident values are created when a procedure is entered and deleted when the procedure exits

In C++ there is a clear distinction between memory values that are *stack resident* and those that are *heap resident*. Stack-resident values are created automatically when a procedure is entered or exited, whereas heap-resident values must be explicitly created using the new operator.

4.2 Stack-Resident Memory Values

An activation record *is sometimes called an* activation frame *or a* stack frame

Both the stack and the heap are internal data structures managed by a runtime system. Of the two, the stack is much more orderly. Values on a stack are strongly tied to procedure entry and exit. When a procedure begins execution, a new section of the stack is created. This stack segment holds parameters, the return address for the caller, saved internal registers and other machine-specific information, and space for local variables. The section of a stack specifically devoted to one procedure is often called an *activation record*.

In Java, only primitive values are truly stack resident. Objects and arrays are always allocated on the heap. Compare the following two example procedures. Each creates a local integer, a local array, and an object instance.

```
void test () // Java
{
    int i;
    int a[ ] = new int[10];
    anObject ao = new anObject();
```

```
       .
       .
       .
}

void test () // C++
{
    int i;
    int a[10];
    anObject ao;
       .
       .
       .
}
```

In the Java procedure only the primitive integer value is actually allocated space on the stack by the declaration. Both the array and the object value must be explicitly created (as heap-resident values), using the new operator. In C++ all three values will reside on the stack, and none require any actions beyond the declaration to bring them into existence.

Procedure invocations execute in a very orderly fashion. If procedure A invokes procedure B and B in turn invokes C, then procedure C must terminate before B will continue with execution, and B in turn must terminate before A will resume. This property allows activation records to be managed efficiently and orderly. When a procedure is called, an activation record is created and pushed on the stack, and when the procedure returns, the activation record can be popped from the stack. A pointer can be used to point to the current top of stack. Allocation of a section of the stack then simply means moving this pointer value forward by the required amount.

The efficiencies of stack memory are not without cost. There are two major drawbacks to the use of the stack for variable storage:

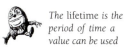
The lifetime is the period of time a value can be used

- The *lifetime* of stack-resident memory values is tied to procedure entry and exit. This means that stack-resident values cease to exist when a procedure returns. An attempt to use a stack-resident value after it has been deleted will typically result in error.

- The *size* of stack-resident memory values must be known at compile time, which is when the structure of the activation record is laid out.

4.2.1   Lifetime Errors

An important fact to remember is that once a procedure returns from execution, any stack resident values are deleted and no longer accessible. A *reference* to such a value (see Chapter 3) will no longer be valid, although it may for a time appear to work. Here are some examples:

```
// WARNING---Program contains an error
char * readALine ()
{
    char buffer[1000]; // declare a buffer for the line
    gets(buffer); // read the line
    return buffer; // return text of line
}
```

This procedure will return a pointer to the array buffer;[1] however, the memory for the buffer will have been deleted as part of the procedure return. The pointer will reference values that may or may not be correct and will almost certainly be overwritten once the next procedure is called.

Contrast this with an equivalent Java procedure:

```
String readALine (BufferedInput inp) throws IOException
{
    // create a buffer for the line
    String line =  inp.readLine();
    return line;
}
```

Although the variable line is declared inside the procedure, the *value* assigned to the variable will be heap resident. Therefore this value will continue to exist, even after the procedure returns.

Function return values are by no means the only way to create dangling references. An assignment to a global variable or a by-reference parameter can do the same thing, as shown in the following:

```
char * lineBuffer; // global declaration of pointer to buffer

// WARNING---Program contains an error
void readALine ()
{
    char buffer[1000]; // declare a buffer for the line
    gets(buffer); // read the line
```

---

[1] The close relationship in C++ between arrays and pointers is discussed in detail in Chapter 3. It should also be noted that gets is a problematic function, for many of the reasons cited in this chapter. Better solutions to this problem are provided by the Stream I/O package described in Chapter 10. However, gets is part of the legacy C++ inherited from C, and is still commonly found in many programs.

```
    lineBuffer = buffer; // set pointer to reference buffer
}
```

Some of the more sophisticated C++ compilers will warn about such errors, but you should not depend on their being caught.

4.2.2   Size Errors

For object-oriented programming, one of the most severe restrictions of stack-based memory management derives from the fact that the positions of values within the activation record are determined at compile time. For primitive values and pointers this is a small concern. However, it is an issue for arrays and objects. For arrays, it means that the array bound must be known at compile time. For objects, it means a limitation on the degree to which values can be polymorphic.

Array Allocations

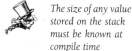
The size of any value stored on the stack must be known at compile time

Stack-resident arrays must have a size that is known at compile time. Often, programmers avoid this problem by allocating an array with a size that is purposely too large. An earlier example, which we repeat here, illustrated this technique. In this case the programmer is reading lines of input from a file and has allocated the character array to hold 200 elements, on the assumption that no line will have more than this number of characters:

```
// WARNING---Program contains an error
char buffer[200]; // making array global avoids deletion error
char * readALine ()
{
    gets(buffer); // read the line
    return buffer;
}
```

Never assume that, just because an array is big, it will always be "big enough"

Problems can occur because array bounds are not checked in C++ at run time.[2] Should an overly long line be encountered in the file, the buffer will simply be exceeded, and the values read will flow over into whatever happens to follow

---

[2] See Chapter 3 for further discussion of this issue. Note that an alternative function, fgets, permits the buffer size to be specified. As a general matter, fgets should be preferred over gets for just this reason. However, the type of error discussed here arises in many situations, so the point is still valid.

the array in the activation record. This will have the effect of changing the values of other variables unpredictably, with generally infelicitous results.

It *is* possible to create arrays with sizes determined at run time by using heap-resident values. This is done as in Java, except that the programmer must explicitly free the memory when it no longer is required (see Section 4.3).

```
char * buffer;
int newSize;
.
:    // newSize is given some value
.
buffer = new Char[newSize]; // create an array of the given size
.
:
.
delete [ ] buffer; // delete buffer when no longer being used
```

The Slicing Problem

Java programmers are used to object values being *polymorphic* (see Chapter 6). That is, a variable declared as maintaining a value of one class can, in fact, be holding a value derived from a child class. In the class hierarchy shown in Figure 4.1,[3] class A is extended by a new class B, which overrides the virtual method whoAmI.[4] In both Java and C++, it is legal to assign a value derived from class B to a variable declared as holding an instance of class A:

```
A instanceOfA; // declare instances of
B instanceOfB; // class A and B

instanceOfA = instanceOfB;

instanceOfA.whoAmI(); // question: what will happen?
```

However, the effect of this assignment will differ in the two languages. The Java programmer will expect that, although the declaration of instanceOfA is class A, the value will continue to be that of a B, and thus the method invoked will be that found in class B.

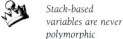 *Stack-based variables are never polymorphic*

This polymorphic behavior conflicts with the stack-based memory allocation model. Note that the values of class B are larger than the values of class A, since

---

[3] Output is here produced using the statement printf, which is one of two output techniques commonly encountered in C++ programs. The topic if I/O libraries is discussed in Chapter 10.

[4] See Chapter 6 for a more complete discussion of the keyword virtual.

Figure 4.1 A Class Hierarchy for Illustrating the Slicing Problem

```
class A {
public:
   // constructor
   A () : dataOne(2) { }

   // identification method
   virtual void whoAmI () { printf("class A"); }
private:
   int dataOne;
};

class B : public A {
public:
   // constructor
   B () : dataTwo(4) { }

   // identification method
   virtual void whoAmI () { printf("class B"); }
private:
   int dataTwo;
};
```

they include an additional data field (namely, the inherited field dataOne and the field dataTwo defined in class B). To maintain the efficiencies of the stack-based memory allocation, these additional fields are simply sliced away when the assignment occurs. Thus the value ceases to be an instance of class B and simply becomes an instance of class A:

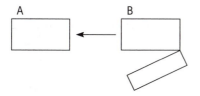

Therefore, it is not surprising that the method executed by the invocation of whoAmI will be that of class A, not that of class B. This is true regardless of whether the method whoAmI was declared virtual.

The message passing rules for pointers and references are different from those for simple variables

Note, however, that slicing does not occur with references or pointers:

```
A & referenceToA = instanceOfB;
referenceToA.whoAmI(); // will print class B


B * pointerToB  = new B();
A * pointerToA = pointerToB();
pointerToA->whoAmI(); // will print class B
```

Slicing occurs only with objects that are stack-resident. For this reason, the majority of objects in many C++ programs are made heap-resident. The Java programmer learning C++ should be aware of several pitfalls when using heap allocation.

4.3   Heap-Resident Memory Values

Heap-resident values are created with the new operator. Memory for such values resides on the *heap*, or *free store*, which is a separate part of memory from the stack. Typically, such values are accessed through a pointer, which will often reside on the stack. The following contrasting code fragments in C++ and Java illustrate this point:

The parentheses are omitted from a new statement if there are no arguments for the constructor

```
void test () // Java
{
    A anA = new A();
    .
    .
    .
}


void test () // C++
{
    A * anA = new A; // note pointer declaration
    if (anA == 0) ... // handle no memory situation
    .
    .
    .
    delete anA;
}
```

Here anA will reside on the stack (in both Java and C++), but the value it references will reside on the heap:

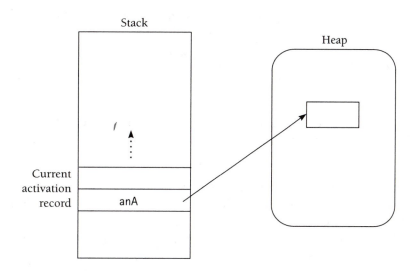

The language Java hides the use of this pointer value, and programmers seldom need be concerned with it. In C++, however, the pointer declaration is explicitly stated.

Not all compilers will throw an exception when memory has been exhausted

In Java, if a memory request cannot be satisfied, an OutOfMemory exception is thrown. Newer versions of C++ will likewise throw a bad_alloc exception. In contrast, earlier versions of the language would simply return a null pointer value when a request could not be satisfied. It is therefore important to test for this condition and take appropriate action (such as throwing an exception yourself) if it occurs.

A garbage collection system searches out and recovers unused memory

A more important difference relates to the recovery of heap-based memory. Java incorporates a *garbage collection system* into its run-time library. The garbage collection system monitors the use of dynamically allocated variables and will automatically recover and reuse memory that is no longer being accessed. However, C++ leaves this task to the programmer. Dynamically allocated memory must be handed back to the heap manager, using the **delete** operator. There are two forms of this operator, both of which have been used in examples presented earlier in this chapter. The deletion of an individual object is performed by simply naming the pointer variable, as in the preceding example. Deleting an array requires the use of a pair of empty square brackets. An example showing this syntax was presented earlier in Section 4.2.2.

Because memory recovery must be an explicit concern of the programmer, four types of errors are common:

- Forgetting to allocate a heap-resident value and using a pointer as if it were referencing a legitimate value.

- Forgetting to hand unused memory back to the heap manager.

- Attempting to use memory values after they have been handed back to the heap manager.

- Invoking the delete statement on the same value more than once, thereby passing the same memory value back to the heap manager.

Uninitialized values in C++ are not only not reported by the compiler, but their initial values are generally garbage

In Java the first type of error, if not caught by the compiler, will generally raise a null pointer exception. C++ compilers are not obligated to try to detect the use of variables before they have been set—and few will. Furthermore, the initial contents of memory are generally not determined. Thus an uninitialized pointer value will sometimes contain a legal memory address even before it has been set, although there is no way to know where in memory it is pointing to. Attempting to read from such a value or assigning to it will cause an unpredictable result.

A memory leak is an allocation of memory that is never recovered

The second type of error is called a *memory leak*. Often such leaks can occur without any harmful effects. However, in a long-running program or if memory allocation occurs in a situation that is executed repeatedly, such leaks will cause the memory requirements for the program to increase over time. Eventually the heap manager will be unable to service a request for further memory, and the program will halt. Leaks are often the result of successive assignments to the same pointer variable:

```
AnObject * a;
.
.
.
a = new AnObject();
.
.
.
a = new AnObject(); // leak, old reference is now lost
```

The third type of error sometimes occurs as the result of an overzealous attempt to avoid the second error. In this case, memory is passed back to the heap manager before all references to the value have been deleted. As part of managing and recycling heap-resident values, the heap manager often stores pertinent information in the value. For example, the heap manager may keep a list of similarly sized blocks of memory and store in each block a pointer to the next element. Thus, after a value is deleted, the contents are often overwritten. Reading from such a value will produce garbage, and writing to such a value will confound the heap manager. Both errors are typically catastrophic.

Depending on the sophistication of the memory manager, the fourth error may or may not be severe. Some heap managers can detect this condition. Other heap managers will not notice the error, but the internal data structures used by the heap manager will be put into an inconsistent state. This, too, can result in unpredicatable errors.

Always match memory allocations and deletions

A simple rule of thumb is that every time the new operator is used, the programmer should be able to identify where and under what circumstances the associated delete directive will be issued. Two techniques are frequently used to help simplify the management of heap values:

- Hide the allocation and release of dynamic memory values inside an object. The object is therefore the "owner" of the heap-resident value, and is "responsible" for memory management. For example, memory management is often tied to the lifetime of the object, which can sometimes be reliably predicted (for example, the object is stack-resident). This technique is applicable only when there is but one pointer to the heap-resident value.

- If it is not possible to designate a single "owner" for a heap-resident value, it is difficult to know who should be responsible for deleting the value once it is no longer being referenced. This problem can be solved by maintaining, as part of the value, a *reference count* that indicates the number of pointers to the value. When this count is decremented to zero, the value can be recovered.

We illustrate each of these techniques by developing a data abstraction for the *String* data type.

4.3.1   Encapsulating Memory Management

String literals in C++, unlike in Java, are very low-level abstractions. A string literal in C++ is treated as an array of character values, and the only permitted operations are those common to all arrays. The String data type in Java is designed to provide a higher level of abstraction. A version of this data structure is provided in the new STL (see Chapter 9). It is also an example commonly found in many introductory C++ texts. The version we present here is skeletal, describing only those features related to memory management. More complete implementations are described in [Budd 98a, Budd 94, Lippman 91, Coplien 92].

The class description for String is shown in Figure 4.2. As is common in C++, the shorter methods (in this case, all but one method) are provided by using inline definitions in the class heading. Longer methods are used in an implementation file, outside the class definition.

Figure 4.2   The Class String (Version One)

```
class String {
public:
   // constructors
   String () : buffer(0) { }
   String (const char * right) : buffer(0)
      { resize(strlen(right)); strcpy(buffer, right); }
   String (const String & right) : buffer(0)
      { resize(strlen(right.buffer)); strcpy(buffer, right.buffer); }

   // destructor
   ~String () { delete [ ] buffer; }

   // assignment
   void operator = (const String & right)
      { resize(strlen(right.buffer)); strcpy(buffer, right.buffer); }

private:
   void resize (int size);
   char *  buffer;
};
```

String variables can be declared with no initialization or can be initialized with a literal string text, a character array (that is, a pointer to a character), or another string value:

```
string a;
string b = "abc";
string c = b;
```

One way to manage dynamically allocated memory is to make an object responsible for managing the memory

The important feature of this string abstraction is that there is a one-to-one matching of **String** objects to dynamically allocated buffers. Every string has one buffer, and every buffer is "owned" by a specific **String**. This buffer is created by the method **resize**:

```
void String::resize(int size)
{
   if (buffer == 0) // no previous allocation
      buffer = new char[1 + size];
   else if (size > strlen(buffer)) {
      delete [ ] buffer; // recover old value
```

```
        buffer = new char[1 + size];
    }
}
```

If one has not yet been allocated, a buffer of the requested size is created. (The one extra character is for the null character inserted at the end of a string by the function **strcpy**.) Otherwise, if the current buffer is too small for the requested number of characters, the current buffer is returned to the heap manager and a new buffer is created.

A string variable can be assigned a value from another string variable:

```
a = b;
```

In this case, a *copy* of the contents of the right-hand side is created:

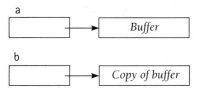

We have shown how the dynamic buffer allocation will take place in the constructor. We have also shown how this buffer may be deleted and replaced with another as the result of an assignment. If we now ask our fundamental question, For every **new** is there a matching **delete**? we realize that we have not yet discussed one remaining case. What happens if a variable of type **String** is destroyed? This will happen, for example, when local variables are recovered at the end of a procedure. To handle this case, C++ provides a mechanism to perform actions immediately before the point of destruction. This capability is provided by a procedure called the *destructor*. The destructor for a class is a nonargument procedure with a name formed by insertion of a tilde before the class name. The destructor shown in Figure 4.2 simply deletes the dynamically allocated buffer. With this facility, we can now match all allocations and deletes, ensuring that no memory leaks will occur.

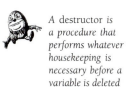
A destructor is a procedure that performs whatever housekeeping is necessary before a variable is deleted

Do not confuse the destructor with the **delete** operator. The **delete** operator is the function used to actually return memory to the heap manager. The destructor is charged with whatever "housecleaning" tasks are necessary before a variable disappears. Often, this housecleaning involves memory management—but not always. In the next section we present a destructor that performs more than memory management.

The concept of a destructor in C++ should also not be confused with the notion of the **finalize** method in Java. Destructors are tied to *variables*, whereas the finalize method is tied to a *value*. The destructor will be invoked when a variable is about to be destroyed—for example, as soon as it goes out of scope when a procedure returns—or when the variable itself is dynamically allocated and has been the target of a delete. The finalize method in Java is invoked when the value holding the method is about to be recovered by the garbage collector. There is no guarantee in Java when this will occur, if ever. Thus programmers cannot make assumptions concerning behavior in Java based on the execution of code in the finalize method. In this regard, the C++ programmer is on slightly safer ground, as the rules for when a destructor will be invoked are carefully spelled out by the language definition.

An Execution Tracer

Constructors and destructors can be used for a variety of nested activities

A clever example that illustrates the use of constructors and destructors is an execution tracer. The class Trace takes as argument a string value. The constructor prints a message using the string, and the destructor prints a different message using the same string:

```
class Trace {
public:
    // constructor and destructor
    Trace (string);
    ~Trace ();
private:
    string name;
};


Trace::Trace (string t) : name(t)
{
    cout << "Entering " << name << endl;
}


Trace::~Trace ()
{
    cout << "Exiting " << name << endl;
}
```

To trace the flow of function invocations, the programmer simply creates a declaration for a dummy variable of type Trace in each procedure to be traced:

```
void procedureOne ()
{
    Trace dummy("Procedure One");
```

```
    .
    .
    .
    procedureTwo(); // proc one invokes proc two
}

void procedureTwo ()
{
    Trace dummy("Procedure Two");
    .
    .
    if (x < 5) {
        Trace dumTrue("x test is true");
        .
        .
        .
    }
    else {
        Trace dumFalse("x test is false");
        .
        .
        .
    }
    .
    .
    .
}
```

The ability to declare variables local to a block allows the programmer to use trace variables to follow the effect of conditional or loop statements. By their output, the values of type Trace will indicate the flow of execution. A typical output from this program might be:

```
Entering Procedure One
Entering Procedure Two
Entering x test is true
.
.
.
Exiting x test is true
Exiting Procedure Two
Exiting Procedure One
```

The auto_ptr Class

The relationship between a string value and the underlying buffer is a pattern that is repeated many times in programs. That is, there is an object that must dynamically allocate another memory value in order to perform its intended task.

However, the lifetime of the dynamic value is tied to the lifetime of the original object; it exists as long as the original object exists and should be eliminated when the original object ceases to exist.

To simplify the management of memory in this case, the STL implements a useful type named auto_ptr (see Section A.5 in Appendix A). A simplified version of auto_ptr may be described as follows:[5]

```
template <class T>
class auto_ptr {
public:
    auto_ptr (T *p) : ptr(p) { }
    auto_ptr () : ptr(0) { }
    ~auto_ptr() { delete ptr; }

    void operator = (T* right)
    {
        delete ptr;
        ptr = right;
    }
private:
    T * ptr;
};
```

The actual class is more robust and will handle assignments and copies, but this form illustrates its key features. An auto_ptr object simply holds a pointer value and will delete the memory referenced by the pointer when it itself is destroyed.

A revised string class that used auto pointers would look like:

```
class string {
    .
    .
    .
private:
    auto_ptr<char> buffer;
};

void String::resize(int size)
{
    if ((buffer == 0) || (size > strlen(buffer)))
        buffer = new char[1 + size];
}
```

---

[5] This class description uses templates, which are described in Chapter 9.

In this form, implementing a destructor for the **string** class would not be necessary. The default destructor would invoke the destructor for the auto pointer field, which, in turn, would return the buffer memory to the heap manager.

Auto pointers should be used whenever there is a one-to-one correspondence between objects and an internal heap-allocated memory and the lifetime of the internal object is tied to the lifetime of the surrounding container.

4.3.2   Reference Counts

In many situations, two or more objects need to share a common data area. We could imagine, for example, wanting to change the semantics for the assignment of strings so that two strings would share a common internal buffer. That is, subsequent to the statement

```
a = c;
```

both variables **a** and **c** would reference the same buffer:

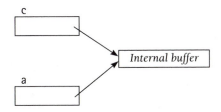

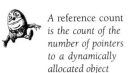

A reference count is the count of the number of pointers to a dynamically allocated object

The difficulty with this interpretation is that we no longer have a single unambiguous object that can be said to "own" the dynamically allocated value and can therefore be charged with disposing of it when it is no longer needed. A solution to this problem is to augment the dynamic value with a count of the number of pointers that reference it. This count is called a *reference count*. Care is needed to ensure that the count is accurate; whenever a new pointer is added the count is incremented, and whenever a pointer is removed the count is decremented.

Figure 4.3 shows a revision of the **String** abstraction that incorporates these changes. The method **resize** has here been replaced with **reassign**, which replaces the current string reference with another. In doing so, it both decrements the reference count on the old string reference and increments the count on the new. Performing the increment first ensures that the procedure will work in the special case where a variable is assigned to itself. If the reference count for the old value becomes zero, the memory for the entire string reference is returned to the heap manager, using the method **delete**. Before recovering the memory, the

Figure 4.3 The Class String (Version Two)

```
class String {
public:
   // constructors
   String () : p(0) { }
   String (const char * right) : p(0)
      { reassign(new StringReference(right)); }
   String (const String & right) : p(0) { reassign(right.p); }

   // destructor
   ~String () { reassign(0); }

   // assignment
   void operator = (const String & right) { reassign(right.p); }

private:
   void reassign (StringReference *);

   class StringReference {
      public:
         int count;
         char * buffer;
         StringReference(const char * right);
         ~StringReference() { delete [ ] buffer; }
   }

   StringReference * p;
}

void String::StringReference::StringReference(const char * right)
{
   count = 0;
   buffer = new Char[1 + strlen(right)];
   strcpy(buffer, right);
}
```

heap manager will execute the destructor for the string reference being deleted.
This destructor in turn will return the buffer to the heap manager:

```
   void String::reassign(String::StringReference * np)
   {
      if (np) // increment count on new value
         np->count += 1;
```

```
    if (p) { // decrement reference counts on old value
       p->count -= 1;
       if (p->count == 0)
          delete p;
    }
    p = np; // change binding
}
```

The structure of the object holding both the reference count and the buffer is defined by a nested class declared within the body of the String class. Note that, although there are superficial syntactic similarities, there are some semantic differences between nested classes in C++ and inner classes in Java. We discuss these differences in more detail in Chapter 5.

The values held by reference counts can be illustrated by tracing the execution of a simple program. Imagine the following:

```
string g; // global string value

void test ()
{
   string a = "abc";
   string b = "xyz";
   string c;
   c = a;
   a = b;
   g = b;
}
```

The following table summarizes the reference counts associated with the values `"abc"` and `"xyz"` as the program executes.

Statement	"abc"	"xyz"
`string a = "abc";`	1	0
`string b = "xyz";`	1	1
`string c;`	1	1
`c = a;`	2	1
`a = b;`	1	2
`g = b;`	2	2
End of execution		
Destructor for c	1	2
Destructor for b	1	1
Destructor for a	1	0

We are left with a single reference (namely, the global variable g) pointing to the value `"abc"`. The value `"xyz"` will have been recovered when the reference count reached zero, that is, when the variable a was deleted.

Test Your Understanding

1. What are some of the advantages of having the programmer control memory management? What are some of the disadvantages?

2. What is a stack-resident value? When is it allocated? When is it deleted?

3. What are characteristics of stack-resident values that are not necessarily characteristics of heap-resident values?

4. Explain the error in the following program fragment:

```
char * secretMessage()
{
    char messageBuffer[100];
    strcpy (messageBuffer "Eat Ovaltean!");
    return messageBuffer;
}
```

5. Explain the slicing problem and state the circumstances under which it will occur.

6. What is a heap-resident memory value? How is this value allocated?

7. What are the four types of errors that can occur in the recovery of heap-resident values?

8. What is a destructor? When is it invoked?

9. What is a reference count?

10. The following statement is legal. It will create a temporary string value for the right-hand expression and then assign the temporary to the left-hand variable, before destroying the temporary. Assume that the reference counting scheme is being used to implement the **string** data type and trace the reference counts on the various internal buffer values.

```
string text = "initial text";
text = "new text";
```

Class Definition

The most obvious area of similarity between Java and C++ is in the structure of a class definition. However, the obvious similarities between the two are superficial; behind them are many syntactic and subtle semantic differences. In this and subsequent chapters, we explore some of these differences.

5.1 Obvious Similarities and Minor Differences

A class definition in Java (Figure 5.1) is similar to a class definition in C++ (Figure 5.2) in that they both begin with the keyword class and both are demarcated by a pair of curly brackets.

Then there are the differences, some of which are minor. Class definitions in C++ are statements and must end with a semicolon. Class definitions in Java have no semicolon. Class definitions in C++ are divided into major sections by the keywords private, protected, and public, which are sectioning commands followed by a colon. Java applies these modifiers to each data field or method individually, omitting the colon. Java uses the keyword extends to indicate inheritance from a parent class, and C++ uses a colon and the keyword public. (In Chapter 6 we point out that the keywords private or protected could also be used here, although the meaning is then slightly different.) Java permits the modifier public to be applied to an entire class, whereas all classes in C++ have this attribute. (The more important difference is between classes that are *not* declared as public in Java. The closest C++ equivalent to them is produced by using a nonpublic namespace, a relatively recent addition to the C++ language. See Section 12.7 for a discussion of namespaces.)

Figure 5.1   A Typical Class Definition in Java

```
class box {

    public box (int v) { val = v; }
    public int value() { return val; }

    private int val;
}
```

Figure 5.2   A Typical Class Definition in C++

```
class box {
public:
    box (int v) { val = v; }
    int value() { return val; }

private:
    int val;
};
```

Once past the minor differences, we enter the realm of more substantive issues. In the following sections we explore many of these issues.

5.2   Separation of Class and Implementation

A class definition in Java is a single unit, and everything related to the class is found between the opening and closing curly braces. In C++ the class definition is the starting point, defining only the structure and interface for the class. Many features associated with the class will be found outside the class definition, sometimes even outside the file in which the class definition appears.

In Java all methods are defined within the class itself. In C++ this is true only for the smallest methods. Furthermore, there is a semantic difference between methods defined within a class and those not.

A method that is provided with a definition as part of the class body is called an *inline* method. Such a method may (at the discretion of the C++ compiler) be expanded inline at the point of call. That is, when the method function is invoked, rather than issuing a function call instruction, the compiler may elect to expand the body of the method directly into the code being produced for the caller.

 Invoking an inline *method does not generate a function call, but rather expands the body at the point of call*

The advantage of expanding a method inline is one of speed, as such a function avoids the overhead of a procedure call statement. However, this advantage is purchased at a price of space and complexity. The code for the caller may become larger, and the code is (internally to the compiler at least, if not for the programmer) more complex. For this reason, inline definitions should be used only for short method bodies. A good rule of thumb is to use inline definitions only for assignment statements and return statements or, at most, a single conditional statement. Never use an inline definition for a code fragment that contains a loop or a recursive function call.

Use inline definitions only for methods that are short

When methods are not defined inline, they must be provided with a definition elsewhere. As methods in different classes may have the same name, the method definition must be tied to the appropriate class. This is accomplished by defining a method using a *fully qualified* function name. The following code illustrates this:

Method definitions in C++ can be separate from the class definition

```
void Link::addBefore (int val, List * theList)
{
   // create a new link
   Link * newLink = new Link(val, this, backwardLink);
   // put it into the appropriate place
   if (backwardLink == 0) // replacing first element in list
      theList->firstLink = newLink;
   else { // inserting into the middle of the list
      backwardLink->forwardLink = newLink;
      backwardLink = newLink;
      }
}
```

The double colon indicates that full qualification is being employed. The prefix indicates the class (Link, in this example), and the text after the double colon indicates the function name (addBefore). This method definition appears outside the class definition. The qualified name can be thought of as similar to a person's full name; the name Tom Smith identifies a unique individual better than simply the first name Tom, which may have many different associations.

5.2.1   Interface and Implementation Files

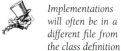
Implementations will often be in a different file from the class definition

A further form of separation in C++ involves the division of a program into multiple files. A class that is used in many files is normally described in an *interface* file. Traditionally, the extension .h is used in the interface file name.

The interface file describes just the bare bones of the services provided by a class but not how the class goes about implementing that behavior. Method bodies are found in a separate file, called the *implementation* file. Traditionally, implementation files are given file names ending in **.cpp** or **.c++**.

In C++ a class need not be defined in a file with the same name

C++ is much less concerned than Java with the relationship between class and file names. It is not necessary for a class to be defined in a file of the same name, although adopting this as a convention certainly makes file management a bit easier.

Every file that must use a class will include the appropriate interface file, using a statement such as the following:

```
# include <libClass.h>
# include "myClass.h"
```

The angle brackets surrounding the file name are used to indicate where the requested interface file is to be found. Angle brackets indicate "system" interface files—those that are provided as part of standard libraries and that are found in the designated location for such libraries. Quotation marks are used for immediate interface files—those that are found in the same directory as the program being compiled.

The include statement differs from the import statement in Java, in that the include statement performs a textual inclusion of the given file at the point where the include statement is written. Note also that no semicolon follows an include statement, whereas a semicolon necessarily follows an import statement in Java.

5.2.2   The inline Directive

Normally, class definitions are found in an interface file, and methods are found in an implementation file. For classes, an exception is made if a class is used in only one file, when it can simply be written in the implementation file. Similarly, method implementations will occasionally be written in an interface file. When they are, an inline directive can be used to indicate that the function can be expanded inline at a point of call, exactly as though the method had been written in a class description.

Inline methods are most often needed to overcome the more stringent naming restrictions in C++. Names in general in C++ must be known to the compiler at the first point they are used. In contrast, Java names can often be defined subsequent to their first use. For example, a method may need to access another feature that is not known at the time the class definition is processed—but is known shortly thereafter. In such cases, the definition of the name is given between the class definition and the description of the method body. If the method body is sufficiently short, it can then be marked as inline. We present an example of this approach later in this chapter.

Template methods (see Chapter 9) are also normally found in an interface file, regardless of their size.

Virtual methods (see Chapter 4) should not be declared as inline, as the compiler is not able to produce inline code even if requested by the user.

5.2.3   Prototypes

Another common feature found in an interface file is a list of function prototypes. In order to perform strong type checking, function type signatures must be known before a function can be invoked. A *function type signature* is a description of the types of all the arguments, as well as the return type for a function.

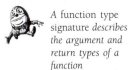

A function type signature describes the argument and return types of a function

A function prototype is simply a function heading, with the function body and, optionally, the argument names removed. Thus the only information conveyed by the prototype is the function name, the argument types, and the result type. The following are some examples:

```
int max (int, int);
int min (int a, int b); // argument names are optional
complex abs (complex &); // can use user defined types
bool operator < (distance &, distance &); // prototype for
                                          // operator
```

Some C++ compilers will issue warnings if a function is defined without a prior prototype directive.

A curious holdover from language C is occasionally encountered. In earlier versions of C, a prototype with an empty argument list such as

```
int fun ();
```

indicated only the existence of a function by the given name. No information concerning the arguments, if any, was implied. Instead, to indicate that the function took no arguments, it was necessary to explicitly indicate the fact, using the keyword void:

```
int fun (void); // no arguments, returns an int
```

The language C++ recognizes both declarations, but unlike in C the assumption is that if no arguments are given, none are required.

5.2.4   External Declarations

A variable used in two or more files must be declared as external

The **extern** modifier to a declaration indicates that a global variable is defined in another file but will be used in the current file:

```
extern int size;
extern char buffer[ ]; // array limits don't have to be given
extern ObjectType anObject;
```

The declaration informs the linker that the value being named is used in two or more files but that it should nevertheless refer to only one object. Such declarations are most generally found in header files, although there is no restriction on their appearing in implementation files.

Another form of the statement is used to indicate that a C++ program is being linked with a function written in a different language:

```
// declare strcmp is written in C, not C++
extern "C" int strcmp (const char *, const char *);
```

5.3   Forward References

Both function and class names must be defined before they can be used

The language C++ resolves names at the point they are used. This means that, when a class name is used (say, in a declaration) the name must already be known to be a class. Similarly, when a function is invoked, a declaration (in prototype at least) for the function must already have been seen. In Java references are resolved only after an entire file has been processed.

Prototypes are used to get around the problem of function definitions. For classes the language permits a *forward declaration*. A forward declaration asserts that a particular name represents a class but gives no further information. Such a declaration permits pointers to be declared to the class but not to invoke methods defined by the class or the creation of instances of the class.

To illustrate, let's assume that we want to implement a linked list abstraction, using two classes: List and Link. Instances of List will simply reference the first Link in the collection. Thereafter each link will point to the next, and to the previous.

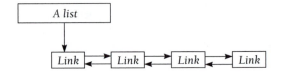

The class List must include a pointer to a Link; however, the class Link might also want to reference features in List. In the following example we illustrate this possibility by writing the method addBefore, which adds a new value immediately before a given link. The code for this method was presented earlier. The solution to the referencing problem is first to provide a forward declaration for the Link class before the definition of List. The forward definition is sufficient to permit the declaration of a data field holding a pointer to an object of type Link, although not the execution of any methods associated with the class:

```
class Link; // forward declaration

class List {
public:
    .
    .
    .
private:
    Link * firstLink; // permitted, since class Link is declared

    void push_front (int val);
};

class Link { // now provide the full link implementation
public:
    // data fields are public
    int value;
    Link * forwardLink;
    Link * backwardLink;

    // constructor defined inline
    Link (int v, Link * f, Link * b)
    {
        value = v;
        forwardLink = f;
        backwardLink = b;
    }

    // prototype, definition given elsewhere
    // requires knowledge of class List
    void addBefore (int val, List * theList);
};
```

This situation—involving a pair of mutually recursive classes—is commonly where an explicitly inline method definition is appropriate. For example, the method push_front in class List is a suitable candidate for inlining, but can only be written once the class definition for Link has been seen because it uses methods from that class:

```
inline void List::push_front (int val)
{
    if (firstElement == 0) // adding to empty list
        firstElement = new Link(val, 0, 0);
    else  // else add before first element
        firstElement->addBefore(val, this);
}
```

5.4   Constructors and Initialization

Constructors *tie together the tasks of creation and initialization*

Constructors in Java and in C++ are designed to serve the same purpose, namely, to tie together the two tasks of creation and initialization, thereby ensuring that no value is created without being initialized and that no value is initialized more than once. In both languages a constructor is written as a method that shares the same name as a class. Beyond these similarities, there are a number of important differences.

5.4.1   Default and Copy Constructors

In C++ two types of constructors are used not only for explicit initialization associated with a declaration statement, but also implicitly for a variety of situations that occur during execution. These two constructor patterns are given special names.

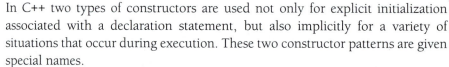
All class definitions should include both a default and a copy constructor

A *default constructor* does not take any arguments. The constructor is invoked with a declaration of an object value and does not specify argument values. It is also used to initialize object data fields when no other arguments are specified.

A *copy constructor* takes an instance of the same class as a constant reference argument. Copy constructors are used to make a copy, or clone, of an object value, a task that in Java is often performed with the clone method. Copy constructors are used internally in the processing of parameters that are passed by value. The copy constructor will be invoked to create the temporary value that will be passed to the function, leaving the original value immune to modification. Copy constructors are also used to create a temporary value when a function returns an object value and (as are all constructors) in the initialization of values newly created by either a declaration or a new operation.

The following class description illustrates both a default and a copy constructor:

```
class box {
public:
   box () // default constructor
      { i = 1; } // give data field some default value

   box (int x) // ordinary constructor
      { i = x; }

   box (const box & a) // copy constructor
      { i = a.i; } // clone argument value
private:
   int i;
};
```

The following three declarations will implicitly invoke the three forms of constructor:

```
box one;        // default constructor
box two(7);     // ordinary constructor
box three(two); // copy constructor
```

5.4.2   Initializers

Data members in Java are initialized in one of two ways. If a data member is initialized with a value that is independent of the constructor arguments, it is often simply written as an initial assignment at the point of declaration. Otherwise, an explicit assignment statement appears in the constructor function definition.

With one minor exception (discussed in Section 5.8), the language C++ does not allow the initialization of data members at the point of declaration. Instead, all data members must be initialized in a constructor function. This can be performed either in an explicit assignment statement or in an *initializer*. The following class definition illustrates the syntax used for initializers, by rewriting the Link constructor presented earlier to use initializers rather than assignment statements:

```
class Link {
public:
    Link(int v, Link * f, Link * b)
        : value(v), forwardLink(f), backwardLink(b) { }
        .
        .
        .
};
```

For primitive data types, such as integers or pointers, an initializer is exactly equivalent to an assignment. For more complex types, such as user-defined types, the situation is different. The rule is that data members are all initialized before the body of the constructor is executed, either by using an initializer or (if no initializers are known) by using the default rules.

Imagine a class box that defines both a default constructor (a constructor with no argument), a copy constructor (a constructor that creates a clone of another value), and an assignment operation. Now consider the following class definition:

```
class A { // class with initialization error
public:
    void A (box & aBox) : boxOne(aBox) { boxTwo = aBox; }
private:
    box boxOne;
    box boxTwo;
};
```

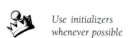
Use initializers whenever possible

The data field boxOne will be initialized with the copy constructor, in one step. Because the data field boxTwo has no initializer field, it will thus first be initialized with the default constructor. After both data members have been initialized, the body of the constructor is executed. During execution, the assignment statement is used to alter the value of boxTwo to match the argument value. Thus the field boxTwo is modified twice, once by the default constructor and once by the assignment operator.

Data members that are declared to be const and data fields that are references are never permitted to be targets of assignment statements. Thus both of these types of objects must be initialized by using initializers instead of in the body of the constructor.

```
class B {
public:
    void B (box & aBox) : boxOne(aBox), boxTwo(aBox) { }
```

```
private:
    box & boxOne;
    const box boxTwo;
}
```

The last category of initializer is the initialization of parent classes in the constructors associated with child classes. Let's assume that the constructor for a parent class requires an argument value. In Java, the constructor for the child supplies the value by invoking the function **super** in the constructor:

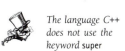

The language C++ does not use the keyword super

```
class bigBox extends box { // Java code

    public bigBox (int x, double d)
    {
        super(x); // initialize parent
        dvalue = d; // initialize self
    }

    private double dvalue; // private data field
}
```

In C++ the same effect is achieved by means of an initializer. The initializer names the parent class and uses as arguments the arguments for the parent class constructor. As in Java, if no appropriate initializer is found, the default constructor for the parent class is invoked:

```
class bigBox : public box { // C++ code
public:
    bigBox (int x, double d) : box(x), dvalue(d) { }

private:
    double dvalue;
};
```

Fields are initialized in the order of declaration

A final item to note is that class members are initialized in the order in which they are declared in the class body, not in the order in which the initializers are listed. (They are deleted by the *destructor* in reverse order. Destructor functions were introduced in Chapter 4.) The programmer might be confused by the result of executing the method **test** on an instance of the following class:

```
class order {  // warning, initialization error
public:
    order (int i) : one(i), two(one) { }
    int test() { return two; }
```

```
private:
    int two; // initialized first
    int one; // initialized second
};
```

The variable two is initialized with the as yet uninitialized value of one, and *then* the value of one is set. The result is that the value held in two is unpredictable garbage.

5.4.3   Order of Initialization

C++ and Java initialize subclasses differently

In C++ the initialization of parent classes occurs before the initialization of child classes. While a parent class constructor is being executed, the object is viewed as an instance of the parent class. This means that methods that are invoked are matched only to functions in the parent class, even if these methods have been declared as *virtual*. (See Chapter 4 for a discussion of the *virtual* modifier.) To see the impact of this, we can once again contrast a simple class written in Java and the equivalent class written in C++. Consider first the following Java classes:

```
class A { // Java classes illustrating initialization
    public A ()
    {
        System.out.println("in A constructor");
        init();
    }

    public void init()
    {
        System.out.println("in A init");
    }
}

class B extends A {
    public B ()
    {
        System.out.println("in B constructor");
    }

    public void init()
    {
```

```
        super.init();
        System.out.println("in B init");
    }
}
```

When an instance of B is created, the constructor for B will be executed. This constructor will automatically invoke the constructor for A. The constructor for A will invoke the method init, which is defined in A but overridden in B. However, the overridden method in B will invoke the method in A. (Note that constructors always use *refinement* semantics, in which the parent class will always be invoked. In contrast, methods use *replacement* semantics, and so the parent function is invoked only if explicitly called.) The output of the sequence would be as follows:

A refinement com-bines the actions of the parent and child

```
in A constructor
in A init
in B init
in B constructor
```

A superficially equivalent C++ program is as follows:

```
class A { // C++ classes illustrating initialization
public:
    A ()
    {
        printf("in A constructor\n");
        init();
    }

    virtual void init()
    {
        printf("in A init\n");
    }
};

class B : public A {
public:

    B ()
    {
        printf("in B constructor\n");
    }
```

```
virtual void init()
{
    A::init();
    printf("in B init\n");
}
};
```

However, in C++ when the function init is invoked in the constructor for A, only the method in class A is used, regardless of whether the virtual keyword is used in the declaration of the function. Thus the output from C++ would be as follows:

```
in A constructor
in A init
in B constructor
```

Note that the init function in B has not been executed. A C++ programmer attempting to overcome this limitation by invoking the init function directly in B would discover another error, namely, that the init function in A would then be invoked *twice*.

5.4.4   Combining Constructors

Java programmers are accustomed to being able to define one constructor using another, as in the following:

```
// Java class with linked constructors
class newClass {
    public newClass (int i)
    {
        // do some initialization
            .
            .
            .
    }

    public newClass (int i, int j)
    {
        this(i); // invoke one argument constructor
        // do other initialization
            .
            .
            .
    }
}
```

In C++ you cannot invoke one constructor from within another

This feature has no direct C++ counterpart. Programmers often will try to use a fully qualified name, as in the following:

```
class box { // error---does not work as expected
public:
    box (int i) : x(i) { }
    box (int i, int j) : y(j) { box::box(i); }

    int x, y;
};
```

Creating a two-argument box and printing the resulting value of x and y will demonstrate that the fully qualified call on the one-argument constructor had no effect. In reality, this function created an unnamed temporary, initialized it, and then destroyed it.

Two common methods demonstrate the proper solution to this problem. If the only difference between two constructors is the assignment of a default value, a *default argument value* can be used:

```
// C++ class with default arguments in constructor
class newClass {
public:
    newclass (int i, int j = 7)
    {
        // do object initialization
        .
        :
        .
    }
};
```

Although only one function is defined, it can be used with either one argument or two. In the one-argument case, the default value (here, 7) is automatically supplied for the second argument.

Another common solution to this problem is to factor the common initialization into a separate method, which is then declared as **private**:

```
// C++ class with factored constructors
class newClass {
public:
    newClass (int i)
    {
        initialize(i); // do common initialization
    }
```

```
     newClass (int i, int j)
     {
        initialize(i);
        .
        :   // then do further initialization
        .
     }

private:
     void initialize (int i)
     {
        .
        :   // common initialization actions
        .
     }
};
```

Even if the initialize method is declared public or protected, as well as virtual, it cannot be overridden because it is invoked from within a constructor function (see Section 5.4.3).

5.5   The Orthodox Canonical Class Form

Always define the four functions in the OCCF

Several authors of style guides for C++ have suggested that almost all classes should define four important functions. This has come to be termed the *orthodox canonical class form* (OCCF). The four important functions are:

- A default constructor. This is used internally to initialize objects and data members when no other value is available.

- A copy constructor. This is used in the implementation of call-by-value parameters.

- An assignment operator. This is used to assign one value to another.

- A destructor. This is invoked when an object is deleted.

Even if empty bodies are supplied for these functions, writing the class body will at least suggest that the program designer has *thought* about the issues involved in each of these functions. Furthermore, appropriate use of visibility modifers, described in the next section, give the programmer great power in allowing or disallowing different operations used with the class.

5.6 Visibility Modifiers

For the most part, the visibility modifiers public, protected, and private operate the same in C++ as they do in Java. However, there are some differences. In C++ the modifiers designate a section of a class definition, rather than being applied item by item as they are in Java. The modifiers cannot be applied to entire classes in C++. One way to get the effect of a nonpublic class in C++ is to declare a class inside a *namespace* (see Section 12.7).

There is a minor difference in the meaning of the keyword protected. Protected fields in Java are open both to subclasses and to other classes declared within the same package. The C++ language has no notion of packages, so the term applies only to subclasses.

A subclass is permitted to change the visibility of attributes inherited from a parent class

The C++ language allows a subclass to change the visibility of a method, even one that is declared as virtual and is being overridden. Consider the following code fragment:

```
class parent {
public:
    virtual void test () { printf("in parent test\n"); }
};

class child : public parent {
private:
    void test () { printf("in parent test\n"); }
};

parent * p = new child;
p->test();
```

A variable of type pointer to parent is nevertheless holding a value of type child. The method test is defined in both classes. When invoked, the method executed will be that found in the child class, not that found in the parent class. That much, except for the funny keyword virtual that we discuss in Chapter 6, should come as no surprise to the Java programmer.

What *is* surprising is that the method test was executed, despite the fact that it was declared as private in the class definition. Such a method cannot, after all, be invoked from a variable declared as child, even if it holds the exact same value:

```
child * c = (parent *) p;
c->test(); // compile error, cannot invoke private method
```

Some compilers will produce warning messages when the visibility of methods is changed in this way, but unlike with Java it is not considered a compiler error.

5.7   Inner Classes Versus Nested Classes

C++ and Java both allow classes to be defined inside each other but have different semantics

Both Java and C++ permit class definitions to be nested. A class definition that appears inside another class definition is called an *inner class* in Java and a *nested class* in C++. Despite similar appearances, there is a major semantic difference between the two concepts. An inner class in Java is linked to a specific instance of the surrounding class (the instance in which it was created) and is permitted access to data fields and methods in this object. A nested class in C++ is simply a naming device; it restricts the visibility of features associated with the inner class, but otherwise the two are not related.

To illustrate the use of nested classes let's rewrite the Java linked list abstraction presented earlier, placing the Link class inside the List abstraction:

```java
// Java List class
class List {
   private Link firstElement = null;

   private class Link { // inner class definition
      public Object value;
      public Link forwardLink;
      public Link backwardLink;

      public Link (Object v, Link f, Link b)
         { value = v; forwardLink = f; backwardLink = b; }

      public void addBefore (Object val)
      {
         Link newLink = new Link(val, this, backwardLink);
         if (backwardLink == null)
            firstElement = newLink;
         else {
            backwardLink.forwardLink = newLink;
            backwardLink = newLink;
         }
      }
```

```
   .
   .    // other methods omitted
   .
   }

public void push_front(Object val)
{
   if (firstElement == null)
      firstElement = new Link(val, null, null);
   else
      firstElement.addBefore (val);
}


   .
   .    // other methods omitted
   .
}
```

Note that the method addBefore references the data field firstElement, in order to handle the special case where an element is being inserted into the front of a list. A direct translation of this code into C++ will produce the following:

```
// C++ List class
class List {
private:
   class Link; // forward definition
   Link * firstElement;

   class Link { // nested class definition
   public:
      int value;
      Link * forwardLink;
      Link * backwardLink;

      Link (int v, Link * f, Link * b)
         { value = v; forwardLink = f; backwardLink = b; }

      void addBefore (int val)
      {
         Link * newLink = new Link(val, this, backwardLink);
         if (backwardLink == 0)
            firstElement = newLink; // ERROR !
         else {
            backwardLink->forwardLink = newLink;
```

```
                            backwardLink = newLink;
                }
        }

        .
        .    // other methods omitted
        .
        };


    public:
        void push_front(int val)
        {
            if (firstElement == 0)
                firstElement = new Link(val, 0, 0);
            else
                firstElement->addBefore (val);
        }
        .
        .    // other methods omitted
        .
    };
```

It was necessary to introduce a forward reference for the Link class so that the pointer firstElement could be declared before the class was defined. Also C++ uses the value zero for a null element, rather than the pseudoconstant null. Finally, links are pointers rather than values, so the pointer access operator is necessary. But the feature to note occurs on the line marked as an error. The class Link is not permitted to access the variable firstElement because the scope for the class is not actually nested in the scope for the surrounding class. In order to access the List object, it would have to be explicitly available through a variable. In this case, the most reasonable solution probably would be to have the List method pass itself as argument, using the pseudovariable this, to the inner Link method addBefore. (An alternative solution—having each Link maintain a reference to its creating List—is probably too memory-intensive.)

```
    class List {
        Link * firstElement;

        class Link {
            void addBefore (int val, List * theList)
            {
                .
                .
                .
```

```
                if (backwardLink == 0)
                    theList->firstElement = newLink;
                .
                .
                .
            }
        };
    public:
        void push_front(int val)
        {
            .
            .
            .
            // pass self as argument
            firstElement->addBefore (val, this);
        }
        .
        .   // other methods omitted
        .
    };
```

When nested class methods are defined outside the class body, the name
may require multiple levels of qualification. The following code fragment, for
example, shows how the method addBefore would be written in this fashion:

```
void List::Link::addBefore (int val, List * theList)
{
    Link * newLink = new Link(val, this, backwardLink);
    if (backwardLink == 0)
        theList->firstElement = newLink;
    else {
        backwardLink->forwardLink = newLink;
        backwardLink = newLink;
    }
}
```

The name of the function indicates that this is the method addBefore that is
part of the class Link, which is, in turn, defined as part of the class List.

5.8   Static Initialization

*C++ does not use
the message-passing
syntax for invoking
static functions*

Static items in both Java and C++ are elements defined as part of a class description that exist independently of class instances. A static data field, for example,
will exist as a single value, regardless of the number of instances that have been
created (even if none have been created). Thus a static member function can be

invoked without a receiver. One difference is in the syntax used for the latter operation. In Java the syntax is the same as for message passing, with the class name as the receiver. In C++ a static member function is written as the class name, a pair of colons, and the member function name:

```
d = Math.sqrt (d); // Java---invoke static function sqrt
Date::setDefault(12,7,42); // C++---use qualified name
```

Another way in which C++ and Java differ is the way that static data fields are initialized. In Java they are initialized either as direct assignments in the class body or in a special static initializer block. The following code fragment illustrates both of these examples:

```
class box {
    public box (int v)
    {
        boxCount++;
        value = v;
        if (v == 0)
            zeroCount++;
    }

    private int value;

    // keep track of number of boxes created
    static private int boxCount = 0;

    // also track number of boxes with value zero
    static private int zeroCount;

    static {
        zeroCount = 0; // initialize the zeroCount field
    }
}
```

In C++ there are also two separate mechanisms that can be used. Data fields that are declared either as const or static and are primitive data types can be defined by an initialization of the data field inside the class, as in Java. This syntax, however, is used only for this one situation. All other initializations are performed outside the class body, using a fully qualified name. The syntax used in the latter is similar to that used with initializations in a declaration; an assignment can be used if there is a single argument, or parentheses can be used if there are two or more arguments:

```
class box {
public:
    box (int v) : value(v)
        { boxCount++;  if (v == 0) zeroCount++; }

private:
    static int boxCount = 0;
    static int zeroCount;
};


// global initialization is separate from class
int box::zeroCount = 0;
```

The declaration and use of static methods in C++ is generally similar to the techniques used in Java.

A common use for static data fields in Java is to produce class-specific constants, as in the following example:

```
class coloredBox extends box {
    // define the range of color values
    public static final int Red = 1;
    public static final int Yellow = 2;
    public static final int Blue = 3;

    public coloredBox (int v, int c) { super(v); ourColor = c; }

    private int ourColor;
}
```

The language C++ does not have the keyword final. However, in this case, such fields can be written as static integer constants:

```
class coloredBox : public box {
public:
    // define the range of color values
    static const int Red = 1;
    static const int Yellow = 2;
    static const int Blue = 3;
```

```
        coloredBox (int v, int c) : box(v), ourColor(c) { }

    private:
        int ourColor;
    };
```

Use enumerated data types to describe lists of mutually exclusive alternatives

An even better solution in this situation is to define a new *enumerated data type*. An enumerated type creates a new data type with a specific set of constant elements. This avoids the inadvertent use of integer constants with arithmetic expressions:

```
class  coloredBox : public box {
public:
    enum Colors {Red, Yellow, Blue};

    coloredBox (int v, Colors c) : box(v), ourColor(c) { }

private:
    Colors ourColor;
};
```

To access an enumerated constant value that is defined within a class, a fully qualified name must be used. An example would be coloredBox::Red.

5.9   Final Classes

C++ does not have the Java concept of a final class, a class that cannot be subclassed. One technique that is sometimes used to achieve this effect is to declare all constructors for the class as private; since subclasses cannot then invoke their parent class constructors, the C++ compiler will not permit them to be written. But this introduces a different problem, namely, that such values cannot be created. To get around this, the programmer can write *pseudoconstructors*, which are static functions that do nothing more than invoke a constructor value:

```
class privateBox {
public:
    // pseudoconstructor used for creation
    static privateBox & makeBox(int v) { return privateBox(v); }

private:
    // since constructor is private,
```

```
    // cannot create instances directly
    privateBox (int v) : value(v) { }
    int value;
};
```

The static function is then used each time a value is needed:

```
// make a new box value
privateBox aBox = privateBox::makebox(7);
```

Test Your Understanding

1. What are some of the superficial similarities between class definitions in Java and C++? What are some of the minor differences between them?

2. What does it mean to say that C++ separates class definition and implementation?

3. What is an inline method? How is it declared?

4. How does the compiler treat the invocation of an inline method differently from the invocation of a normal method?

5. What is the advantage to using inline methods? What is a disadvantage?

6. What is a qualified name?

7. What is a prototype? What information omitted from a prototype is found in a function definition?

8. What is indicated by a declaration that uses the extern modifier?

9. Why are forward references necessary in C++ but not in Java?

10. What two tasks are tied together by a constructor?

11. What is a default constructor? What are some of the conditions under which it will be invoked?

12. What is a copy constructor? What are some of the conditions under which it will be invoked?

13. What types of items can be found in an initializer list?

14. In what order will data fields be initialized?

15. What is a default argument? In what situations can default arguments be used to replace two overloaded function bodies with a single function?

16. What four methods are necessary for a class to be said to satisfy the orthodox canonical class form?

17. What error is being exhibited by the following C++ class definition?

```
class A {
public:
   void a () { ... }

   class B {
   public:
      void b () { a(); }
   };
};
```

18. How is a nested class in C++ different from an inner class in Java?

19. How is the initialization of static data fields in C++ different from that of Java?

20. How can final constants in Java be represented in C++?

21. What is the effect of declaring constructor methods as private?

6

Polymorphism

A static type is associated with a declaration; a dynamic type is associated with a value

The *polymorphic variable* is one of the most powerful mechanisms provided by the object-oriented paradigm. Recall that a polymorphic variable is a variable for which the *static type,* the type associated with a declaration, may differ from the *dynamic type,* the type associated with the value currently being held by the variable.

In Java a polymorphic variable can be declared as either a class type or an interface type. If a variable is declared as a class type, the value held by the variable must be derived either from the declared class or from a class that inherits from the declared class. If a variable is declared with an interface type, the value held by the variable must be derived from a class that implements the given interface. The C++ language does not include the concept of interfaces, so the idea of a polymorphic variable is possible only if class inheritance is used. In this chapter, we explain the many other subtle and not-so-subtle differences that exist between polymorphism in C++ and polymorphism in Java.

To discuss polymorphism, we need a class hierarchy. An intuitive hierarchy is provided by a portion of the animal kingdom, which we can represent as follows:

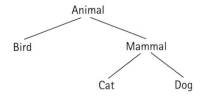

Figure 6.1 Animal Kingdom Class Hierarchy in Java

```
abstract class Animal {
   abstract public void speak();
}

class Bird extends Animal {
   public void speak() { System.out.println("twitter"); }
}

class Mammal extends Animal {
   public void speak() { System.out.println("can't speak"); }
   public void bark() { System.out.println("can't bark"); }
}

class Cat extends Mammal {
   public void speak() { System.out.println("meow"); }
   public void purr() { System.out.println("purrrrr"); }
}

class Dog extends Mammal {
   public void speak() { System.out.println("wouf"); }
   public void bark() { System.out.println("wouf"); }
}
```

Figure 6.1 provides a realization of this class hierarchy in Java. Figure 6.2 gives the corresponding C++ code. We use these classes in various discussions throughout this chapter.

Figure 6.2 Animal Kingdom Class Hierarchy in C++

```
class Animal {
public:
   virtual void speak() = 0;
};

class Bird : public Animal {
public:
   virtual void speak() { printf("twitter"); }
};
```

Figure 6.2 Animal Kingdom Class Hierarchy in C++, (continued)

```
class Mammal : public Animal {
public:
   virtual void speak() { printf("can't speak"); }
   void bark() { printf("can't bark"); }
};

class Cat : public Mammal {
public:
   void speak() { printf("meow"); }
   virtual void purr() { printf("purrrrr"); }

};

class Dog : public Mammal {
public:
   virtual void speak() { printf("wouf"); }
   void bark() { printf("wouf"); }
};
```

6.1   Virtual and Nonvirtual Overriding

A type signature is the type descriptions for each argument and the type description of the return type

Overriding occurs when a method in a parent class is replaced in a child class by a method having the exact same *type signature*. In Java, overriding is the norm, the expected result. In C++, whether overriding occurs is controlled by the programmer, using the keyword virtual.

The issue in overriding is how a method—the actual code to be executed—is bound to a message. If the virtual keyword is omitted, the binding is determined by the *static type* of a variable, that is, by the variables declared type. This is illustrated by the following code fragment:

```
Dog * d = new Dog();
Mammal * m = d;
d->bark(); // wouf
m->bark(); // can't bark
```

Because d is declared as a Dog, the method selected will be that of the Dog class. Because m is declared only as a Mammal, even though it holds exactly

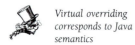
Virtual overriding corresponds to Java semantics

the same value as d, the method executed will be that provided by the class Mammal.

However, if a method is declared as *virtual*, as is the speak method in Figure 6.2, the method invoked may, under the right circumstances, be determined by the *dynamic* (that is, run-time) value held by the class. This is illustrated as follows:

```
d->speak(); // wouf
m->speak(); // also wouf
Animal * a = d;
a->speak(); // and more wouf
```

The method speak for variable d will be that of class Dog, as might be expected. However, m will also use the Dog method. Even a, which is an Animal, will use the Dog method. Thus virtual overridding corresponds to the behavior of overridden functions in Java.

Regardless of the type of value held by a variable, the validity of a message is determined by the static, or declared, type—the same as in Java. Thus, while the variable d will respond to the message bark, the variable a that was declared as Animal, even though it contains the exact same value, is not allowed to perform this operation:

```
d->bark(); // wouf
a->bark(); // compile error, not allowed
```

Because of the C++ memory model (see Chapter 4), virtual, or polymorphic, overriding will occur only when method invocation is used with a pointer or reference, not with stack-based variables. This is illustrated by the following code fragment:

```
Mammal mm;
mm = *d;
mm.speak(); // can't speak
d->speak(); // although dog will wouf
```

Note that here the variable mm is not declared as a pointer, as were earlier variables, but as a simple stack-based value. The Dog value held by d is assigned to the variable mm. During the assignment process, the value loses its dog identity and becomes simply a mammal. Thus the speak method will be that of class Mammal, not that of class Dog.

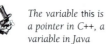
The variable this is a pointer in C++, a variable in Java

The pseudovariable this, the reference to the receiver within a method, is a pointer in C++, whereas it is an object value in Java. Thus implicit messages sent to this can have polymorphic bindings.

If a method is not declared as virtual in a parent class, it cannot subsequently be made virtual in a child class. But, because the keyword is optional in the child class, once declared as virtual by the parent, the method remains virtual in all child class definitions. Note that we have made use of this fact by omitting the virtual keyword from the specification of the method speak in class Cat. Despite this omission, the method remains virtual.

6.1.1   Impact of Virtual on Size

 When classes contain virtual methods, instances will hold a hidden pointer to a virtual method table

When a class description contains a virtual method, an internal table, called the virtual method table, is created for the class. This table is used in the implementation of the dynamic binding of message to method required by the virtual method. In order to do so, each instance of a class must contain an additional hidden pointer value, which references the virtual method table. The programmer can see this effect by adding or removing the virtual keyword from a class description and examining the size of an instance of the class:

```
class sizeTest {
   public:
       int x, y;
       virtual void test () { x = 3; }
};

sizeTest x;
// size will be 8 if not virtual, larger if virtual
printf("%d\n", sizeof(x) );
```

6.1.2   Obtaining Type Information from a Dynamic Value

In Java all objects recognize the method getClass() and in response will yield a Class object that describes the dynamic type of the value. Using the Class value, we can obtain various bits of information about the value—for example, a string that describes the dynamic type:

```
Animal a = new Dog();
// following will print class Dog
System.out.println("class is " + a.getClass().getName());
```

The function typeid *is a recent addition to C++*

The equivalent feature in C++ is the function **typeid**. It returns a value of type **typeinfo**, described by the include file of the same name. The string representation of the name of the class is yielded by the method **name**:

```
Animal * a = new Dog();
// will print the class Dog
println("class is %s\n", typeid(*a).name());
```

Note that it is necessary to dereference the variable **a**, since **typeid** must act on the value that **a** points to, not the pointer value itself.

Being a relatively recent addition to C++, the **typeid** facility is one of the few places in the standard library that will generate an exception on error. Should the pointer value in the preceding expression be null, a **bad_typeid** exception will be thrown.

6.2   Abstract Classes

An *abstract class* is a class used only as a parent class for inheritance; it cannot be used to create instances directly. The language Java includes an explicit keyword **abstract** to indicate this situation. The language C++ does not use this keyword. Instead, an abstract class is simply a class that includes a pure virtual method. A *pure virtual method* is a method that is declared as virtual but does not contain a method body. Instead, the method is "assigned" the null value. An example occurs in Figure 6.2:

A pure virtual method must be overridden in subclasses

```
class Animal {
public:
    virtual void speak() = 0;
};
```

As with abstract classes in Java, it is not possible to create an instance of a class that contains a pure virtual member. An attempt to do so will produce a compile-time error message.

As we noted at the beginning of this chapter, the C++ language does not provide the **interface** facility. Sometimes classes that consist entirely of pure virtual methods are used in the same manner as interfaces:

An interface can be simulated by pure virtual methods

```
class KeyPressHandler { // specification for key press event
                        // handler
public:
    virtual void keyDown (char c) = 0;
};
```

```
class MouseDownHandler { // specification for mouse down event
                         // handler
public:
   virtual void mouseDown (int x, int y) = 0;
   virtual void mouseUp (int x, int y) = 0;
};
```

Since C++ supports multiple inheritance (see Section 12.8), a class can implement several such interfaces:

```
class EventHandler : public KeyPressHandler, public
                           MouseDownHandler {
public:
   void keyDown (char c) { ... }
   void mouseDown (int x, int y) { ... }
   void mouseUp (int x, int y)( { ... }
};
```

In Java the keyword final is in some ways the opposite of abstract, serving to indicate methods or classes that cannot be overwritten. There is no equivalent feature in C++, although as we noted in the previous chapter, in some cases declaring the constructor for a class as protected can have a similar effect.

6.3   Downcasting (Reverse Polymorphism)

Downcasting reverses the assignment to a polymorphic variable; hence, the term reverse polymorphism

A polymorphic variable can have a dynamic type that is a subclass of its static, or declared, type. For example, a variable can be declared as a pointer to an Animal but actually be maintaining a pointer to a Cat. Often the programmer is required to form an assignment that depends on the dynamic type, rather than the static type. For example, the polymorphic Animal variable needs to be assigned to a variable of type Cat.

The Java programmer can test the dynamic type of a variable by means of the operator instanceof and perform the transformation by using a cast operator:

```
Animal a = ... ;
if (a instanceof Cat)
   Cat c = (Cat) a;
```

Alternatively, the Java programmer can explicitly catch the exception that is thrown if the conversion is illegal:

```
Animal a = ... ;
try {
    Cat c = (Cat) a;
} catch(ClassCastException & e) { ... }
```

There is no direct C++ equivalent to the instanceof operation. Furthermore, although the syntax of the cast operation is taken directly from C++, the Java programmer should be aware that the semantics of the equivalent operation in C++ are slightly different. The Java cast operator performs a run-time check to ensure the validity of the conversion and issues an exception if illegal. The C++ cast is entirely a compile-time operation, and no check is made at run time. If the cast is improper, no indication is given to the programmer, and an erroneous outcome will likely result:

C++ does not per-form a run-time check to ensure the validity of cast con-versions

```
Animal * a = new Dog();
Cat * c = (Cat *) a;
c->purr();  // behavior is undefined
```

Such errors can sometimes be hidden due to the interaction of the cast operation and the rules for virtual and nonvirtual method invocation. Note, for example, that if we had *not* declared the method purr as virtual, the proper Cat method would have been invoked (because the static type is Cat), despite the fact that the actual value held by variable c is a dog. The behavior when the method *is* declared as virtual is more difficult to predict; on many machines, it will produce a segmentation fault.

The RTTI is a recent addition to the language C++

To get around this problem, the language C++ provides a different type of cast, called a *dynamic cast*. The dynamic cast is part of a suite of functions, called the run-time type information system, or RTTI. The dynamic cast operator is a templated function (see Chapter 9). The template argument is the type to which conversion is desired. Unlike the normal cast, the dynamic cast operator checks the validity of the conversion. If the conversion is not proper, a null value is yielded. Thus the result is either a properly type-checked value, or null. The programmer can then test the resulting value to determine whether the conversion took place. In this way the dynamic_cast operator combines the features of both the instanceof operator and the cast operator in Java:

Testing a pointer in an if statement is the same as testing whether the pointer is null

```
Cat * c = dynamic_cast<Cat *>(a);
if (c)
    printf("variable was a cat");
else
    printf("variable was not a cat");
```

If dynamic_cast is used with object values, instead of pointers, a failure results in a bad_cast exception being thrown, rather than a null pointer. The dynamic cast operation works only with polymorphic types, that is, pointers (or references) to classes that contain at least one virtual method.

A static_cast is similar, but performs no dynamic check on the result. This operator is most often used to convert one pointer type, for example, a void * pointer, into another type:

```
void * v = ...;

// we know from elsewhere that v is really a cat
Cat * c = static_cast<Cat *>(v);
```

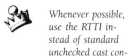 *Whenever possible, use the RTTI instead of standard unchecked cast conversions*

A static_cast is not restricted to polymorphic types. Two other types of cast (const_cast, and reinterpret_cast) have also been added to C++, but their use is uncommon, and we do not describe them here. However, programmers are encouraged to use these newer, more type-safe facilities instead of the older cast mechanism.

6.3.1 Simulating the Dynamic Cast

Because the RTTI is a relatively new addition to the language C++, not all compilers will support this feature. Thus it may be necessary to achieve the effect of the dynamic_cast operator without actually using it. Before the introduction of RTTI, one common programmer's trick was to encode explicit *is-a* methods in class hierarchies. For example, to test animal values to see if they represent a dog or cat, we can write methods such as:

```
class Mammal {
public:
    virtual bool  isaDog() { return false; }
    virtual bool  isaCat() { return false; }
};

class Dog : public Mammal {
public:
    virtual bool  isaDog() { return true; }
};

class Cat : public Mammal {
public:
    virtual bool  isaCat() { return true; }
};

Mammal * fido;
```

A test such as fido→isaDog() can then be used to determine whether the variable fido is currently holding a value of type Dog. If so, a conventional cast can safely be used to convert the quantity into the correct type.

By returning a pointer rather than an integer, we can extend this trick to combine both the test for subclass type and the conversion, which is more closely similar to the dynamic_cast operator in the RTTI. Since a function in the class Mammal is returning a pointer to a Dog, the class Dog must have a forward reference (see Section 5.3). The result of the assignment is either a null pointer or a valid reference to a Dog. The test on the result must still be performed, but we have eliminated the need for the cast. This is shown as follows:

```
class Dog; // forward reference
class Cat;

class Mammal {
public:
    virtual Dog *  isaDog() { return 0; }
    virtual Cat *  isaCat() { return 0; }
};

class Dog : public Mammal {
public:
    virtual Dog *  isaDog() { return this; }
};

class Cat : public Mammal {
public:
    virtual Cat *  isaCat() { return this; }
};

Mammal * fido;
Dog * lassie;
```

A statement such as:

```
lassie = fido->isaDog();
```

can then *always* be performed. It will result in the variable lassie holding a non-null value only if fido indeed held a value of class Dog. If fido did *not* hold a dog value, a null pointer value will be assigned to the variable lassie:

```
if (lassie)
    .
    :   fido was indeed a dog
    .

else
    .
    :   assignment did not work
    .

    .
    :   fido was not a dog
    .
```

Although the programmer can implement this technique for performing downcasting (sometimes called reverse polymorphism), it requires adding methods to both the parent and the child classes. If many child classes are inheriting from a common parent class, the mechanism can become unwieldy. If making changes to the parent class is not permitted, use of this technique is not possible.

6.4   Name Resolution

Name resolution is matching a function body to a function name

As part of object-oriented method invocation, a message selector must be bound to the appropriate function body. The Java and C++ techniques used for this purpose are similar, but not identical. Consider, for example, the following two class definitions in Java:

```
class Parent {
    public void test (int i)
        { System.out.println("parent test"); }
}

class Child extends Parent {
    public void test (int i, int i) {
        System.out.println("child two arg test"); }
    public void test (Parent p) {
        System.out.println("child object test"); }
}
```

The name space for the class Parent introduces a new function, test, that takes a single integer argument. The class Child builds on this name space and adds to it two other definitions for the function test. Each of these definitions can be easily distinguished from the original by the number or type of arguments, so there is no possibility of confusion. If we now provide an invocation such as:

```
Child c = new Child();
c.test(3);
```

the compiler selects the function with matching arguments—in this case, the function inherited from the class Parent.

Now consider an equivalent C++ program:

```
class Parent {
public:
    void test (int i) { printf("parent test"); }
};


class Child : public Parent {
public:
    void test (int i, int i) { printf("child two arg test"); }
    void test (Parent & p) { printf("child object test"); }
};
```

If we try to invoke the function inherited from the parent, we get a compiler error:

```
Child * c = new  Child();
c->test(3); // generates compiler error
```

The explanation for this behavior is that the language C++ maintains separate but linked descriptions of each of the various name scopes. In this case, there are at least three different name scopes: the global scope, the scope for class Parent, and the scope for class Child. To resolve a name, such as test, the compiler performs a two-step process. Step 1 is to search for the first enclosing scope in which the name is defined. In this case, it is the scope for Child. Step 2 then is to try to match the name with a function *defined in that scope*. In this case, there are only two possibilities, neither of which will work. Being unable to find a matching function, the compiler reports an error.

 Redefine any inherited names that are overloaded with different type signatures

To circumvent this, the C++ programmer should redefine any inherited names that are being overloaded with new meanings. This can be done with a simple inline function, as in the following code fragment:

```
class Child : public Parent {
public:
    void test (int i) { Parent::test(i); } // redefine inherited
                                           // method
    void test (int i, int i) { printf("child two arg test"); }
    void test (Parent & p) { printf("child object test"); }
};
```

Now all three methods will be defined in the Child scope and hence will be available for use.

6.5   A Forest, Not a Tree

In Java all objects descend ultimately from the base class Object. This has the advantage of ensuring that every object possesses some minimal functionality, namely, the methods provided by class Object. These operations include the ability to get the class of an object, convert an object into a string representation, test an object for equality against another object, and compute the hash value for an object.

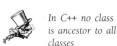

In C++ no class is ancestor to all classes

Classes in C++ are not part of a single hierarchy. If a class is not defined as inheriting from another class, it is the root of its own hierarchy and provides only the behavior defined by the class description. Thus a typical C++ program contains a number of different class hierarchies, each independent of the others.

In Java the class Object is often used to declare universal generic objects, or values that can hold any other object type. As C++ does not have a single root class, there is no exact equivalence. Frequently, template classes (see Chapter 9) eliminate the need for generic Object variables. However, when they cannot be avoided, void pointers can often be made to serve the same purpose. A variable declared as a pointer to a void value can be assigned any other pointer type, regardless of the type of object the pointer references:

```
Animal * a = new Dog();
void * v = a; // assign v pointer to an animal
```

Just as cast must be used to downcast an Object value in Java, dynamic_cast (see Section 6.3) should be used to convert a void pointer value back into the original type.

```
Dog * dd = dynamic_cast<Dog *>(v);
```

Note, however, that dynamic_cast works only if the pointer references a class that contains at least one virtual method.

6.6   Virtual Destructors

A *destructor* (see Chapter 4) is a method that is invoked immediately before a variable is to be deleted. When polymorphic variables are used, a concern is whether a destructor function should be declared as virtual. To illustrate, let's add destructor functions to the classes presented earlier in Figure 6.2:

```
class Animal {
   virtual ~Animal () { printf("goodbye animal"); }
      .
      .
      .
};
   .
   .
   .
class Cat : public Mammal {
   ~Cat () { printf("goodbye cat"); }
      .
      .
      .
};
```

Now imagine that we create and delete a polymorphic variable, as follows:

```
Animal * a = new Cat();
delete a;
```

If the destructor in Animal is declared virtual, as shown, both the destructors in class Animal and class Cat will be executed. If the virtual designation is omitted, only the method in class Animal will be performed. If the destructor is omitted from Animal altogether, the method from class Cat will not be performed, whether or not it is declared virtual.

Declare a virtual destructor if a class has any virtual methods

A good rule of thumb is to declare a destructor as virtual if there are any other virtual methods. A destructor should be provided in this case, even if it performs no useful actions; otherwise, destructors from child classes may not be executed.

Note also one more difference between destructors and finalize methods in Java. A finalize method should always explicitly invoke the finalize method that it inherits from its parent class. A destructor will do this automatically, and no explicit call is required.

6.7   Private Inheritance

Undoubtedly, you have noticed how the keyword public is used to indicate inheritance in C++ in contrast to use of the keyword extends in Java. While public inheritance is the most common form, protected or private inheritance can also be performed. When one of these other forms is used, the visibility of data fields and methods is the maximum of their declared modifiers and the modifier used for inheritance. That is, if inheritance is protected, fields declared as public in the parent class become protected in the child class. If inheritance is private, fields declared either as public or protected in the parent become private in the child class.

To understand the significance of this distinction, imagine the public features of a parent class as flowing through a child class, to become public features of the child class as well:

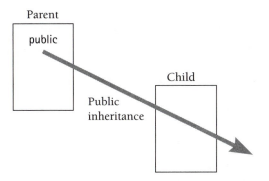

In a **private** inheritance, the **public** (and **protected**) features of the parent class are available for use in the child class but do not become part of the child class interface. In effect, they do not flow through the child class but instead are stopped at that level:

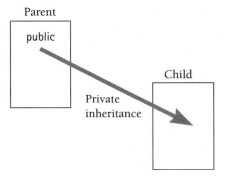

To illustrate why you might want to use this feature, imagine that you need to build a stack abstraction and that you have already a list class that you want to use as the underlying container. One possibility is to simply use inheritance, and derive the stack from the list:

```
class Stack : public List { // assume that elements are integers
public:
    push (int val) { addToFront(val); }
    pop () { removeFirstElement(); }
    top () { return firstElement();
}
```

A problem with this abstraction is that it is too powerful: It provides the user of the stack with too many operations. In particular, there is no way to keep the user from accessing the List operations, even when their use is not appropriate. For example, someone might add or remove an element directly from the bottom of a stack.

 Use private inheritance when the child class is not a more specialized form of the parent class

By specifying a private inheritance, the programmer avoids this potential misuse. The features of the parent class List, even if they are declared public or protected, are not passed through to become part of the Stack interface. Thus the only features are those explicitly described:

```
class Stack : private List {
public:
    push (int val) { addToFront(val); }
    pop () { removeFirstElement(); }
    top () { return firstElement();
}
```

But if public inheritance permitted too many operations to become attached to the new abstraction, simply declaring a private inheritance can be too restrictive. You may want to permit some operations. For example, the methods that check the size of the list are still appropriate for the stack abstraction. You can specify that these new features should continue to be part of the Stack abstraction by means of the using keyword. It permits items in the parent class to be selected and attached to the interface for the child class, while filtering out all other operations:

```
class Stack : private List {
public:
    push (int val) { addToFront(val); }
    pop () { removeFirstElement(); }
    top () { return firstElement(); }
    using isEmpty();
    using int size();
};
```

6.8   Inheritance and Arrays

In a number of situations, we could argue that Java semantics are an improvement over C++ semantics, most often because C++ semantics are incomplete or undefined. However, there is one curious situation in which Java semantics seem more confused than their C++ counterpart. This concerns an interaction between inheritance and arrays. Let's assume that we have declared an array of **Dog** values. Java permits this array to be assigned to a variable that is declared as an array of the parent class:

```
Dog [ ] dogs = new Dog[10]; // an array of dog values
Animal [ ] pets = dogs; // legal
```

In effect, Java is asserting that the type **Dog[ ]** (that is, array of dogs) is a subtype of the type **Animal[ ]**. To see the confusion that can then arise, imagine the following assignment:

```
pets[2] = aCat; // is this legal?
```

On the face of it, reassigning an element in the array to now hold a **Cat** value would certainly seem to be legal. After all, the array is declared as an array of animals, and a **Cat** is an animal. But recall that the array in question shares a reference with an array of dog values and that by performing this assignment we actually convert one element in the **Dog** array into a cat.

To prevent this, Java actually performs a run-time check on assignments to arrays of objects. C++ involves a simpler approach, simply asserting that, even though a **Dog** may be an **Animal**, there is no inheritance or subtype relationship between an array of **Dog** and an array of **Animal**.

6.9   Overloading

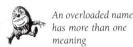

An overloaded name has more than one meaning

A function is said to be *overloaded* when two or more function *bodies* are associated with a single function *name*. Overriding is one form of overloading; however, overloading can occur without overriding. We presented an example of this in an earlier section, which included the following class definition:

```
class Child : public Parent {
public:
    void test (int i) { Parent::test(i); } // redefine inherited
                                            // method
    void test (int i, int j) { printf("child two arg test"); }
    void test (Parent & p) { printf("child object test"); }
};
```

These three versions of the test function are distinguished by the compiler by the number and type of arguments used in the function invocation. Constructor functions are often overloaded in this way; however, any function can be so defined.

The Java programmer should be aware that almost all C++ operators can also be overloaded. For example, if we wanted to provide a meaning for the operations of "adding" two cats or two dogs, we could do so as follows:

```
Dog * operator + (Dog * left, Dog * right)
{
    // return a new Dog value
    // that is the sum of the parents
    return new Dog();
}

Cat * operator + (Cat * left, Cat * right)
{
    return new Cat();
}
```

These functions would permit a dog value to be added to another dog, or a cat to a cat but would not permit a cat to be added to a dog. Operators can be defined either as ordinary functions (as shown here) or as member functions. We discuss this in detail in Chapter 7.

Test Your Understanding

1. What is a polymorphic variable?

2. Using the concepts of static and dynamic type, explain the effect of the modifier virtual.

3. How can you print the name of the class for an object value being held by a polymorphic variable?

4. What is a pure virtual method?

5. What is a downcast?

6. What do the initials RTTI stand for?

7. What is a dynamic_cast? How does it differ from a normal cast?

8. Explain how the name resolution algorithm used in C++ differs from that in Java.

9. How are exceptions tied to function names in C++? How is this different from Java?

10. What are some of the advantages that Java derives from having all object types inherit from the same base class (namely, Object)?

11. What is a virtual destructor? When is such a concept important?

12. How does private inheritance differ from normal inheritance?

13. What is an overloaded name? How is it different from an overridden method name?

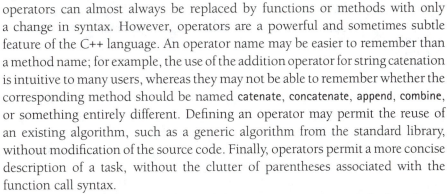

7

Operator Overloading

Almost all operators in C++ can be overloaded with new meanings

Operator overloading might at first appear to be only syntactic sugar, since operators can almost always be replaced by functions or methods with only a change in syntax. However, operators are a powerful and sometimes subtle feature of the C++ language. An operator name may be easier to remember than a method name; for example, the use of the addition operator for string catenation is intuitive to many users, whereas they may not be able to remember whether the corresponding method should be named catenate, concatenate, append, combine, or something entirely different. Defining an operator may permit the reuse of an existing algorithm, such as a generic algorithm from the standard library, without modification of the source code. Finally, operators permit a more concise description of a task, without the clutter of parentheses associated with the function call syntax.

Operators may not look like functions but can hide function invocations

But the programmer must be careful; many operators are invoked implicitly or have effects that may not be obvious at first glance. And a surprising amount of what might be thought of as simple syntax is actually formed from operators that can be overloaded. For example, there is a world of difference between:

```
aFun (x, 3);
```

and

```
aFun ((x, 3));
```

The former invokes the function aFun with two arguments. The latter, perhaps surprisingly, invokes aFun with only one argument. Whereas the comma in the first line is simply a separator, the comma in the second function call is actually an operator (see Section 7.12), one that normally discards the left argument and

Figure 7.1   Overloadable Operators in C++

+	—	*	/	%	
^	&	|	~	!	&&
||	++	--	<<	>>	,
<	<=	==	!=	>	>=
=	+=	-=	*=	/=	%=
&=	|=	^=	<<=	>>=	
[ ]	( )	->	new	delete	

returns as result the right argument. However, like other operators, the comma operator can be overloaded to give it new meanings.

You cannot overload the meaning of operators if all arguments are primitive data types, nor can you change the precedence or associativity of operators

User-defined operators are permitted only if one or both of the arguments are user-defined data types (or pointers or references to such data types) or enumerated data types. For example, changing the default meaning of the addition operator when used with integer arguments is not permitted, but changing the meaning of this operator when used with **rational** values (where **rational** is the data type developed in Chapter 14) is possible.

The C++ language has a predefined set of operators, and the user is not allowed to create any new operators. The set of valid operators is shown in Figure 7.1. Furthermore, the precedence and associativity among operators is fixed by the language and cannot be changed. Thus, for example, a multiplication operator will always be performed prior to an addition operator in an expression in which they both occur.

7.1   Overloaded Functions or Methods

Operators can be defined either as functions or as member functions

Operators can be overloaded in one of two ways. They can be defined as simple functions, independent of any class definition, or they can be defined as member functions in a class description. These two forms are illustrated by Figures 7.2 and 7.3, which define the less-than relational operator using each of the different techniques. The comparison operator is a binary operation, requiring two argument values. When overloaded as an ordinary function, both arguments are explicitly shown as parameter values. When overloaded as a member function, the left argument is implicitly taken to be the receiver, and only the right argument is declared in the parameter list.

Figure 7.2   Comparison Defined as an Ordinary Function

```
class box {
public:
   box (int v) : value(v) { }
   int value;
};


// define meaning of comparison for boxes
bool operator < (box & left, box & right)
{
   return left.value < right.value;
}
```

A few operators, such as the various forms of assignment, are required to be defined as member functions. For most operators, however, the programmer has the choice of defining the operator either as an ordinary function or as a member function.

To decide which option is preferable, you should keep two points in mind.

- An ordinary function is normally not permitted access to the private portions of the class, whereas a member function is allowed such access. (The word *normally* is used, since a concept known as a *friend function* can override this restriction. We discuss friend functions in Chapter 12.) For this reason, we made the value field public in Figure 7.2 but private in Figure 7.3.

Figure 7.3   Comparison Defined as a Member Function

```
class box {
public:
   box (int v) : value(v) { }

   // define meaning of comparison for boxes
   bool operator < (box & right)
      { return value < right.value; }
private:
   int value;
};
```

- Implicit conversions, say, from integer to float or integer to rational, will be performed for both right and left arguments if the operator is defined in functional form, but only for the right argument if the operator is defined as a member function.

Thus the member function form is preferable if the left argument is modified, as in assignment, or if the data fields to be compared are not easily accessible. The functional form is preferable if the data fields being compared are easily accessible, and if the left argument is not modified or conversions are permitted on both arguments.

7.2   The Simple Binary Operators

Probably the most commonly overloaded operators are the binary arithmetic operators: +, −, *, /, and %. They can be defined either as a two-argument ordinary function or as a one-argument unary method. In the latter case, the receiver is used as the left argument, and only the right argument is written as a parameter.

An example that illustrates the redefinition of the + operator is found in the case study presented in Chapter 14. The following code is used to define the addition of two fractional values:

```
const rational operator + (const rational & left, const
                                  rational & right)
{
    // return sum of two rational numbers
    rational result (
       left.numerator() * right.denominator() +
          right.numerator() * left.denominator(),
       left.denominator() * right.denominator());
    return result;
}
```

Unary operations, such as negation, are either defined as a one-argument ordinary function or as a no-argument member function.

Always return a constant value, unless you want the result to be a target for an assignment

By returning a constant value (indicated by the **const** keyword), we prevent the resulting value from being used as the target of a subsequent assignment:

```
rational a(2,3), b(7,8);
(a + b) = b; // error: constant result cannot be reassigned
```

In Java, the + operator is overloaded for string arguments, providing a string catenation facility. C++ provides a similar overloading for the **string** data type (see Chapter 8). However, note that the Java version is even more robust than the C++ version. In Java any value, primitive or object type, can be used with the catenation operator. In C++ only strings can be catenated to strings using the + operator. One technique for converting primitive data values into strings is provided by the string stream facility (see Section 10.2.2).

7.3   The Comparison Operators

Comparison operators are defined in a manner analogous to the arithmetic operators, except that the results are typically boolean, rather than values. The following is the less-than operator defined for the rational data type described in Chapter 14:

```
bool operator < (const rational & left, const rational & right)
{
    // less than comparison of two rational numbers
    return left.numerator() * right.denominator() <
        right.numerator() * left.denominator();
}
```

Although there are six comparison operators, it is usually necessary to define only two: the less-than operator and the equality comparison operator. Template definitions in the standard library define the remaining four operations in terms of these two, as in the following example:

```
// define greater than in terms of less than
template <class T>
bool operator > (T & left, T & right)
    { return right < left; }
```

The result incurs the overhead of an extra function call but saves coding. Should efficiency be a major concern, all six operators can be defined directly.

7.4   The Increment and Decrement Operators

If the increment operator is over-loaded, you should define both the prefix and postfix forms

As with their integer counterparts, the increment and decrement operators generally alter their argument value, in addition to producing a result. A second unusual characteristic of these operators is that there are two versions of each—a prefix version that produces a change before the result is determined and a postfix version that yields the original value prior to the modification. To distinguish these two cases, the C++ language introduces an extra argument to the postfix version of the operator. The value of this argument is not used; indeed, it need not even be given a name. The following code, for example, illustrates the definitions of these operators for our **box** data type:

```
class box {
public:
    box (int v) : value(v) { }

    // prefix versions, ++aBox
    int operator ++ () { value++; return value; }
    int operator -- () { value--; return value; }

    // postfix versions aBox++
    int operator ++ (int)
    {
        int result = value; // step 1, save old value
        value++; // step 2, update value
        return result; // step 3, return original
    }

    int operator -- (int)
    {
        int result = value;
        value--;
        return result;
    }

private:
    int value;
};
```

Whenever you have a choice, always invoke the prefix form of the increment operator, as it is usually simpler

Note that the prefix increment operator is more efficiently implemented than is the postfix version. This is typically true. In general, a prefix operation should be used whenever the programmer has the choice of either form (as, for example, in the increment field of a **for** loop).

Usually these operators return either a value or a reference to the underlying object. The following rewritten version of the **box** abstraction illustrates this point:

```
class box {
public:
    .
    .
    .
    const box & operator ++ () { value++; return *this; }
}
```

As we showed in the case of simple binary operators, returning a constant value prevents the result from begin used as the basis for a subsequent increment or as the target of an assignment:

```
box mybox(3);
mybox++++; // error---cannot increment constant value
mybox+++= 7; // error---cannot assign to constant value
mybox++ = 7; // error---cannot assign to constant value
```

Unlike Java, the order of evaluation for increments, decrements, and binary operations is left unspecified in C++. The following statement could produce either 10 or 11, depending on whether the increment is performed before or after the left argument is evaluated:

```
int i = 5;
int x = i + ++i;   // ambiguous result
```

Avoid expressions whose meanings are not completely clear

Expressions with ambiguous meanings, such as the preceding example, should be avoided.

An implementation of the increment and decrement operators for the rational number case study is described in Section 14.3.3.

7.5   The Shift Operators

The left and right shift operators, << and >>, are overloaded in exactly the same fashion as the binary arithmetic operators. An important use of these operators is in the stream I/O package, described in Chapter 10. When streams are used, the << is redefined to mean stream output, while >> is redefined to mean stream input. Having these operators return a stream as their value allows complex output expressions to be written:

```
cout << "m " << m << " n " << n << " average " << (n+m)/2.0
     << '\n';
```

Output operators for a new data type are usually described by using the existing output operations on component values. For example, the following code fragment describes the output operation for the rational number data type, described in Chapter 14:

```
ostream & operator << (ostream & out, const rational & value)
{
    // print representation of rational number on an output stream
    out << value.numerator() << '/' << value.denominator();
    return out;
}
```

Note that this result is not declared as const. In fact it cannot be declared as const if we want to embed the invocation in large expressions.

Avoid the right shift of signed integer values

C++ does not have the >>> operator found in Java. The effect of this operator is achieved as a right shift of an **unsigned** integer value. The effect of a right shift of a **signed** integer value holding a negative integer is implementation dependent. In some systems, it may fill with the sign bit, as in Java; in other systems it may fill with a zero bit. In general, this situation should be avoided.

7.6   The Assignment Operator

The assignment, comma, and address-of operators will be constructed automatically if the programmer does not specify an alternative

The assignment operator is one of three operators that will be provided automatically by the compiler, should the programmer not override it. (The others are the address-of operator and the comma operator.) Nevertheless, because the default interpretation is sometimes incorrect, it is considered good practice by many C++ programmers to always provide a precise definition for assignment as part of any class definition.

The default definition of assignment simply recursively applies the assignment operation to each data field, thereby copying each data field into the new structure. For example, consider the following class definition:

```
class box {
public:
    box () {  value = 0; }
    box (int i) { value = i; }

    int value;
};

box a(7);
box b;
b = a;
```

The default interpretation for the assignment arrow is to copy the data fields (in this case, the single data field named value), using whatever rules are appropriate for the particular types. This is satisfactory for primitive types, such as integers and characters.

Always redefine the assignment operator in classes that include a pointer value

Generally, this becomes unsatisfactory when pointer values are involved. For example, in Chapter 4 we described a string abstraction in which each string value maintained a pointer to an internal array of character values. The design intended that each string would have its own internal data array. However, the default assignment operator would have simply copied the pointer value, thereby creating two pointers to the same array. To overcome this, the assignment operator was overridden so as to create a new data area (see Figure 4.2).

The assignment operator can be defined either as a member function, as in the string example, or as an ordinary binary function. The following code fragment illustrates this second possibility with creation of two different assignment operators for the box data type:

```
// const result prevents a second assignment
const box & operator = (box & left, const box & right)
{
   left.value = right.value;
   return left;
}

const box & operator = (box & left, int right)
{
   left.value = right;
   return left;
}
```

Generally, the return type is declared either as void or as a reference to the left expression. Declaring the result type of the assignment operator as void ensures that an assignment can be used only as a statement, not embedded in an expression. However, returning a value permits a sequence of assignments to be performed in one expression. When we use these definitions, we can manipulate our box values as follows:

```
box c;
c = a;
b = 2 + (a = 3);
```

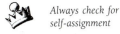
Always check for self-assignment

A common error is to overload the assignment operator but then overlook the possibility that a value might be assigned to itself. Always make certain that an identity assignment will work as expected. For example, in the string data type described in Section 4.3.2, a value associated with the right-hand side is incremented before the value associated with the left-hand side is decremented. Taking these actions in the opposite order would potentially cause a memory error.

```
a = a; // make certain this works
```

An easy way to handle self-assignment is to do nothing in this situation:

```
const string string::operator = (const string & right)
{
    if (this == & right) // check for self assignment
        return right;
    .
    .
    .
}
```

Despite the use of the assignment symbol, constructors do not use the assignment operator

Note that the assignment operator is not used in a declaration, although a superficial consideration of syntax might lead you to believe so:

```
box d = c; // uses copy constructor
```

Such a declaration will use the appropriate constructor, perhaps even creating an internal copy constructor, as in this case. When a class defines both a copy constructor and the assignment operator, the meanings should be similar to avoid confusion.

If addition and assignment are both overloaded, then += should be overloaded as well

An overloaded definition for the assignment operator will not automatically imply a definition for the binary compound-assignment operators. If a binary operator, such as the addition operator +, is overloaded, and if the assignment operator is overloaded, the addition assignment operator += should be overloaded as well (see Section 7.7).

The combination of assignment and polymorphism may create some unintuitive situations. Imagine, for example, that we define a new subclass of class **box**:

```
class bigbox : public box {
public:
    bigbox (int i, double d) : box(i), dvalue(d) { }
    void operator = (bigbox & right) {
        value = right.value;
        dvalue = right.dvalue;
        }
protected:
    double dvalue;
};
```

If we now create instances of the two classes, it is legal to assign a box variable a bigbox value (the operator used will be that defined in class box), but not the reverse:

```
box a(3);
bigbox b(3, 4.0);

a = b; // legal, but sliced, box assignment,
b = a; // not legal, argument must be a bigbox
```

7.7   The Compound Assignment Operators

For primitive data types, the operators +=, *=, and the like combine the operations of addition and assignment. When both addition and assignment are redefined for a user-data type, these operations should be defined as well.

As with the assignment operator, the result of this expression should either be void (which has the effect of not allowing the operator to be embedded in an expression) or a reference to the updated left-hand expression.

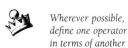

Wherever possible, define one operator in terms of another

An easy way to ensure consistent behavior between an overloaded operator and the compound assignment operator is to define one in terms of the other. If the += operator and a copy constructor are defined, for example, the + operator can be easily implemented:

```
AnObject operator + (const AnObject & left, const AnObject
                                              & right)
{
    AnObject clone(left); // copy the left argument
    clone += right; // combine with right argument
    return clone; // return updated value
}
```

Alternatively, the += operator can be defined in terms of + and =:

```
const AnObject & operator += (AnObject & left,
                                const AnObject & right)
{
    AnObject sum = left + right;
    left = sum;
    return left;
}
```

Here, the reference returned as a result is returned as **const** in order to prevent it from being the target of another assignment operation.

7.8   The Subscript Operator

The subscript operator is often defined for classes that represent a container abstraction. In this case, the subscript represents a key and the value returned is the element associated with the key. An example is the **vector** data type in the STL (Chapter 9), which is a safer abstraction built on top of the underlying C++ array data type. One reason for overloading this operator would be to perform a range test on the index value, something that is not done by the C++ language for ordinary arrays. The following simple example illustrates how this can be done:

```
class safeArray {
public:
    safeArray (int s) { size = s; values = new int[size]; }

    int & operator [ ] (unsigned int i)
    {
        assert(i < size);
        return values[i];
    }
private:
    unsigned int size;
    int * values;
};
```

*The real **vector** data type does not check subscript ranges*

We used the **assert** macro package to check the validity of the index expression (see Section 11.2). By declaring the index value as **unsigned**, we guarantee that it will always be greater than or equal to zero, so we only need check that it is less than the vector size. Rather than using **assert**, another possibility would have been to throw an exception. Because the operator returns a reference, it can be used for both the left and right sides of an assignment arrow:

```
safeArray v(10);
v[2] = 7;
v[3] = v[2] + 12;
```

Defining the subscript operator so that it returns a value, rather than a reference, produces the situation in which the subscript can be used only as a

When returning a reference, make sure that the value will continue to exist after the function exits

value, not as the target for an assignment. Returning a reference declared as const will have a similar effect. As with all references, care should be taken to ensure that the value being referenced will continue to exist even after the operator returns (see Chapter 4).

Unfortunately, the subscript operator can be defined only as a unary function. As a result, in situations that require multiple levels of subscript, the programmer must define them as a sequence of objects, each of which defines its own subscript operator, or use the parenthesis operator, which can be defined for any number of arguments.

7.9   The Parenthesis Operator

The parenthesis operator is the only operator for which the number of arguments is not specified by the language syntax. The parenthesis operator provides the implementation for the syntax normally associated with a function invocation. However, as with all operator overloadings, when it is redefined the meaning applied to this operation is determined by the programmer.

A function object is an object that can be used as though it were a function

Defining the parenthesis operator results in an object that can be used as though it were a function. Such a value is sometimes called a *function object* (see Section 9.3.4). Function objects are used extensively in the STL, described in Chapter 9. For example, let's consider the following definition:

```
class LargerThan {
public:
    // constructor
    LargerThan (int v) { val = v; }

    // the function call operator
    bool operator () (int test)
       { return test > val; }

private:
    int val;
};
```

We can create an instance of this class in the normal manner, using a declaration statement:

```
LargerThan tester(12);
```

The variable tester is now a value, but we can use it as if it were a function:

```
int i = ... ;
```

```
if (tester(i)) // true if i is larger than 12
```

A temporary object can be created by simply naming the class and any arguments to the constructor

If the only need for such a value is as an argument to a generic function, it is often created as a nameless temporary value, by simply naming the class and constructor arguments in the argument list for the generic function:

```
list<int>::iterator found =
    find_if (aList.begin(), aList.end(), LargerThan(12));
```

The STL includes a template class definition for a function object named lesser, which defines a function object for the template type. The function defined by lesser takes two arguments and returns the boolean result obtained by comparing the two values. This particular function occurs frequently in many of the generic algorithms found in the STL. The case study presented in Chapter 15 illustrates the use of function objects, including lesser.

Because the parenthesis operator can be defined with any number of arguments, whereas the subscript operator is restricted to just a single argument, the parenthesis operator is sometimes used for subscripting operations in multidimensional structures (e.g., a matrix).

7.10   The Address-of Operator

The address-of operator is notable for being one of three operators provided automatically for the programmer. That is, it can be applied to an object value, even if the class definition for the object type omits any discussion of the operator. (The other operators that share this characteristic are the assignment operator and the comma operator.) The following code fragment illustrates this point:

```
class box {
public:
    box () { i = 7; }
private:
    int i;
};

box a;
box * b; // b is a pointer to a box
b = & a;  // b now points to a
```

Nevertheless, as with all operators in C++, the programmer is free to overload the address-of operator. The following code, for example, changes the return type for the address operator so that the address yielded is that of an internal variable, rather than the address of the object itself:

```
class box {
public:
    box () { i = 7; }
    int * operator & () { return & i; }
private:
    int i;
};


box a;
box * b;
b = & a; // error, types don't match
int * c;
c = & a; // c now points to internal value in a
```

It is rare to find a use for overloading the address-of operator

There are not many circumstances in which overloading the address-of operator and producing a different value makes sense. However, overloading the operator so that it yields a value of type **void** produces a class of objects that cannot have their address computed, which sometimes is useful.

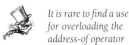

7.11   The Logical Connectives

Short-circuit evaluation means that in some situations only the left argument is evaluated, and the right argument is not even examined

When used with boolean or integer arguments, the operators **&&** and **||** provide the logical connectives *and* and *or*, respectively. However, they also provide one more important feature: A *short-circuit evaluation* of the result is used. That is, if the logical result of the operation can be determined by examining only the left argument, the right argument is left unevaluated. This behavior is important in many situations. For example, it permits the **&&** operator to be used as a guard to protect an out-of-bounds array access:

```
int i;
int a[10];
    .
    .
    .
    // don't exceed array bounds if i is too large
if ((i < 10) && (a[i] != 0))
```

There is no way to overload the logical operators and preserve the short-circuit evaluation

Unfortunately, when overloaded, the && and || operators lose this short-circuit behavior. They are then treated simply as ordinary functions, and for ordinary functions all arguments are evaluated (in an indeterminate order) before execution of the function commences.

7.12   The Comma Operator

The comma operator, like the assignment and address operators, is generated automatically for classes that do not include an explicit redefinition. The comma operator is used for sequencing, and as with the short-circuit evaluation of *and* and *or*, the left argument is explicitly evaluated before the right. The default meaning is to discard the left value, yielding as the result the value of the right argument.

The for statements in Java and C++ use the same syntax and achieve a similar result but use different mechanisms

The comma operator is most commonly encountered in the initialization section of a **for** statement. The following statement is written the same way in both Java and C++ and has the same effect, but it achieves the effect by two different routes:

```
int i, j;
for (i = 0, j = 1; x[i] != 0; i++)
    if (x[i] == x[j]) j++;
```

In Java the for statement grammar permits a statement list to appear in the initialization section, thereby allowing the two assignments shown. The language C++ permits only a single expression. However, the comma operator is used to combine the two assignments into one expression, thereby matching the grammar.

Mistakenly typing a comma instead of a period can be a very subtle programming error

As the preceding example shows, the comma operator has a lower priority than does the assignment operator. The following expression will assign to the variable x the value 7, but the result of the entire expression is the value 12:

```
x = 7,12;
```

As the right argument in a comma expression can be any data type, the implicit meaning is perhaps best described as a templated argument:[1]

---

[1] Although methods that have template arguments independent of their class definition are legal according to the C++ standard, their implementation is complex. For this reason, many compilers do not permit this feature. See Chapter 9 for a more complete description of the template facility in C++.

```
class box {

    template <class T>
    const T & operator , (T & right) { return right; }

};
```

However, even this characterization is not quite correct. As we noted in relation to the logical connectives, an overloaded operator is interpreted by using function semantics, whereby all arguments are evaluated prior to the function invocation. Furthermore, even the order of evaluation for functions is purposely left undefined (see Section 2.8.1). Thus an overloaded version of the comma operator can never have the same short-circuit semantics as the original.

The following code fragment illustrates changing the comma operator so that a box value can be used only with another box value, and the result is the integer quantity stored by the second box:

```
class box {
public:
    box (int v) : val(v) { }
    int value () { return val; }

    int operator , (box & right) { return right.value(); }

private:
    int val;
};
```

7.13   The Arrow Operator

A smart pointer is an object that can be used in the manner of a pointer

The arrow, or member access operator, can be overloaded for certain types of objects. Doing so is useful in creating objects that have a "pointerlike" behavior. The arrow operator can be defined only as a member function (not an ordinary function), and the return type must either be a pointer to a class type or an object for which the member access arrow is itself defined. Objects that can be used like pointers are termed smart pointers. Although it seems odd at first, the address-of operator is a unary operator, which depends only on the receiver (the left argument) and totally disregards the field being denoted by the right argument.

The following example illustrates the use of this operator. The object will count the number of times that the underlying valueis accessed by the arrow operator. The object maintains a pointer to a value, as set by the constructor.

```
class countPointer {
public:
    countPointer (Window * w) { count = 0; win = w; }
    Window * operator->() { count++; return win; }

private:
    Window * win;
    int count;
};
```

The countPointer object can be used in the same manner as the underlying pointer value:

```
Window * x = new Window( ); // create the underlying value

countPointer p(x); // create a counting pointer value

p->setSize(300, 400); // invoke method in class window
```

When the arrow operator is executed, the overridden method is first executed. In the preceding example, this increments the counter. Then the arrow operator is applied *once more* to the result produced by the overloaded operator. This is why the result of an overloaded operator must be a value that itself understands the arrow operator.

7.14   Pointers to Members and Pointers to Member Functions

A variation on the arrow operator is provided by the pointer-to-member operator .* and the pointer-to-member-function operator .->*. The use of these operators is rare, so we do not discuss them here.

7.15   Conversion Operators

The semantics for conversion from a user-defined data type to another data type can be specified with a conversion operator. In a conversion operator, the name

Conversions from user types are defined by conversion operators; conversions to user types are defined by using constructors

of the operation is the type to which the value will be converted. Since the result type is specified by the name, no other result type is given in the function header.

The following code fragment, for example, describes the conversion of a rational number (Chapter 14) into a double precision floating point value:

```
operator double (const rational & val)
{
    return val.numerator() / (double) val.denominator();
}
```

This operator will be invoked for situations in which a value is converted from one type to another, as with a cast:

```
rational r (2, 3);
double d;
d = 3.14 * double(r); // cast converts fraction to double
```

When written as a member function, the argument is omitted and the entire method should be declared as **const**:

```
class rational {
    .
    .
    .
    operator double () const
       { return numerator() / (double) denominator(); }
    .
    .
    .
};
```

Conversion in the other direction—from primitive types to object types—is generally performed using a constructor. We discuss this in Section 7.18.2.

7.16   Memory Management Operators

It is possible to overload the memory management operators **new** and **delete**, obtaining even more control over these tasks than is provided by the default implementations. (They already provide considerably more control over memory management than the Java programmer will be used to.) For example, we could overload them so that allocation was performed by removing a value from a linked list, and deletion simply returned the allocated item to a linked list. (This technique will often be faster than using the memory manager, albeit more complicated.)

7.17   Disallowing Operations

An operator declared as private *can be used only within a class definition*

One way to disallow the application of operators to a class of values is to declare the operators as private. For example, declaring the assignment operator as private creates a data type that can be initialized (using a constructor) but not modified by an assignment:

```
class box {
public:
    box (int v) : val(v) { }
    int value () { return val; }
private:
    void operator = (box & right) { }
}

box aBox (2); // create a new box
box bBox (3); // and another

aBox = bBox; // error---assignment is private
```

The same trick can be applied to constructors. Declaring all constructors as private creates a class of objects that can be created only by other instances of the class or by friends (we introduce the concept of a *friend* in Chapter 12).

Interestingly, an even stronger restriction is created if a destructor is declared as private. Doing so creates an object that cannot be declared as an automatic variable (e.g., as a data field or as a local variable); for if the object cannot legally be destroyed, it will not be created. However, such a value can be allocated by using the new operator. But once allocated, the value can never be deleted and returned to the free store.

7.18   Implicit Functions and Invocations

Implicit function definitions *and* implicit function invocations *are invoked without the programmer directly requesting it*

Implicit function definitions and *implicit function invocations* are actions that take place within the compiler without any explicit direction from the programmer. The discussion is divided into two parts. In Section 7.18.1, we discuss function definitions that can, under certain circumstances, be created automatically as part of a class definition. This is followed by in Section 7.18.2 a discussion of implicit function invocations.

7.18.1   Implicitly Created Operations

Let's consider the following simple class definition, one that both inherits from class box and has a data field of type box:

```
class emptyBox : public box {
private:
    box aField;
};
```

*The default con-
structor, copy con-
structor, destructor,
assignment operator,
address operator,
and comma oper-
ator will all be given
implicit meanings
unless overridden by
the programmer*

Even in the absence of explicit definitions, a large number of functions and operations can be used with an emptyBox data type. In fact, the preceding definition can be considered to be equivalent to:

```
class emptyBox : public box {
public:
    // constructors
    emptyBox () : box() , aField() { }
    emptyBox (const emptyBox & right)
        : box(right), aField(right.aField) { }

    // destructor
    ~emptyBox()
    {
    // implicit deletion of aField
    // implicit call on parent class destructor
    }
    // operators
    const emptyBox & operator = (const emptyBox & right)
    {
        aField = right.aField;
        box::operator = (right);
        return *this;
    }

    emptyBox * operator & () { return this; }

    template <class T>
    const T & operator , (const T & right) { return right; }

private:
    box aField;
};
```

To disallow the use of an implicitly defined operator, such as assignment, the operator must be explicitly defined and declared as private (see Section 7.17).

Implicit Constructors

The implicit copy constructor and implicit assignment simply copy the bits from the right side to initialize the left side

If no constructors are specified, an implicit *default constructor* will be created. This default constructor will first invoke the default constructor for the parent class if the current class was formed by using inheritance. Then the function will recursively apply default initialization rules (e.g., invoking other default constructors) for every data field. Primitive data types, including pointers, are left uninitialized. Often, for pointers this behavior is not desirable (see Section 4.3.2). Remember that this default constructor is created *only* if no other constructors are declared. Creating a constructor, even one that requires argument values, will stop the creation of this function.

An implicit copy constructor is created if no other copy constructor is specified, even if other constructors have been defined. This copy constructor first invokes the copy constructor for the parent class if inheritance is being used. Next, each field is copied from the argument value, using the copy constructor appropriate for the field type. Primitive data types, including pointers, are copied bitwise. Again, for pointers this may often be undesirable.

Implicit Destructors

The destructor created for a class type will first invoke destructors for every data field and then invoke the destructor for the parent class. Fields are destroyed in the opposite order listed in the class body—the last field first and the first field last. Note that this also is the opposite of the order of initialization. An implicit destructor is never considered virtual.

Implicit Assignment Operator

The assignment operator created implicitly, if no alternative is defined, takes as an argument a value of the same type as the class and recursively assigns each data field from the corresponding fields in the argument object. If there is a parent class, the assignment operator for the parent class is then invoked.

If all data fields in the class permit assignment from const objects, the argument to the implicit operator will be declared const. Otherwise, it will not be so marked, and forming assignments by using constant objects will not be legal.

Implicit Address and Comma

The implicit address-of operator simply returns a reference to the current object. A const value is returned if the receiver is constant; otherwise, a reference to a nonconstant value is formed. The implicit comma operator simply returns a reference to the argument object.

7.18.2   Implicit Function Invocations

Implicit function invocations can greatly increase a program's execution time

A copy constructor is always invoked to pass a by-value object

The C++ programmer should be aware that many operations are performed automatically, behind the scenes, without any explicit reference to a function invocation appearing in the code. It is easy to remember, for example, that a constructor will be invoked for every declaration. Less easy is to remember that copy constructors will be executed every time a by-value parameter is used or that doing so will construct a temporary value that will eventually be handed by a destructor. Assignments and implicit conversions are also sources of hidden operations. All take their toll on execution time, and if care is not taken the cost can be considerable.

The following, for example, is a simple class definition. The class includes a default constructor, an integer constructor, and a copy constructor. We have included a destructor for completeness (and so that we can point out when it will be invoked), although in this case it does nothing. An assignment operator copies one value into another. A conversion operator converts a value of the **box** data type into an integer. An addition operator for **box** values is defined as an ordinary function, outside the class definition.

```
class box {
public:
    box () { value = 0; }
    box (int i) { value = i; }
    box (box & a) { value = a.value; }

    ~box() { } // destructor

    void operator = (box & right) { value = right.value; }

    operator int () { return value; }

private:
    int value;
};

box operator + (box & left, box & right)
{
    return box(((int) left) + (int) right);
}
```

Now let's consider the following simple program:

```
int foo (box abox)
{
    box bbox;
    bbox = abox + 1;
    return bbox;
}


int main()
{
    box mybox(3);
    mybox = 4;
    mybox = foo (mybox + 1);
    return 0;
}
```

The following program fragment describes the sequence of operations invoked by each statement. Note how few actually correspond to symbols explicitly shown in the source program:

```
box mybox(3);
    // integer constructor
mybox = 4;
    // integer constructor to create temporary
    // assignment of temporary to variable
    // destructor on temporary
mybox = foo (mybox + 1); // start of statement
    // integer constructor to create temporary
    // binary addition of boxes
box operator + (box & left, box & right)
return box(((int) left) + (int) right); // inside addition
                                        // operator
    // conversion of left box to integer
    // conversion of right box to integer
    // integer constructor for temporary
    // return from addition operator
mybox = foo (mybox + 1); // continuation of statement
box bbox; // inside function foo
    // default constructor to create variable
bbox = abox + 1; // start execution
```

```
        // integer constructor to create temporary for constant
        // binary addition operator for boxes
box operator + (box & left, box & right)
return box(((int) left) + (int) right); // inside addition
                                        // operator
        // conversion of left box to integer
        // conversion of right box to integer
        // integer constructor for temporary
bbox = abox + 1; // continue execution
        // assignment for boxes
        // destructor for temporary
        // conversion from box to integer
        // destructor for local variable bbox
        // return from function
        // destructor for temporary argument
mybox = foo (mybox + 1); // continuation of statement
        // integer constructor converting result to box
        // assignment operation
        // destructor of temporary value
        // destructor of variable mybox
```

The use of a constructor as a way to convert from a primitive type to an object type can sometimes cause problems. For example, imagine a string data type with a constructor that takes an integer value and returns a string with the given number of positions:

```
class string {
public:
    // constructors
    string (char * c) ...
    string (const string & s) ...
    string (int i) ...
};
```

You might be surprised at the effect of the following statement. Instead of converting the character constant into a string, the character is being treated as an integer value. The integer will then be used to create a string with a number of positions equal to the ASCII index of the character literal:

```
string aString = 'a';
```

The use of constructors as implicit conversion operators can be avoided by means of the explicit modifier. A constructor that is declared as explicit will not be used as conversion, but only in conjunction with declaration statements:

```
class string {
public:
    // constructors
    string (char * c) ...
    string (const string & s) ...
    explicit string (int i) ...
};
```

Test Your Understanding

1. To give an existing operator a new meaning, what must be true of the argument values?

2. Explain the difference between overloading an operator as a method and overloading the same operator as a function. When would you want to choose one over the other?

3. How is the definition of *prefix increment* differentiated from the definition of *postfix increment*?

4. Why should the prefix version of an increment operator be used instead of the postfix version whenever you have a choice between the two?

5. What are the possible outcomes of the following program fragment?

```
    i = 7;
    j = ++i + i++;
    k = j++ + ++j;
```

6. How can the effect of the Java operator >>> be simulated?

7. What is the default behavior of an assignment operator on a class value if you do not override the operator?

8. Why would you want to have a non-void return type for an assignment operator?

9. Why would you want to have a subscript operator return a reference rather than a value?

10. What is the unique feature of the parenthesis operator?

11. What is a function object?

12. What three operators are provided "for free," even if they are not defined as part of a class description?

13. Both the following assignments are legal, but neither likely has the intended effect. Explain what values will be held by the two variables following the statements:

```
double pi = (3,14159); // comma, not period
double piTwo;
piTwo = 3,14159;
```

14. What is a conversion operator? When is it invoked?

15. How can you make applying the assignment operator to an object value illegal?

16. What will be the effect of declaring a destructor as private?

17. Which operators are implicitly created as part of every class definition?

18. What is the meaning of the **explicit** modifier when used with a one-argument constructor?

8

Characters and Strings

Next to numbers, strings are perhaps the most common data values manipulated by computer programs. Almost any application that must send or receive textual information to or from a user will use character values. C++ and Java both provide a variety of tools for manipulating characters and strings of character values. In this chapter we describe those facilities and contrast the C++ and Java approach to strings.

8.1 Characters and Literals Strings

A char in C++ is normally an 8-bit quantity, whereas in Java it is explicitly a 16-bit value. We use the word *normally* here because the language definition provides only an 8-bit lower bound on size; in theory a compiler could use a larger unit, although few do. The char data type can be declared either as signed or unsigned; a signed char can represent values between −128 and 127, whereas an unsigned char can represent values 0 through 255. A relatively recent addition to the C++ language is the data type wchar_t, which represents a *wide character*, or 16-bit character similar to the Java char data type.

8.1.1 Character Literals and the cctype Library

Character literals are formed as in Java. Character literals defined by an ASCII integer value are written '\u012' in Java, where 012 can be replaced by any

Recent changes to C++ have changed the names of many libraries. Legacy code may still use the older names

hexadecimal number less than 65535 (or FFFF in hex). In C++ such values are written either as '\123', if the value is less than 256, or as L'1234', if the value is larger than 255. The type associated with the first form is char and with the latter is wchar_t.

There is no equivalent to the Java wrapper class **Character**. One of the major uses for this class is as a source for functions that classify character values. Similar functions are found in the standard C++ library described by the header file cctype.[1] These include:

isalpha(c)	True if c is alphabetic
isupper(c)	True if c is uppercase
islower(c)	True if c is lowercase
isdigit(c)	True if c is decimal digit char
isxdigit(c)	True if c is hexadecimal digit
isalnum(c)	True if c is alphabetic or numeric
isspace(c)	True if c is white space (space; tab or newline)
isprint(c)	True if c is a printable character (8-bit only)

8.1.2   String Literals

A literal string value has type *array of character* in C++, whereas it has type string in Java. Most often, this type is almost immediately converted into type *pointer to character*, using the close equivalence of arrays and pointers in C++ (see Chapter 3). The pointer data type, and pointer operations, are often used to declare string values, and as the argument type in functions that manipulate string values:

```
char * text = "A Literal Text";

int vowelCount (char const * p)
{
    // procedure to count vowels in text
    int sum = 0;
    while (1) { // will break out of loop in switch statement
        switch (*p++) { // switch on character value
            case '\0': return sum;
```

---

[1] The name cctype is of relatively recent origin. The historical name for this header file was ctype.h, and many vendors still supply it only under that name. See Appendix A.

```
         case 'a': case 'e': case 'i': case 'o': case 'u':
             sum++;
             break;
         }
     }
   return sum;
}
```

Always remember the null character at the end of a string literal

String values in C++ are always terminated with a *null character*, that is, a character with integer value zero. The user of a string value must remember this extra character and ensure that any character storage area maintains space for it.

8.1.3   The cstring Library

Language C, the predecessor to C++, provided a library of functions for manipulation of character array values. These functions are still commonly used in C++ programs. The library was described by the header file string.h, which should not be confused with the header file string. More recently, the C++ standards committee has changed the name of the file to cstring; however, most vendors still supply the file with the original name. The string header file describes the more recent string data type, which we examine in Section 8.2. Among the functions provided in the cstring library are:

strcpy(dest, src)	Copy characters from source to destination
strncpy(dest, src, n)	Copy exactly *n* characters
strcat(dest, src)	Append characters from source onto destination
strncat(dest, src, n)	Append only *n* characters
strcmp(s1, s2)	Compare strings s1 and s2
strncmp(s1, s2, n)	Compare first *n* characters in s1 and s2
strlen(s)	Count number of characters in s

Here dest, src, s1, and s2 are pointers to char, and n is an integer value.

A comparison of two character pointers is legal, but the interpretation is generally not what you might expect. Comparison between pointer values is determined by the relative placement in memory of the locations being pointed to. To determine a lexicographic comparison of two character pointer values, an explicit comparison function must be used.

The comparison function returns an integer value that is less than zero if the first string is lexicographically smaller than the second, equal to zero if they are equal, and larger than zero if the first string is larger than the second. An implementation of this function illustrates the close connection between integers, pointers, strings, and arrays in the C++ language:

```
int strcmp (const unsigned char * p, const unsigned char * q)
{
    while (*p && (*p == *q)) { p++; q++; }
    return *p - *q;
}
```

Let's consider the test condition in the while loop. While the pointer p is referencing a non-null value and the value that p is referencing is equal to the value that q is referencing, continue the execution. Execution will halt either when the first argument reaches the end or when the two strings differ. The latter condition includes, as a special case, the second string halting (i.e., encountering a null character) before the first.

When the while loop terminates, the values referenced by the two pointers are treated as integer values. If the two strings are equal, they will both be pointing to null characters, and the subtraction will yield a zero value. If the loop terminates while both pointers reference non-null values, the subtraction will be either positive or negative, depending on the location of the two characters in the alphabet. (This feature depends on the ASCII ordering of character values.) If the loop terminates because either pointer encountered a null value, the subtraction will be either negative or positive, depending on whether it was the first or second string that terminated early.

Always verify that the destination buffer is large enough

An important feature to remember when working with the string functions is that they do not allocate space for the result, nor does C++ perform validity checks on subscript or pointer values. The following code fragment will almost certainly cause unexpected errors:

```
char buffer[20];
char * text = "literal";

strcpy(buffer, text); // copy literal into buffer
for (int i = 0; i < 5; i++)
    strcat(buffer, text); // append literal to buffer
```

The strcat function continues to catenate the literal text into the buffer, overwriting whatever data values happened to follow the buffer text in memory. Always remember that string values contain a terminating null character and are thus one character larger than you might expect. The error in the following program fragment is less obvious, but it is no less serious in that it will overwrite a position in memory outside the range of the declared variable:

```
char buffer[7];
strcpy (buffer, "literal"); // error!---copies eight values,
                            // not seven
```

8.2   Constant and Mutable Values

An immutable value *cannot be changed*

String literals in Java are immutable, they cannot be modified. The same is not true in C++. The following approach makes a literal miserable:

```
char * text = "literal  "; // note space at end
text[0] = 'm'; // change l to m
text[2]--; // t becomes s
strcpy (text + 6, "ble"); // replace l with ble
```

Immutable strings can be formed with the **const** modifier. Note, however, that this modifier can imply multiple meanings, depending on its placement, and the actual meaning may not be intuitive. Placing the **const** value at the front creates a pointer to a constant literal. Such a value cannot be modified, but it *can* be reassigned to a new constant string:

```
const char * a = "literal";
a[2] = 'z'; // error---cannot modify a
a = "new literal"; // ok---can change to new constant value
```

Placing the **const** in the middle of the declaration creates a value that is a constant pointer to a nonconstant object. The pointer itself cannot be changed, but the value it references can:

```
char * const b = "literal";
b[2] = 'z'; // ok---can change what it points to
b = "new literal"; // error---cannot change pointer itself
```

A value that cannot be changed and cannot be reassigned can only be formed by using two occurrences of the **const** modifier:

```
const char * const c = "literal";
c[2] = 'z'; // error---cannot be modified
c = "new literal"; // error---cannot change pointer itself
```

8.3   The **string** Data Type

The string data type is a recent addition to C++ and is still not widely used

The problems associated with the use of character pointers for strings in C++ is a situation that calls out for a high-level data abstraction. Indeed, most early textbooks in C++ described just such values (see [Budd 94, Coplien 92, Lippman 91]). Because of the differences among many implementations, the C++ language standards committee decided to add a common data abstraction to the C++ standard library. The **string** data type is a recent addition to the C++ language. It is still relatively little used, although its use is expected to increase over time as programmers become more aware of its utility. The **string** abstraction is similar to a combination of the **String** and **StringBuffer** data types in Java.

Strings can be created and initialized in the manner you might expect:

```
string a;
string b = "initial text";
string c("more text");
string d(b); // copy of b

a = "some text"; // assignment to a
```

Table 8.1 compares the functionality of the C++ **string** data type to that of **String** and **StringBuffer** in Java. An empty space in the Java column indicates that no corresponding feature is provided.

Like the **vector** data type (see Chapter 9) string values maintain an internal buffer that holds the actual values. This buffer can be accessed with the member function **c_str**. It returns a value of type constant pointer to string.

Subscript index values are not checked for validity

As with the vector data structure, subscripts are generally not checked for validity in the **string** data type. An alternative function, **at**, does check argument values and will throw an **out_of_range** exception if the index is not legal.

The substring operation in C++ is an integer pair that represents a starting position and a length, whereas the equivalent test in Java uses a pair that represents starting and ending positions. The **replace** function in C++ replaces a contiguous region of a string, whereas the similarly named function in Java replaces all occurrences of a specific character with another character.

Some of the functionality provided by the Java **String** class has no direct equivalent functionality in the C++ library but can be easily simulated. For example, the method **startsWith** tests whether one string is a prefix to another. In C++ this test could be performed as follows:

```
// see if string b is prefix to a
if (a.substr(0, b.length()) == b) ...
```

Table 8.1 Comparison of string functionality in C++ and Java

Operation	C++	Java
Number of characters	length()	String.length()
Readjust length	resize(newsize, pad)	StringBuffer.setLength(newsize)
Assign	s = s2	
Append	s += s2	StringBuffer.append(s2)
Catenation	s + s2	String.concat(s2)
Character access	s[index]	String.charAt(index)
Insertion	insert(location, s2)	StringBuffer.insert(location, s2)
Removal	remove(location, length)	
Replacement	replace(location, length, s2)	
Substring	substring(location, length)	String.substring(start, end)
Comparison	s < s2	
Comparison	strcmp(s.c_str, s2.c_str)	String.compareTo(s2)
Equality comparison	s == s2	String.equals(s2)
Substring search	find(text, start)	String.indexOf(s2)
Character search	find_first_of(text, start)	

8.4 Example Program—Split a Line into Words

We illustrate the use of the operations provided by the string abstraction by developing a procedure that takes a line of text and splits it into individual words. Here a *word* is defined by a string of separator characters, also passed as an argument. We use the list data type, which we discuss in Chapter 9. The procedure is as follows:

```
void split
    (const string & text, const string & separators,
         list<string> & words)
// split a string into a list of words
// text and separators are input,
// list of words is output
{
    int textLen = text.length();

    // find first nonseparator character
    int start = text.find_first_not_of(separators, 0);
```

```
// loop as long as we have a nonseparator character
while ((start >= 0) && (start < textLen)) {
    // find end of current word
    int stop = text.find_first_of(separators, start);
    // check if no ending character
    if ((stop < 0) || (stop > textLen)) stop = textLen;
    // add word to list of words
    words.push_back (text.substr(start, stop - start));
    // find start of next word
    start = text.find_first_not_of (separators, stop+1);
    }
}
```

The procedure begins by finding the first character that is not a separator, using the member function find_first_not_of. This function returns the index of the first position that holds a character not found in the list of separators, returning an illegal index value if no such character can be found. The loop therefore cycles as long as the result of the search remains in bounds as a legal index value.

Starting at the given position, the member function find_first_of is then used to find the first character that is from the list of separator values. A special case must be recognized for the situation in which no such character can be found, that is, when the final word ends the original text string. We are guaranteed only that if no such value is found the result will be an illegal index, so we use the if statement to ensure that this value is changed to the size of the text array should no such character be located.

The substr member function is then used to extract the word between the two boundaries. As we demonstrate in Chapter 9, the function push_back is used to append this value to the end of the list of words. Then a search is performed for the start of the next word, and the loop continues.

To illustrate use of this function, imagine that we have a text and want to find the lexicographically largest and smallest words in that text. We could do so by using the following program:

```
int main()
{
    string text = "it was the best of times, it was the worst
                        of times.";
    list<string> words;
    string separators = " .,!?:";
    split(text, separators, words);
```

```
      string smallest = words.front();
      string largest = words.front();

      list<string>::iterator current;
      list<string>::iterator stop = words.end();
      for (current = words.begin(); current != stop; ++current) {
         if (*current < smallest)
            smallest = *current;
         if (largest < *current)
            largest = *current;
      }
      cout << "smallest word " << smallest << endl;
      cout << "largest word " << largest << endl;
      return 0;
   }
```

The result would indicate that the smallest word was **best** and that the largest word was **worst**.

Test Your Understanding

1. How many bits does the C++ language specify for the **char** data type?

2. What are the functions described in the **cctype** header file used for?

3. What is the type associated with a string literal in C++?

4. What is the null character? How is it used in character strings?

5. What are the functions described in the **cstring** header file used for?

6. Explain why the following will probably not have the intended effect:

   ```
   char * x = "here now";
   char * y = "there now";
   if (x < y) ...
   ```

7. Explain why the following will eventually result in a program error:

   ```
   char buffer[10];
   strcpy(buffer, "now is the winter of our discontent");
   ```

8. What are some of the ways that the **string** data type in C++ differ from the **String** data type in Java?

9

Templates and Containers

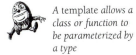

A template allows a class or function to be parameterized by a type

The template mechanism in C++ is perhaps one of the more complex features of the language that has no correspondence in Java. A *template* allows a class definition or function to be parameterized by types or values, in much the same way that a function definition can be executed with a variety of different values. The template mechanism is performed at compile time, permits a great deal of type checking to be performed statically, and eliminates many of the run-time casts that typically populate Java programs (and consume Java execution time).

A major use of templates is as a tool to develop a rich set of data structure, or container, abstractions. In this chapter we first explain the template mechanism, contrasting it to various techniques in Java. We then conclude the chapter with a description of the Standard Template Library (STL). The STL is the primary data structure library used in C++ programs.

9.1   Template Classes

Template classes are perhaps best explained with an example. Let's consider the following definition, which is a generalization of the **box** data structure we developed earlier:

```
template <class T> class box {
public:
    box ( ) { }
    box (T v) : val(v) { }
    box (box<T> & right) : val(right.val) { }
```

```
        T value() { return val; }

        void operator = (T right) { val = right; }
        void operator = (box<T> & right) { val=right.val; }

    private:
        T val;
    };
```

The new **box** is a template class. In other words, the type **box** itself is incomplete and cannot by itself be used to create instances. Instead, the parameter (T, in this case) must be filled in with a specific type before an instance can be created. A class template gives the programmer the ability to define a data type in which some type information is purposely left unspecified—to be filled in at a later time. One way to think of this is that the class definition has been parameterized in a manner similar to a procedure or function. Just as several different calls on the same function can all pass different argument values through the parameter list, different instantiations of a parameterized class can fill in the type information in different ways.

Within the class body the variable T can be used as a type name. Thus we can declare variables of type T, have functions that return a T value, and so on. (Note that T is simply an identifier and that any other identifier name could have been used.)

To create an object, we must first specify a value for T. For example, the following code fragment creates a box that will hold an integer and a box that will hold a double precision value:

```
box<int> ib;
box<double> db;
ib = 7;
db = 3.14;
box<int> ibtwo = 4; // can be initialized in constructor
ib = ibtwo;
int x = ib.value();
```

The types associated with template classes are scrupulously checked at compile time. An attempt to use a value incorrectly will result in a compile time error:

```
ib = 2.7; // error---cannot assign real to int
```

Probably the most common use for template classes, although by no means the only one, is to create container classes. The STL, described in Section 9.3, is one such collection of classes. For example, the list data structure represents the abstraction of a linked list but does not itself specify the particular type of elements it will contain. Instead, the element type is specified by a template parameter:

```
list<int> ilist; // create a list of integers
list<double> dlist: // create a list of real numbers
list<Animal *> alist; // create a list of pointers to animals

ilist.push_front(7); // add an element to front of list
int x = ilist.front(); // extract first element from list
```

Contrast this with the way collections are implemented in Java. In Java, the values held by a collection class are stored in variables declared as Object. There are two main problems with the Java approach:

1. It means that nonobject values, such as primitive types (integers and the like), cannot be stored in Java collections. This is the primary reason that the language Java provides wrapper classes, such as Integer.

2. It means that when a value is removed from a Java collection, it must be cast back to the appropriate type. Note that there are no cast operations in the preceding example. When we remove an element from the list ilist, the compiler already knows that it is an integer, not a double or an animal or any other sort of value.

On the one hand, with templates the language allows creation and manipulation of truly reusable, general-purpose components with a minimum of difficulty but retention of type safety—an important goal of strongly typed languages. On the other hand, Java can easily maintain heterogeneous collections, that is, collections of values of various types. Such collections are more difficult to represent in C++.

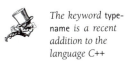

The keyword type-name *is a recent addition to the language C++*

The keyword class in the template parameter list is somewhat misleading, since the value can be any type quantity, not simply a class value. (The slightly more descriptive keyword typename can be used instead of class; however, this is a recent change to C++ and as yet is not supported by many compilers.) For example, we created box values using the int type as a template parameter, which is not a class type. Other primitive values can also be used as template parameters. For example, the following code fragment creates a bit array with a given number of bit values:

```
template <int s> class bitSet {
public:
    set (int index) { ... }
    test (int index) { ... }

    void operator = (bitSet<s> & right);

protected:
    // assume 16 bits per word
    int data [ (s + 15)/ 16 ];
};
```

To manipulate a bit array, we simply fill the template argument value with an integer quantity:

```
bitSet<25> a;
a.set(17); // set position 17
if (a.test(i)) ...
```

A bit array can be assigned to another bit array of the same size, but not to an array with a smaller number of values:

```
bitSet<25> b;
bitSet<30> c;


a = b; // ok, will execute assignment operator
a = c; // produces compile time error; sizes don't match
```

9.1.1   Template Methods

When template methods are written separately from the class definition, they must also be parameterized by the template argument:

```
template <int s>
void bitSet<s>::operator = (bitSet<s> & right)
{
    // first compute the data vector size
    int max = (s + 15) / 16;
    // then copy all the data fields into our array
    for (int i = 0; i < max; i++)
        data[i] = right.data[i];
}
```

Note that the class name bitSet has been qualified by the template argument s. This is not simply a method in class bitSet, but is a method in bitSet<s>.

9.2 Template Functions

In addition to classes, ordinary functions can also be given template definitions. In the following simple example, a function determines the maximum of two quantities:

```
template <class T>
T max (T left, T right)
{
    // return largest value
    if (left < right)
        return right;
    else
        return left;
}
```

Template function types will be inferred from the argument values and need not be specified by the programmer

The function max can be used with any data type that implements the < operator. As the < operator can be overloaded for user-defined data types, this is potentially an infinite set of possibilities:

```
int i = max(3, 4);
double d = max(3.14, 4.7);

// assume comparison has been defined for class AnObject
AnObject a, b;
AnObject c = max(a, b);

// mixing types will not work
int i = max(2, a); // will produce compiler error
```

Note that explicitly declaring the types that will be used with an invocation of a template function is not necessary, as it is with template classes. Instead, the necessary types are *inferred* from the types given by the arguments. If a single unambiguous meaning is not possible, as in the last statement shown in the preceding example, the compiler will produce an error message.

Errors in template functions are often difficult to trace back to the originating statement

Template functions are not expanded until they are used, at which point an instance of the function with the correct argument types will be created.

Often, template functions operate by using other template functions, continuing through many levels of function invocation. An error, for example, using argument values that do not support all the necessary operations (e.g., using max with arguments that do not recognize the < operator), will be reported in relation to the expanded template function, not in reference to the function invocation that caused the template to be expanded. Because of this, an error in a template function may be very difficult to trace back to the originating statement.

9.3   The Standard Template Library

The Standard Template Library (STL) is a collection of useful container classes for common data structures, such as lists and stacks. It includes the following:

vector	Resizeable array
list	Linked list
deque	Double-ended vector
set and multiset	Ordered set
map and multimap	Keyed dictionary
stack	Last-in, first-out collection
queue	First-in, first-out collection
priority queue	Ordered access collection

Manipulation of the containers is facilitated by a tool called an iterator. An *iterator* is a generaization of a memory pointer, used to access elements in a container without knowledge of the internal representation for the container, similar to the class Enumeration in Java. Finally, the STL is unique in providing a large collection of generic algorithms, which are functions manipulated by means of iterators and not tied to any single container.

9.3.1   Containers

Space does not permit discussion of all the STL classes. Instead, in this section we simply contrast the containers that are most similar to the standard containers in Java and outline the major areas of difference.

Vectors

The vector data type has lowercase v, unlike the Vector data type in Java

Like the Java Vector data type, the class vector (note the lowercase v) represents a dynamically resizable array. Unlike the Java class, the C++ class must be provided with a template parameter that describes the element type:

Table 9.1 Comparison of Vector Methods

Operation	C++	Java
Creation	vector<T> v;	v = new Vector();
	vector<T> v(int size);	
	vector<T> v(size, initial value);	
	vector<T> v(oldvector);	
Element access	v[index]	elementAt(index)
First element	front()	firstElement()
Last element	back()	lastElement()
Size	size()	size()
Empty test	empty()	isEmpty()
Set size	resize(newsize)	setSize(newsize)
Capacity	capacity()	capacity()
Set capacity	reserve(newsize)	ensureCapacity(newsize)
Add to front	push_front(value)	insertElementAt(value, 0)
Add to back	push_back(value)	addElement(value)
Insert at position	insert(iterator, value)	insertElementAt(value, position)
Change at position	v[position] = value	setElementAt(value, position)
Remove last element	pop_back()	*None*
Remove from position	erase(iterator)	removeElementAt(position)
Copy	vector<T> v(oldvector);	clone()
Create iterator	begin()	elements()
	end()	

```
vector<int> a;
vector<double> b(10); // initially 10 elements
```

Note that data structures are generally declared as ordinary variables. It is not necessary to use the **new** operator to allocate a container class except in special circumstances, such as when the container must outlive the context in which it is declared.

Table 9.1 compares methods in the **vector** data type to their Java equivalents. The C++ class provides a variety of constructors, including some that set the initial size and one that sets the initial size and provides a default initial value.

Element access and modification in the C++ version are both provided by the subscript operator; in Java two different methods are used for these two activities. In the methods that refer to an internal position within the vector, the Java methods generally use an integer index; the C++ versions use an iterator value (see Section 9.3.2). A copy, or clone, is formed in Java with an explicit method; in C++ the same action is performed with a copy constructor.

Like arrays and strings, vectors do not check for out-of-range index values

One important difference between the Java abstraction and the C++ version is that attempting to access an element that is out of range will always raise an exception in Java; however, the C++ data abstraction performs no run-time checks. Thus an out-of-range index value might not be detected, and garbage values would be returned on access or an unknown location modified on element set. An alternative method, at, does perform a run-time range check and generates an out_of_range error for illegal index values.

The Java class provides one method (contains) that can be used to determine whether a specific value is held by the container and another method (removeElement(val)) to remove an element by giving its value rather than its position. The C++ version has no similar methods, although one of the generic algorithms (see Section 9.3.3) can be used for this purpose. If this operation is common, using the set data abstraction is preferable to using a vector.

Linked list

The list proves most of the same features as the vector data type but adds methods that allow insertions and removals from both the front and back of the container. In addition, insertions or removals from the middle are performed in constant time, rather than the $O(n)$ time required by the vector data type.

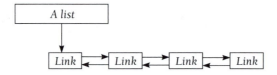

Deque

The deque is an interesting data abstraction that can be thought of as a pair of vectors placed back to back, moving in opposite directions. This arrangement permits efficient (constant time) insertion at either end but slows linear insertion in the middle. However, the deque is a more space-efficient structure than a list.

Set

A set in mathematics does not imply order, but the set data type maintains its values in order

The **set** data type maintains elements in order and thereby permits very efficient (i.e., logarithmic) time insertion, removal, and inclusion tests for values. Internally, it is implemented by a balanced binary tree.

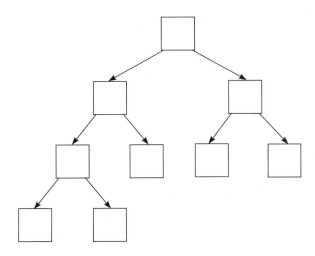

Map

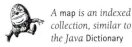

A map is an indexed collection, similar to the Java Dictionary

A **map** is a key/value structure, similar to the Java **Dictionary** or **Hashtable** data types. The **map** data type is parameterized by two template arguments, one for the key type and a second for the value type. Operations on maps are implemented with a data type called a **pair**, which is a key/value combination. Iterators, for example, yield pair values. The key element in the pair is obtained by using the function **first**, and the value field is found by using the method **second**. An optional third argument (required in some C++ compiler implementations) is a function object used to compare key values to each other. (We discuss function objects in Section 9.3.4.)

The case study in graph manipulation in Chapter 15 illustrates the use of the **map** data type.

Stack and Queue

A **stack** is a linear structure that allows insertions and removals from one end only. A **queue** inserts elements from one end and removes them from the other.

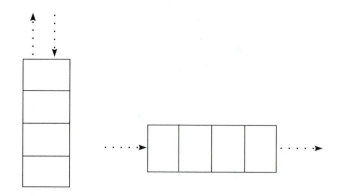

An adapter *is a*
software component
that changes the
interface to another
component

The stack and queue data structures in the STL are interesting in that they are *adapters*, built on top of an underlying data type such as a vector or a linked list. The template argument used in the constructor specifies the underlying container:

```
stack< vector<int> > stackOne;
stack< list<anObject *> > stackTwo;
queue< deque<double> > queueOne;
```

Note the separating space between the two angle brackets. Many C++ compilers will report spurious compiler errors if the space is omitted (confusing the angle brackets for the right shift operator). The method names for the stack abstraction are similar to those used by the Java Stack class.

Priority Queue

The priority queue data type provides rapid access to the largest element in a collection and its rapid removal. Like the stack, it is built as an adaptor on top of another container, typically a vector or a list. Two template arguments are used with a priority queue. The first is the underlying container, while the second is a function object that is used to compare elements.

9.3.2   Iterators

The concept of an iterator in the STL is similar in purpose to the idea of an Enumeration in Java but differs in the particulars of use. This is perhaps best illustrated by an example. Imagine that v is a vector of integer values. We could compute the sum of the values in Java by using the following code fragment:

```
int sum = 0;
for (Enumeration e = v.elements(); e.hasMoreElements(); ) {
    Object val = e.nextElement();
    Integer iv = (Integer) val;
    sum += iv.intValue();
}
```

The same idea, using iterators, would be written as follows:

```
int sum = 0;
vector<int>::iterator start = v.begin();
vector<int>::iterator stop = v.end();
for ( ; start != stop; ++start)
    sum += *start;
```

Several differences should be noted. Because the STL containers use template definitions, it is not necessary to cast the object to the proper type after it has been removed from the container. The template property of the STL also means that containers can store primitive types, such as integers, and do not need the wrapper classes necessitated by the Java version. A different iterator data type is provided by each container; thus to create an iterator first requires specifying the container type. Most important, although enumerations work as a single value, iterators must always be manipulated in pairs, with a beginning and an ending iterator.

One way to understand iterators is to note that they are designed to be equivalent—and compatible with—conventional pointers. Just as pointers can be used in a variety of ways in traditional programming, iterators are also used for various purposes. An iterator can be used to denote a specific value, just as a pointer can be used to reference a specific memory location. However, a *pair* of iterators can be used to describe a *range* of values, analogous to the way in which two pointers can be used to describe a contiguous region of memory.

Imagine, for example, an array that is being used to represent a deck of playing cards. Two pointer values can be used to denote the beginning and ending of the deck:

cards	cards+1	cards+2		cards+50	cards+51	cards+52
card[0]	card[1]	card[2]	•••	card[50]	card[51]	

If we need to represent the beginning and ending of the memory space, we can use the values **cards** and **cards+52**. In the case of iterators, however, the values being described are not necessarily physically in sequence. Rather, they are logically in sequence because they are derived from the same container, and the second follows the first in the order that elements are maintained by the collection:

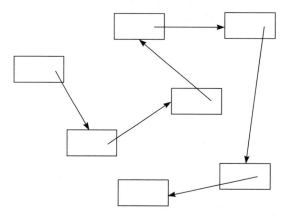

The convention used by the container classes in the STL is to return, in response to the member function named begin(), an iterator that accesses the first element in the collection. An iterator denoting the end of the collection is yielded by the member function end().

Conventional pointers can sometimes be *null*; that is, they point at nothing. Iterators, as well, can fail to denote any specific value. Just as it is a logical error to dereference and use a null pointer, it is an error to dereference and use an iterator that is not denoting a value.

Iterators produced by containers often come in pairs. The beginning iterator is returned by the function begin, *and the ending iterator by the function* end

When two pointers that describe a region in memory are used in a C++ program, the convention is *not* to consider the ending pointer to be part of the region. This is shown in the cards array, wherein the array extends from cards to cards+52, even though the element at cards+52 is not part of the array. Instead, the pointer value cards+52 is the *past-the-end* value—the element that is the next value *after* the end of the range being described. Iterators are used to describe a range in the same manner. The second value is not considered to be part of the range being denoted. Instead, the second value is a *past-the-end* element, describing the next value in sequence after the final value of the range. Sometimes, as with pointers to memory, this will be an actual value in the container. At other times, it may be a special value, specifically constructed for the purpose. The value returned by the member function end() is usually of the latter type, being a special value that does not refer to any element in the collection. In either case, it is never legal to try to dereference an iterator that is being used to specify the end of a range. (An iterator that does not denote a location, such as an end-of-range iterator, is often called an *invalid* iterator.)

An examination of a typical algorithm will help illustrate how iterators are used. The generic function named find() can be used to determine whether a value occurs in a collection. It is implemented as follows:

```
template <class iterator, class T>
iterator find (iterator first, iterator last, T & value)
{
    while (first != last && *first != value)
       ++first;
    return first;
}
```

The following code fragment shows how we could use this algorithm to search for a value being held by a conventional C++ array:

```
int data[100];
    .
    .
    .
int * where = find(data, data+100, 7);
```

Alternatively, the following procedure declares a new variable and then searches for the value 7 in a list of integers, assigning the resulting iterator to the variable:

```
list<int>::iterator where = find(aList.begin(), aList.end(), 7);
```

The resulting value is the end-of-list iterator (equal to the value returned by the function end()), or it represents the location of the first 7 in the list.

When iterators are used as pairs, the second iterator must always be reachable from the first

As with conventional pointers, the fundamental operation used to modify an iterator is the increment operator, ++. When the increment operator is applied to an iterator that denotes the final value in a sequence, it will be changed to the "past-the-end" value. An iterator j is said to be *reachable* from an iterator i if, after a finite sequence of applications of the expression ++i, the iterator i becomes equal to j.

Ranges can be used to describe the entire contents of a container, by constructing an iterator to the initial element and a special "ending" iterator. Ranges can also be used to describe subsequences within a single container. Whenever two iterators are used to describe a range, the algorithms assume, but do not verify that the second iterator is reachable from the first. Errors can occur if this expectation is not satisfied.

The find() algorithm illustrates three requirements for an iterator:

- An iterator can be compared for equality to another iterator. They are equal when they point to the same position but otherwise are not equal.

- An iterator can be dereferenced with the * operator to obtain the value being denoted by the iterator. Depending on the type of iterator and variety of underlying container, this value can also sometimes be used as the target of an assignment in order to change the value being held by the container.

- An iterator can be incremented so that it refers to the next element in sequence, using the operator ++.

Iterators are possible because these characteristics can all be provided with new meanings in a C++ program. The reason is that the behaviors of the given functions can all be modified by *overloading* the appropriate operators (see Chapter 7).

Two primary categories of iterator are constructed by the containers in the STL. The types list, set, and map produce *bi-directional* iterators. These iterators recognize the increment and decrement operators (the latter moving the iterator *backward* one element) but cannot be randomly accessed. In contrast, the types vector, string, and deque generate *random access* iterators, which permit the subscript operator and the addition of integer values to an iterator (analogous to adding an integer value to a pointer, as with the expression cards+52). Some of the generic algorithms depend on this subscripting ability and therefore cannot be used with lists or sets.

9.3.3   Generic Algorithms

A generic algorithm is a software algorithm that can be used with many different collection classes

One of the most interesting features of the STL is the separation between the container abstractions themselves and algorithms that can be used with the containers. By separating the two and providing a rich collection of algorithms that work only through iterators, the same algorithms can be used with a variety of different containers or indeed with normal arrays and regular memory pointers. These functions are called *generic algorithms* because they are generic to a wide variety of uses. Again, the template mechanism is the key to generic algorithm specialization for use in any particular situation.

We presented one example of a generic algorithm in the find procedure described earlier. This algorithm performs a linear search to locate a value within a collection. Other algorithms are used to initialize the elements in a container, to perform a variety of searches, to transform the values in a container in place, to remove elements, or to reduce a collection to a single value.

An algorithm that produces an in-place transformation is the function random_shuffle. It randomly rearranges the values in the collection. Using this function, we could randomly shuffle the card values described earlier as follows:

```
random_shuffle (cards, cards+52, randomizer);
```

The randomizer used by this algorithm must be a random number generator, written in the form of a function object.

9.3.4   Function Objects

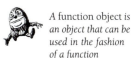

A function object is an object that can be used in the fashion of a function

Functions are not really first-class values in C++ (or in many other languages, for that matter). You cannot have a variable that holds a function, for example[1]. Yet many of the generic algorithms must be specialized by passing a function as an argument.

The STL gets around this problem in an interesting manner. Function invocation is considered by C++ to be just another operator—in this case, the parenthesis operator. Like almost all operators, it can be overloaded by a class. Thus the programmer can make an *object* that can be used as if it were a *function*. One example is the random number generator used in the preceding example, which could be written as follows:

```
class randomInteger {
public:
    unsigned int operator () (unsigned int max) {
        // compute rand value between 0 and max
        unsigned int rval = rand();
        return rval % max;
    }
};
```

```
randomInteger randomizer; // create an instance of class
```

The parenthesis operator defines a "functionlike" interface that takes a single integer argument. Using this value, and a real system–provided random number generator named rand,[2] the function computes a positive random number between 0 and the maximum value.

Another example will further illustrate this idea. The generic algorithm find_if locates the first element in a collection that satisfies a predicate supplied by the user. Suppose that we want to find the first value larger than 12. We could write a special "larger than 12" function, but let's generalize this to a "larger than x"

---

[1] It is important to be precise here. In C++ you can have a pointer to a function, but that is not the same as having a function value.

[2] See Section A.8 in Appendix A for a discussion of the standard libraries.

function, where the value *x* is specified when an instance of the class is created. We can do so as follows:

```
class LargerThan {
public:
    // constructor
    LargerThan (int v) { val = v; }

    // the function call operator
    bool operator () (int test)
        { return test > val; }

private:
    int val;
};
```

Creating an instance of LargerThan gives us a functionlike object that will test an argument value to determine whether it is larger than the value specified by the constructor. Using this instance, we could find the first element in a list that is larger than 12 by using the following function invocation:

```
LargerThan tester(12); // create the predicate function
list<int>::iterator found =
    find_if (aList.begin(), aList.end(), tester);
if (found != aList.end())
    printf("element is %d", *found); // found such a value
else
    printf("no element larger than 12");
```

The find_if generic algorithm takes a collection specified by a pair of iterators and returns an iterator that indicates the first element that matches the specification, returning the end-of-range iterator if no such element is found. By testing the result against the ending iterator, we can tell whether the search was successful. If it was, we can dereference the resulting iterator to find the actual value.

If the only use for a function object is as an argument to a generic algorithm, as in the preceding example, the creation of the function object can often be replaced by the creation of a *nameless temporary variable* value. Such a value can be created by simply naming the class type for the temporary value along with the arguments to be used in the constructor to initialize it:

```
LargerThan(12) // creates an instance of LargerThan
```

The creation of this temporary value can be performed directly in the argument list for the generic algorithm, yielding a concise description:

```
list<int>::iterator found =
    find_if (aList.begin(), aList.end(), LargerThan(12));
```

Another common use for function objects is in the template parameter list for containers. For the map and priority_queue data types, as well as others, an optional template argument describes the algorithm to be used in comparing elements. This algorithm must be described as a function object. For example, in Chapter 15 we present a case study that uses a map to represent a graph data type. For keys this data type uses primitive C++ strings (i.e., pointers to characters). Since the default implementation of pointer comparison is not what we desire in this case, another algorithm must be defined. This is provided by the following class description:

```
class charCompare { // compare two character literal values
public:
    bool operator () (const char * left, const char * right) const
    {
        return strcmp(left, right) < 0;
    }
};
```

A charCompare compares the strings that two character pointer values reference. The desired data type is then declared as a structure that uses character pointers as keys, holds integers as values, and uses the charCompare function object to compare key values:

```
typedef map <const char *, unsigned int, charCompare> cityInfo;
```

Working together, containers, iterators, algorithms, and function objects provide a set of powerful tools that can be used in almost any nontrivial program.

Test Your Understanding

1. How is the description of a template class different from the description of a normal C++ class?

2. How is the creation of an instance of a template class different from the creation of a normal C++ value?

3. Using a container class in Java frequently necessitates the use of run-time casts. How does the template mechanism eliminate the need for these casts?

4. What is a template function? How are the template argument types for a template function determined?

5. What do the initials STL stand for?

6. In what ways does the vector data type in C++ differ from the Vector data type in Java? In what ways are they similar?

7. Why are the stack, queue, and priority_queue data types known as adaptors?

8. What is a past-the-end value? How is such a value used in an iterator loop?

9. What is a generic algorithm?

10. What is a function object? How is such a value created? How is it used in conjunction with generic algorithms?

10

Input/Output

Programs should use one I/O library or the other, but never both in the same program

The techniques used in the input and output (I/O) facilities of Java are an evolutionary descendant from those developed in C++. It is therefore not surprising to find some similarities, but there also are a great number of differences. Input and output in C++ is also complicated by the existence of two competing systems. The Standard I/O Library, or stdio, is an earlier system inherited from C. The newer C++ specific library is called the Stream I/O Library. As both are commonly found in C++ programs,[1] you need to have at least a passing acquaintance with each system.

All three libraries share the concept of an input console, with values flowing into the program from the standard input and values flowing out of a program from the standard output or the error output (Figure 10.1). In addition, all libraries provide a way to read from files, sockets, or other sources of input and output. In this chapter we first describe the older Standard I/O Library and then the newer Stream I/O Library.

10.1 The stdio Library

The Standard I/O Library is inherited from the original language C. It is therefore widely known and available and is based on stable and well-exercised libraries. However, because it uses no object-oriented features, it is not as extendable or

---

[1] Occasionally programmers even try to mix the two systems in a single program—usually a recipe for confusion and disaster, as both libraries buffer their input and output operations.

Figure 10.1   Visualizing the Standard Input and Output Channels

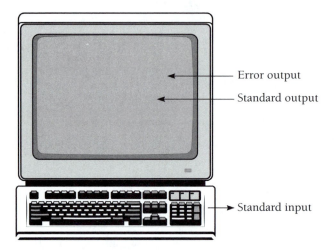

adaptable as the newer Stream I/O Library. Because it is likely to be encountered in the wealth of existing code, a C++ programmer should be aware of the **stdio** library and be somewhat familiar with its use. However, for developing new programs the Stream I/O system is preferred.

The Standard I/O Library is indicated by the include directive **cstdio**:[2]

```
# include <cstdio>
```

The Standard I/O Library is based on the concept of *files*. Console input is provided by the file **stdin**, while console and error output is provided through the files **stdout** and **stderr**. Basic character-based input and output to the standard console is provided by the routines **getchar** and **putchar**:

```
int c = getchar(); // read a single input character
putchar('x'); // print a single character
```

Note that **getchar** returns an integer value, not a **char**. The integer constant **EOF** (normally −1) is returned to indicate the end of input.

A null-terminated string value (see Chapter 8) can be written by using the function **puts**. The function **gets** reads a line of input from the standard input.

gets reads until it encounters an end-of-line character, even if this exceeds the length of the buffer it was given

---

[2] If you are somewhat familiar with C++, you may be surprised by this name. Until relatively recently, the header file was named **stdio.h**. The latest revision of the C++ language definition changed the name. However, in order to accommodate the legacy code program compiler, vendors probably will continue to support both names for the foreseeable future.

A line is a sequence of characters terminated by a newline character. The gets algorithm assumes but does not verify that the buffer passed as argument is sufficient to hold the input line. Hence:

```
char * text = "please enter your name:";
puts(text); // print the text string

char buffer[120];
gets(buffer); // read a line of input
```

Other files can be opened with the function fopen. This function returns a file pointer, which is a value of type FILE:

```
FILE * fp = fopen("mydata.dat", "r");
if (fp == NULL)
    puts("file cannot be opened");
```

After opening a file, always verify that the open was successful

The second argument indicates the mode for the file, which can be read, write, or append. Modifiers can also be applied to the mode, but they are somewhat platform-specific. Consult the reference manual for your platform for more details. This function will return the pointer constant NULL if an error occurs during file processing. It is a good idea to always check for this condition.[3]

Input from or output to a file can be performed by using the functions fgetc or fputc. The stream to be used as a target or source is supplied as the second argument:

```
fputc('z', fp); // write character to fp
int c = fgetc(fp); // read character from fp
char * msg = "unrecoverable program error";
fputs(msg, stderr); // write message to standard error output
```

The fputc function will return the constant EOF upon encountering an error. However, programmers often ignore the return value.

10.1.1   Formatted Output

Formatted output is generated by the function printf. The first argument in this function is a string that represents the formatting specification. Literal text is

---

[3] The constant NULL was introduced in the Standard I/O Library as a representation for a null pointer value and is still often encountered in program listings. Later refinements to the language definition encouraged the use of an integer zero value for this purpose. Generally, all occurrences of NULL can be safely replaced by a zero value.

printed as it appears. Values to be replaced are indicated by a percent sign, followed by a conversion character. The most common conversion characters are the following:

%d   Integer decimal value

%o   Integer printed as octal

%x   Integer printed as hexadecimal

%c   Integer printed as character

%u   Unsigned integer decimal value

%f   Floating point value

%g   Floating point value

%s   Null terminated string value

%%   Percent sign

For example, the following code fragment will print two integer values and one floating point value:

```
int i = 3;
int j = 7;
double d = i / (double) j;
printf("the value of %d over %d is %g", i, j, d);
```

The function fprintf is similar but requires a file pointer as the first argument:

```
char * fileName = ...;
if (fopen(fileName, "r") == null)
    fprintf(stderr,"Cannot open file %s\n", fileName);
```

The sprintf function writes into a character buffer rather than to a file:

```
char buffer[180];
sprintf(buffer, "the value is %d\n", sum);
```

Always verify that formatting commands match the argument types

The printf facility works only for formatting primitive values, such as integers and floats, and is not easily extendable to user-defined data types. It is largely for this reason that the new Stream I/O Library is preferred. A danger with the printf approach is that argument types are not checked, and a mismatch between the formatting directive and the actual argument type will generally produce garbage:

```
double d = 23.5;
printf("the value is %d\n", d); // error -- float printed as int
```

The function scanf is used to format values as they are read from a file. The formatting directives are the same, but the arguments must generally be pointer values. They can be produced by using the address-of operator (see Chapter 3). Thus:

```
scanf("%d %f", &i, &f); // read an int, then a float
```

As with printf, no error checking is performed to ensure that the actual argument types supplied match the formatting directive. This functionality, too, has been superseded by a more object-oriented, more robust input facility in the Stream I/O Library.

Other functions provided by the Standard I/O Library include facilities for reading or printing an entire structure and the ability to seek to an arbitrary position within a file. We do not describe these features here.

10.2 The Stream I/O Facility

Whenever possible, use the Stream I/O Library rather than the Standard I/O Library

The standard I/O printing facility is fine for printing primitive data types, but it performs no argument type-checking, and it does not extend well to user-defined types. As we noted in Section 10.1, formatting directives are written in the form of a two-character sequence, where the first character is % and the second character indicates the type of value to be printed. For example, %d is used to print integer (decimal) numbers, %s to print character strings, %c to print individual characters, and so on. The following statement prints the value of the two integers n and m and their average:

```
printf("n %d m %d average is %f\n", n, m, (n+m)/2.0);
```

The problem with this approach is that the meaning of the formatting directives was fixed when the printf function was written. If a new data type is created, such as the rational number data type described in Chapter 14, it is not possible to add a new formatting directive to indicate how formatting should take place. To print a rational number, we would need to access directly the numerator and denominator fields to print them as integers. Doing so, however, conflicts with the protected status of these fields, as well as with our desire to treat the rational number abstraction as a single entity.

A solution that offers better possibilities for extendability, as well as improved error detection, is to use the ability to overload function names in C++. Let's assume, for example, that the system provides a single function, say, print, that can be used to print values on an output device. Various implementations of print, each differing in the type of argument they take, could be provided to print characters, integers, floating point values, and so on. When a new data type is created, such as our rational number abstraction, it would be necessary only to add yet another overloaded version of the **print** function. This solution will work; the only difficulty is that printing long sequences of values combined with literal text is somewhat clumsy. For example, to produce the output corresponding to the single **printf** statement given previously would require the following sequence of seven statements:

```
print("n ");
print(n);
print(" m ");
print(m);
print(" average is ");
print((n+m)/2.0);
print('\n');
```

Nevertheless, the use of overloading seems to be a useful mechanism provided by the language, which permits a programmer to define output easily for new data types. The key to overcoming the clumsy nature of the overloaded **print** function, perhaps, is the ability to overload *expressions*, not statements. To do this, the Stream I/O Library introduces a new data type, the *stream*, and in particular the data abstraction **ostream**, which stands for "output stream." We can think of streams as representing a file, although it is more accurate to say that a stream can copy onto a file.

To use the stream I/O facility, the programmer must first include the appropriate header file:

```
# include <iostream>
```

Note the omission of the .h extension. This omission is common in many of the more recently written libraries.[4]

Next, the operator **<<**, which for integer arguments is used to produce a left shift, is redefined to indicate data flowing onto a stream. Let's assume that, when the second (right) argument is a character, the single character value is copied to the file associated with a stream. (The details of how this is done are implementation-dependent, and we ignore them here.) We can overload the **<<** operator to print a variety of other data types by reducing the problem to that of printing individual characters. Figure 10.2 illustrates the printing of signed and unsigned integer values.

The fact that each of these operator functions returns a pointer (reference) to the **ostream** value is significant. Since the **<<** operator is left-associative, complicated formatting can be written as a single expression. The global variable **cout** is

When overloading the stream output operator, always return the stream as the function result

---

[4] However, not all compiler vendors seem to have caught on. In some systems, the file is still named iostream.h.

Figure 10.2   Various Overloaded Versions of the << Operator

```
ostream & operator << (ostream & out, const int value)
{ // print signed integer values on a stream

   unsigned int usvalue;
   if (value < 0) {
      // print leading minus sign
      out << '-';
      usvalue = - value;
   }
   else
      usvalue = value;
   // print nonnegative number
   out << usvalue;
   return out;
}


inline char digitCharacter(unsigned int value)
{
   // convert nonnegative integer digit into printable digit
   // assume value is less than 9
   return value + '0';
}


ostream & operator << (ostream & out, const unsigned int value)
{
   // print unsigned integer values on a stream
   if (value < 10)
      out << digitCharacter(value);
   else {
      out << (value / 10); // recursive call
      out << digitCharacter(value % 10); // print single char
   }
   return out;
}
```

the stream associated with a standard common output device. Thus the following expression can be used to print the value of two numbers and their average:

```
cout << "n " << n << " m " << m << " average " << (n+m)/2.0
       << '\n';
```

More significantly, a programmer can easily provide formatting capabilities for a new data type. For example, to output rational numbers the programmer need only define the following operator:

```
ostream & operator << (ostream & out, const rational & value)
{
    // print representation of rational number on an output stream
    out << value.numerator() << '/' << value.denominator();
    return out;
}
```

The programmer can then intermix primitive and user-defined types:

```
rational frac(3,4);
cout << "fraction of " << 3 << " and " << 4 << " is " << frac
        << endl;
```

The variable cerr is similar, but it writes to the standard error output.

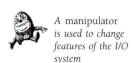
A manipulator is used to change features of the I/O system

The value endl, used in the preceding example, is an I/O stream *manipulator*. In this case, the purpose is to signal the end of end and flush the output buffer. Simply printing a newline character is not guaranteed to flush the output. Other manipulators modify various printing parameters—for example, the precision used in printing floating point values. Despite appearances, a manipulator is not actually a simple value but a function. A simplified version of the endl manipulator is as follows:

```
ostream & endl (ostream & out)
{
    // write the end-of-line character
    out << '\n';
    // then flush the buffer
    out.fflush();
    // then return the buffer
    return out;
}
```

The function is invoked as a consequence of yet another overloaded version of the stream output operator:

```
ostream & operator << (ostream & out, ostream & (*fun)(ostream &))
{
    // simply execute function
    return fun (out);
}
```

Study this approach carefully to understand how seemingly innocuous C++ statements can actually hide implicit function invocations.

10.2.1   Stream Input

Stream input always ignores white space

There is a corresponding data type istream for input streams. Just as the global variable cout represents the standard output, the global variable cin represents a standard input device. A characteristic of stream input is that "white space" characters (spaces, tabs, and newlines) are ignored during input. If intval is declared as an integer variable, the expression

```
cin >> intval;
```

reads an integer value into the variable. As with the << operator, the >> operator returns the value of the left argument. When used in situations where a boolean value is expected, such as if or while statements, the boolean result generated is used to indicate end of file. Thus a loop that would read values repeatedly from the input until end of file was reached could be written as follows:

```
while (cin >> intval) {
    // process intval
    .
    .
    .
}
// reach this point on end of input
    .
    .
    .
```

An easy way to remember the stream I/O operations is to visualize them as arrows. The input operator, >> x, points data into x, while the output operator, << x, copies data out of x.

10.2.2   String Streams

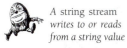

A string stream writes to or reads from a string value

A *string stream* writes to or reads from a string value, rather than from an output device. To use this facility, the programmer must first include the sstream header file. The data type ostringstream creates an output stream. Values are buffered in an internal string, which can be accessed with the member function str.

This facility is useful for formatting complex output because stream operators not only perform catenation, but they also automatically convert the right argument from numerous primitive data types into character values. In this sense, a string stream can be used as a replacement for the string catenation operator **+** commonly used in Java. This is illustrated by the following example:

```
# include <sstream>

int n = ...;
int m = ...;

ostringstream formatter;

formatter << "the average of " << n << " and " <<
    m << " is " << ((n + m)/2.0);

string s = formatter.str();
```

User-defined output stream operators, such as the **rational** number output operator described earlier, also will work with string streams.

An **istringstream** is the corresponding input stream. A simple use for it is to break a string of text into white-space separated parts:

```
string text = "Isn't this a wonderful feature";
istringstream breaker(text);
string word;

while (breaker >> word)
    cout << word << endl; // print each word on a separate line
```

10.2.3   File Streams

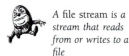

A file stream is a stream that reads from or writes to a file

File streams, that is, streams that are attached to files, are separated from the other stream functions in the Stream I/O Library. To use file streams, the programmer must first include the appropriate header file:

```
# include <fstream>
```

The **fstream** header file includes the **iostream** header, so it is not necessary to include both. Again, note omission of the **.h** extension.

The classes **ifstream** and **ofstream** are used to create streams that are attached to input and output files, respectively. The constructor for the class is a string that represents a filename. A conversion operator changes a file stream into a boolean value, whereby the value indicates the success or failure of the file-opening operation. Using these classes, we can open a file as follows:

```
char fileName = "outfile.dat";
ofstream ofd(fileName); // create file for output
if (! ofd) {
    cerr << " cannot open file " << fileName
}
else {
    ofd << "first line in file"
    .
    .
    .
}
```

The method getline returns a line of input. Other operations can be used to set the state of the file or control the formatting of numeric values. In general, file operations in C++ throw far fewer exceptions than do corresponding operations in Java.

10.3   An Example Program

A simple program can illustrate the use of the stream I/O facilities. The program reads words and determines the average word and sentence length. Words are read one by one until the end of input. As each word is read, the final character is tested to determine whether it is a period. If so, the sentence count is incremented. The program code is as follows:

```
# include <iostream>
# include <string>

int main()
{
    int wordCount = 0;
    double totalWordLen = 0;
    double totalSenCount = 0;
    string word;

    while (cin >> word) {
        int wordLen = word.length();
        wordCount++;
        if (word[wordLen-1] == '.') {
            totalWordLen += (wordLen-1);
```

```
                    totalSenCount++;
                }
                else {
                    totalWordLen += wordLen;
                }
            }

        cout << "total number of words " << wordCount << endl;
        if (wordCount > 0)
            cout << "average word length " << totalWordLen /
                                                wordCount << endl;
        cout << "total number of sentences " << totalSenCount << endl;
        if (totalSenCount > 0)
            cout << "average sentence length " << wordCount /
                                                totalSenCount << endl;

        return 0;
    }
```

After all words have been read, the statistics on the input are printed.

Test Your Understanding

1. Which include file is necessary for use of the facilities of the Standard I/O Library?

2. What names are attached to the standard input, standard output, and error output in the Standard I/O Library?

3. What task is performed by the function printf?

4. What is the danger in the following use of printf?

    ```
    double pi = 3.14159;
    printf("Pi is %d\n", pi);
    ```

5. Why is the printf approach to formatted output not easily extendable to user-defined data types? How is this problem overcome in the Stream I/O Library?

6. Which include file is necessary for use of the facilities of the Stream I/O Library?

7. What names are attached to the standard input, standard output, and error output in the Stream I/O Library?

8. What is a string stream?

9. Which include file is necessary to open a file stream?

10. Using string streams, show how to overload the addition operator to provide catenation with string values and primitive types, similar to the way the + operator works in Java:

```
string operator + (string & left, int right)
{
    // compute and return new string
    .
    .
    .
}
```

11. Using templates, show how the various functions produced for Question 10 can be defined at the same time with a single template function.

Exception Handling

Exception handling, a new feature in C++, is still not widely used

Exception handling has been part of the language Java since the beginning. Thus Java programmers are used to working with methods that will throw an exception as a natural way to handle an unusual situation. The same is not true for C++ programmers. Exception handling is a relatively new addition to the C++ language, and prior to the introduction of the feature, programmers dealt with unusual situations in a number of different ways. Thus in reading and writing C++ code the programmer must not only be aware of the differences between the exception handling mechanisms in the two languages, but also have some knowledge of the alternative techniques that have been used to address similar problems.

11.1   Flags and Return Codes

When functions return an error flag, the result should always be checked

One of the easiest ways to signal that an error has occurred in the processing of a function or method is by returning a special value as the function result. An example of this occurs in the file open function in the Standard I/O Library. The routine fopen is suppose to return a *file pointer*, a pointer to an internal structure that manages information about currently open files. If for any reason (e.g., protection violations and incorrect names) the file cannot be opened, a null pointer value is returned:[1]

---

[1] Earlier versions of the Standard I/O Library defined the symbolic name NULL to represent the null pointer value, and this value is still used in conjunction with the library.

```
FILE * fp = fopen("myData", "r"); // open file for read
if (fp == 0)
    .
    .   // handle error case
    .
else
    .
    .   // handle correctly opened case
    .
```

Routines that yield integer results often return a zero value on error. An example is fwrite, a function that writes a stream of bytes to a file and returns the number of bytes actually transmitted. Of course, it could be that the user originally specified the writing of zero bytes. In this case, a zero return value may or may not indicate an error, illustrating a major problem with this approach.

The stream I/O system is based on a variation on this idea. It does not return an error status flag directly, but rather it yields a value that can be converted into a boolean value that indicates the error:

```
istream fin("filename.dat"); // open file
if (! fin) { // convert to boolean and test
    .
    .   // handle error case
    .
}
```

Sometimes the common use patterns cause the introduction of two or more mechanisms to address the same problem. For example, the output routine fputc will return the integer constant EOF when an error is encountered. However, this return value is almost always ignored by most programmers. So an alternative function, ferror, was introduced to permit an inquiry into the error status of a file pointer:

```
FILE *fp = fopen("rahrah.dat", "w"); // open file
fputc('O', fp); // write a few characters
fputc('S', fp);
fputc('U', fp);
if (ferror(fp)) // did an error occur in any of the previous?
    .
    .   // handle error case
    .
```

Errno should always be checked after calling any function in which it might be set

Not all flags are returned as function results. Several routines return an error indication by means of the global integer value errno. Examples include many of the standard mathematical routines:

```
# include <errno> // include errno definition
 .
 .
 .
double x = ...;
errno = 0; // clear out error flag
double d = sqrt(x);
if (errno == EDOM) // test global status flag
    .
    .   // handle error case
    .
```

A disadvantage of this approach is that several functions that might set the global flag could appear in the same expression. Worse, perhaps a function might *clear* the global flags:

```
// is sqrt evaluated first or is g?
double d = sqrt(x) * g();

// worse, what happens if g clears
// a flag that was set by sqrt ?
double g ()
{
    errno = 0;
    return 3.14159 * sin(42);
}
```

Here, an error in the square root function can be masked by the function g clearing the error flag.

11.2   The Assertion Library

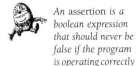

An assertion is a boolean expression that should never be false if the program is operating correctly

One mechanism used to obtain run-time diagnostic information is the assertion package. This library is defined in the **cassert** header file (see Appendix A). An *assertion* is simply a boolean expression that can be evaluated at run time. Should the value evaluate to false, a diagnostic error message is printed and the program is halted by calling the STL function **abort**. The format for the diagnostic information is implementation-dependent, but it typically includes the text of the assertion that failed and the filename and line number at which the assertion appears:

```
# include <cassert> // include assertion package
     .
     .
     .
assert (size != 0); // check size before dividing
double val = sum / size; // do calculation
```

Never turn off assertion checking

The assertion mechanism is hampered by the fact that assertion checking can be turned off at the discretion of the programmer simply by defining the macro NDEBUG. Many programmers use assertions during program development and then, for the sake of efficiency, turn them off when a program goes into production. Another reason sometimes cited for removing assertions from production code is that the error message produced by the assertion facility is mystifying to end users. Unfortunately, errors occur in production programs as well as in programs under development, and such a short-sighted policy not only makes tracing these errors more difficult, but also tends to make programs fail in even more mysterious ways.

11.3   The setjmp and longjmp Facility

Avoid the setjmp facility in new code, as exceptions provide the same functionality

Almost by definition exceptional situations are problems that cannot be handled locally. That is, the part of the program that detects an unusual error is most likely not the same part of the program that is best prepared to handle the problem. Prior to the introduction of exceptions in C++, many alternative mechanisms were proposed to address this quandary. One of those that made it into the language is known as the setjmp facility. The premise of the setjmp idea is that errors often occur many levels deep in the processing of functions and methods and that, rather than unwinding the sequence of function calls, it would be better to simply jump back to an earlier point in execution to handle the error.

To use the setjmp facility, the programmer first creates an instance of the data type jmp_buf, which is defined in the header file csetjmp (see Appendix A):

```
# include <csetjmp> // include setjmp library
     .
     .
     .
jmp_buf Processing_Failed; // create a jump buffer
```

At an outer level of execution, the programmer then writes a call to the routine setjmp, passing as argument the jump buffer. The first time this routine is called it will return a zero, or false, value. Execution then continues with whatever actions the program is performing:

```
if (setjmp(Processing_Failed)) {
.
.    // handle error case
.
} else {

    .
    .
    .

    doProcessing(); // handle program execution
}
```

At some point during the execution of the program, an unrecoverable error might be encountered. Rather than tracing back through the sequence of function invocations, the programmer can invoke the routine longjmp, passing as an argument the jump buffer and a nonzero integer value:

```
void doProcessing()
{
    ObjectType anObject;   // declare an object value
    .
    .    // go through several layers of function call
    .
    doMoreProcessing();
}

void doMoreProcessing()
{
    .
    .
    .
    if (somethingWrong)
        longjmp (Processing_Failed, 13);
}
```

At the point the longjmp function is executed, control is passed back immediately to the setjmp statement, and the integer result specified by the second argument to longjmp is used as the result value. Execution then continues for the setjmp function a *second time*, this time returning a nonzero, or true, value. If the function result is tested by an if statement, as in the preceding example, a different sequence of execution ensues.

The effect is as though multiple levels of procedure call were erased in one action—applying both to control and to data. That is, suppose that some of the intervening levels of call create data values, as in the object anObject declared in the preceding example. Prior to the invocation of the longjmp function, we can view the activation record stack as follows:

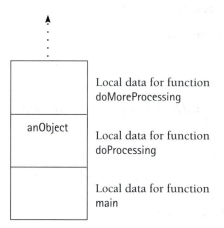

Execution of the longjmp function simply erases the data values, and execution of the program continues with the procedure that invoked the setjmp:

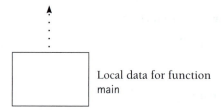

This erasure takes place without the need to invoke the destructors for the given data values.[2] For this reason—and because many programmers find the "action at a distance" processing of jump buffers to be unintuitive—use of the facility is now discouraged and true exception handling is favored.

Prior to the addition of exception handling as a fundamental part of the language C++, the setjmp/longjmp facility was used as a basis for the implementation of several experimental exception handling libraries. See Hanson [Hanson 97] for one example.

11.4   Signals

Various events, such as the user hitting a break key, a floating point exception, a loss of carrier on a phone line, a segmentation violation, or a bus error, are

---

[2] This is probably a consequence of the fact that the setjmp concept predated the idea of destructors.

reported to the program by means of a *signal*. Normally, the effect of a signal is to terminate the program. However, the user can specify a *signal handler*, which is a procedure that will respond to certain signals.

A signal handler is simply a procedure that takes as an argument a single integer value. This integer is used to encode the type of signal being processed:

```
# include <signal.h> // include signal definitions

void handler (int a)
{
     // handle the signal
  .
  :  //
  .
     // reset the signal handler
   signal (a, handler);
}
```

The programmer establishes the association between a signal and a handler, using the procedure signal. The header file signal.h has various symbolic constants that represent different signal categories; SIGINT, for example, represents a terminal interrupt (usually generated by the user hitting the *break* key):

```
signal (SIGINT, handler);
```

A signal handler is removed once a signal has been processed. To maintain the handler for subsequent signals, the handler can itself call signal to reset itself, as shown in the preceding example.

If the signal handler does not stop the program (usually by invoking the library routines exit or abort), then after the signal handler returns, execution will continue from the point in the program where the signal was raised.

11.5   Exception Handling

The most recent definition of the language C++ includes a full exception handling mechanism—one that interacts well with the data model and avoids the problem noted in the earlier discussion of the setjmp facility. There are, however, several differences between this mechanism and the facility provided by Java. These differences apply both to syntax and to semantics. In the following sections, we will describe some of the more notable of these differences.

11.5.1   Exception Types

Exceptions in C++ need not be a subclass of Throwable

Both Java and C++ include the concept of creating an actual value as part of the process of throwing an exception. In Java, this value must be a subclass of Throwable, and it is typically also a subclass iof the further class Exception. In C++ there is no such restriction. The value thrown in conjunction with an exception can be any type, even a built-in type such as an integer. Of course, the information provided by an integer data value may be much less than that which could be provided by another type, but the point is that the language does not dictate the argument type.

The STL does provide a class hierarchy in the header file **stdexcept**. That class hierarchy can be described as follows:

```
exception
    logic_error
        length_error
        domain_error
        out_of_range
        invalid_argument
    runtime_error
        range_error
        overflow_error
        underflow_error
    bad_alloc
    bad_cast
    bad_exception
    bad_typeid
```

However, there is no requirement that user-defined exception types be fit into this structure.

Because exceptions can be any data type, the Java idiom for a "catch-all" exception handler does not work:

```
// Java Catch-All Example
try {
.
:  //
.
}
.
:  //
.
catch (Exception e) { // catch all exceptions
}
```

Instead, C++ permits ellipses to be used as the catch argument. Any uncaught exceptions will match this pattern. Unfortunately, we cannot associate a variable with this pattern, so any information passed along with the exception is lost:

```
// C++ Catch-All Example
try {
  .
  .  //
  .
}
catch ( ... ) { // catch all exceptions
  .
  .  //
  .
}
```

Generally ellipses are used to perform a cleanup action before the exception is re-sent, using a bare **throw** statement:

```
try {
  .
  .
  .
}
catch ( ... ) { // catch all exceptions
   // perform cleanup actions
   throw; // pass action on to higher level
}
```

11.5.2   Rethrowing Exceptions

In Java, a **catch** clause can rethrow an exception, leaving to surrounding statements the detection and further processing of the value:

```
try { // Java Rethrow Exception Example
  .
  .   //
  .
}
catch (exception e) {
   // perform some action
   throw e; // resend exception
}
```

As we showed in the example in Section 11.5.1, C++ allows simply an unadorned **throw** statement in this case, which is interpreted to throw the same value as the current **catch** clause.

11.5.3   No finally Clause

The finally clause in Java permits a section of code to be executed regardless of whether an exception is thrown:

```
try { // Java Finally Clause Example
   .
   .
   .
}
catch (IOError & e) {
.
.   // handle this error
.
}
catch (RunTimeError & e) {
.
.   // handle this error
.
}
finally {
.
.   // common code
.
}
.
.   // next statement
.
```

The statements in the try block are executed. If no errors occur, the finally block and then the following statements are executed. If an exception is thrown during evaluation of the try block, the exception handler is invoked, followed by the finally block. Even if the exception handler performs a return, or passes on the exception (see the previous section), the finally block will be executed. Simply put, there is no way to leave the try block without executing the finally code.

There is no similar facility in C++. One approach would be to catch the exception with ellipses, perform the common code, and then rethrow it—but doing so doesn't handle the situation where no error occurs. A better alternative recognizes that destructors are always invoked for local variables that cease to exist when their local scope is eliminated, whether by normal execution or by an exception. Using this fact, we can create a dummy class and variable whose sole purpose is to launch a destructor when the try block is executed:

```
class CleanUp {
   ~CleanUp ()
   {
```

```
        .
        .   // put common cleanup code here
        .
    }
};


    .   //
    .
    .

try {
    CleanUp dummy;
    .   //
    .
    .
}
catch (IOError & e) {
    .   //
    .
    .
}
catch (RunTimeError & e) {
    .   //
    .
    .
}
    .   // continue with execution
    .
    .
```

Note that one difference between this version and the Java version is that here the cleanup code is performed before the catch clauses. This could be changed by creating a new dummy block to surround the try statement and moving the declaration of the dummy statement to this block.

There are many variations on this idea (see [Meyers 96]). Often they include placing useful behavior in the constructor for the class, in addition to using the destructor. An STL class auto_ptr can be used to avoid having to write special-purpose classes when the only clean-up operation is the deletion of dynamically allocated memory. (See Section 4.3.1 for a discussion of auto_ptr.)

11.5.4   References as Exceptions

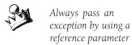

Always pass an exception by using a reference parameter

Like the binding of an argument to a parameter, the binding of a thrown value to an exception handler is basically a form of assignment. The majority of rules for assignment in C++ apply to exception handlers as well. This includes the slicing problem described in Chapter 4. To avoid the slicing problem, exception handlers should declare their variables by reference, as we have shown in all the examples in this chapter.

11.5.5   Exception Class Clonability

Always write a copy constructor for any user-defined exception class

In both Java and C++, the value thrown is an object. However, in Java the value is generally a newly created heap-based object, formed using the **new** operator. In C++ the object is often a nameless temporary value, formed by simply naming the class and any arguments used by the constructor. Behind the scenes the created object may be moved or copied, so it is important that any user-defined exception classes be cloneable. If the class possesses data values, for example, they should be copied:

```
class ParseException {
public:
    // constructors
    ParseException (string & why) : reason(why) { }
    ParseException (ParseException & why)
          : reason(why.reason) { }

    // operators
    void operator = (ParseException & why)
          { reason = why.reason; }
    operator string () { return reason; }

private:
    string reason;
}


    .
    :    // throw an error, creates a temporary value
    .
throw ParseException("missing expression");
```

Defining a string conversion operator makes it easy to generate a formatted error message from the exception value. Another possibility is to define a stream output operator for the class.

11.5.6   No Need to Document Exceptions

In Java a method must document any exception that it might create or inherit by declaring the set of exceptions in a **throws** clause. While C++ has a similar

In C++ a function need not declare the possibility of throwing an exception in the function header

facility, there is one vital difference. In C++, if a function is mute concerning the exceptions it can throw, we assume that it can throw anything:

```
int f () throw (range_error); // will only throw range error
int g (); // can possibly throw anything
```

To indicate that a function throws no exceptions, we must specify an empty throw list:

```
int h () throw (); // throws no exceptions
```

Thus the absence of any named exceptions is actually a bad sign, since it means anything is possible. This decision in the design of C++ was made to preserve backward compatibility with older code that predated introduction of the exception handling facility; otherwise, a huge amount of legacy code would have required modification.

Always document a potential exception by placing a throw list in the function header

The idea that nothing means everything can often be confusing because an examination of the program may not reveal the possibility of an exception being thrown. Consider the following class definition:

```
class Parent {
public:
    virtual void test (int i) { printf("parent test"); }
};

class Child extends Parent {
public:
    virtual void test (int i)
    {
        throw "executed child test";
    }
};
```

A polymorphic variable of type pointer to Parent that happens to contain a value of type Child will throw an exception when the method test is invoked. However, this possibility would not be obvious from an examination of the method in class Parent.

This problem can be compounded by the fact that in many implementations of C++ an exception that is not caught by a handler will sometimes simply produce a segmentation fault. In Java, methods are not allowed to throw exceptions unless they are explicitly declared as part of the type signature of the method, which must match the signature inherited from the parent class.

Another example will illustrate the lax handling of exception handling specifications in C++. Let's assume that we have a function f, described as throwing a string value:

```
void f () throw (string)
{
    .
    :   //
    .
    g();
}
```

Among other things, it is perfectly legal for f to invoke g, a function that says nothing about exceptions and thus is allowed to throw anything:

```
void g ()
{
    // why not throw an irrational value?
    throw 3.14159;
}
```

The function g will throw a double. Since it is not caught by f, it will pass through and hence need to be handled by whatever invoked f. To protect against this, the caller of f will need to check for all exceptions, not simply the documented ones.

Again, the rationale for this decision is backward compatibility. Otherwise, it would never be possible to invoke preexception-handling facilities from within functions that explicitly declared their expectations. Nevertheless, the result makes catching and processing all possible exceptions extremely difficult.

11.5.7   Standard Exceptions

Only a handful of exceptions can be generated by functions in the STL, including the following:

Name	Thrown by
bad_alloc	The operator new
bad_cast	Dynamic cast operator
bad_typeid	The typeid function
out_of_range	Bitset subscript, vector function at
invalid_argument	Bitset constructor

Test Your Understanding

1. What are some of the hazards of using a function result to encode both a value and a status flag?

2. How can the assertion mechanism be turned off?

3. What is a jump buffer used for?

4. What does the returned value from set_jmp indicate?

5. How do longjmp and the destruction of local variables interact?

6. Why can't a catch-all exception clause be written as it is in Java?

7. How can a finally clause be simulated in C++?

8. Why should catch clause variables be declared as references?

9. Why is the absence of a throw clause on a function prototype interpreted to mean that the function can throw any exception type?

12

Features Found Only in C++

The language C++ includes a number of features that have no equivalent in Java, many of which we have discussed already. Table 12.1 summarizes these features and indicates by section number where in the text they are discussed. In this chapter we describe some of the features found only in C++ that we have not discussed elsewhere.

12.1 Global Variables

A global variable is a variable that is declared outside the scope of any class or function

The C++ language permits the declaration of variables outside the scope of any class or function. Such values are known as *global variables*:

```
int top = 0; // global variable, top of stack
int data[100]; // data area for stack

int push(int val) { data[++top] = val; }

int pop() { return data[top--]; }
```

Only a single copy of a global variable will ever exist, in contrast to variables declared inside functions. (In a recursive function many copies of the same variable may exist.) A global variable exists as long as a program executes. Globals can be initialized, as in the preceding example. Initialization occurs prior to the start of execution for the main procedure.

Global variables can be declared **static**, in which case they are accessible only within the file in which they are declared. A global variable that is not **static** can

Table 12.1   Features Found in C++ but Not in Java

Feature	Location	Feature	Location
Assertions	Section 11.2	Name spaces	Section 12.7
const keyword	Section 12.4	Operator overloading	Section 7.1
Default arguments	Section 12.5	Pointers	Section 3.2
delete keyword	Section 4.3	Preprocessor	Section 12.2
Destructor	Section 4.3.1	Private inheritance	Section 6.7
Dynamic cast	Section 6.3	Pure virtual method	Section 6.2
Enumerated values	Section 2.3	Qualified names	Section 5.2
Explicit constructors	Section 7.18.2	References	Section 3.7
Friends	Section 12.6	Stack-resident memory	Section 4.1
Functions	Section 2.8	Standard Template Library	Section 9.3
Generic algorithms	Section 9.3.3	Structures	Section 2.6
Global variables	Section 12.1	Template classes and functions	Section 9.1
goto statement	Section 12.9	typedef	Section 12.3
inline	Section 5.2.2	Unions	Section 2.6
Iterators	Section 9.3.2	Unsigned and signed variables	Section 2.1
long double	Section 2.1	virtual overridding	Section 6.1
Multiple inheritance	Section 12.8	void * pointers	Section 3.4.3

be used in all parts of a program. (The designer of C++ now deprecates this use of the term **static** and suggests that the *name space mechanism* (see Section 12.7) is a better solution to this particular problem [Stroustrup 97].)

A global variable used in two or more files must be declared as **extern** in all but one of the files. A value declared as **extern** cannot at the same time be initialized:

```
extern int top; // top is declared and initialized in another file
```

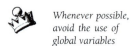

Whenever possible, avoid the use of global variables

Although common in C and C++ programs, global variables are dangerous and error prone. For example, it is difficult to determine where global variables are set and where they are used. Whenever possible, global variables should be eliminated and replaced with values that are managed by a class object. (This approach will, of course, be second nature to the knowledgeable Java programmer.)

12.2   The Preprocessor

The processing of a C++ program includes an initial step prior to analysis by the compiler. A similar initial processing is not normally part of the Java language.

In this initial step, called *preprocessing*, the text of a C++ program is scanned, and directives that begin with a hash mark are processed. The major categories of these directives are:

```
# include <filename>
# define name value
# undef name
# if test
# ifdef name
# ifndef name
# else
# endif
```

The include directive indicates that the text of the associated file should be included textually at the point indicated. The included file is then scanned by the preprocessor and combined with the current file. The resulting text file is then passed to the compiler, which is thereafter unaware of the differing sources of the input.

Include files are normally used to incorporate header files that are used by many files within a project or by many different projects. Examples include the header files that define functions in the standard library:

```
# include <cstdio> // include Standard I/O Library
# include "rational.h" // include my own header file
```

Two different tokens are used to surround the filename. When angle brackets are used, the "system library" directory is searched first. This procedure is commonly used for standard library files. When quotation marks are used as delineators, the current directory is searched first, before the system directory. This form is commonly used for programmer-defined header files.

The #include directive differs from the #import statement in several respects. First, it is not a statement and therefore does not end with a semicolon. Second, it performs a textual inclusion, which is not true of the Java statement.

A #define directive creates a symbolic constant, associating the given text with the name:

```
// limit of 12 elements
# define MAX 12
```

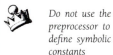

Do not use the preprocessor to define symbolic constants

Thereafter, all occurrences of the text MAX outside of comments and literal strings will be replaced with the given definition. This is one way to create symbolic constants, or meaningful names that represent a less obvious value. However, this feature is now rarely used by C++ programmers; instead, they favor explicit symbolic constants that can be more easily checked for type errors by the compiler:

```
const int max = 12; // limit of 12 elements
```

It is also possible to produce macros that require arguments, using #define; however, such use is generally now also discouraged. A remaining valid use of the #define construct is to create names that can be tested with #ifdef.

The #undef command "undefines" a name. That is, it removes the name from the table of definitions; thereafter, the name will simply be recognized as text.

Two statements can be used to include conditionally or not include text in a program. The #if construct requires an expression, which must be something that can be evaluated at compile time. If the expression evaluates to a nonzero result, all the text between the if statement and the closing #end or #else will be included; otherwise, the text will be discarded. The #ifdef form is similar but is successful if the following name has been defined by a previous #define directive. The #ifndef is successful if the following name has *not* been defined. Finally, the #else works as in Java, inverting the previous conditional test.

A common idiom is found in header files to prevent the contents of a file from being scanned by the compiler twice, should the file happen to be included more than once. A conditional test will be performed on a unique token name. If the token has not yet been defined, the body of the file will be processed, which includes defining the token name. Thereafter, the token will be defined on all successive inclusions of the file, and the text will be discarded:

```
// see if file has already been scanned
# ifndef FOOCLASSDEFINITION
// if not, then define symbol now, so later
// inclusions will skip this file
# define FOOCLASSDEFINITION
    .
    .      // contents of file
    .
# endif
```

12.3   typedef Statement

Use typedef to give a contextually meaningful name to an existing data type

A typedef statement defines a name as an alias for an existing data type. The syntax is similar to a declaration. The typedef keyword precedes the declaration, and the name being defined is used in place of a variable name. Thereafter the name can be used in the manner of a type:

```
typedef double fahrenheit; // define alias for double
fahrenheit currentTemp; // declare a new variable
```

The replacement of typedef names takes place very early in the processing of a C++ program, so two types that expand to the same base are considered to be the same:

```
currentTemp *= 2.3; // can combine with doubles
typedef double celsius; // define new alias
celsius newTemp = 42; // declare another variable
currentTemp += newTemp; // can combine, both doubles
```

A typedef statement is often used to eliminate confusing syntax. For example, the following declaration clearly involves a pointer to a function that takes a character as an argument and an array. But is it declaring an array of pointers or a function that returns an array?

```
int (*fun)(char *)[10];
```

The intent can be made clear by dividing the task into two separate steps:

```
typedef int (* funPtr)(char *); // funPtr---pointer to a function
funPtr fun[10];  // declare array of pointers to functions
```

A typedef statement is also frequently used to shorten a compound type name. For example, in the case study presented in Chapter 15, a type is used that can be defined as:

```
map <const char *,
   map< const char *, unsigned int, charCompare>,
      charCompare> aGraph;
```

Breaking this into several parts not only makes it more understandable, but it also yields convenient names that can be used to describe the individual parts:

```
typedef map <const char *, unsigned int, charCompare> cityInfo;
typedef map <const char *, cityInfo, charCompare> graph;

graph aGraph;  // declare a new graph value
```

12.4   The const Keyword

The keyword const is used to define a quantity that does not change. A modifier placed inside a declaration it can be applied to variables, arguments, and member functions.

Applied to variables, it provides a way of creating symbolic constants:

```
const int maxCharCount = 80; // upper limit on character
```

Applied to an object value, it indicates that the object will not be changed in any fashion. This is stronger than the Java notion of final and means only that the object will not be reassigned. (A Java variable that is final and is assigned a box value can still change the internal state of the box; a C++ variable that is declared const cannot. However, every rule needs an exception. A data field declared as mutable inside a const object can still be modified. Such use is not common, so we do not discuss it here.)

Applied to arguments, particularly by-reference arguments, it indicates that the value will not be modified inside the function:[1]

```
int foo (const box & aBox)
{
    // contents of aBox cannot be changed
    .
    .
    .
    aBox.value = 17; // error---compiler will issue error message
    .
    .
    .
}
```

Applied to a member function, the keyword indicates that the function does not change the receiver:

```
class string {
public:
    .
    .
    .
    // computing length does not alter string
    int length() const;
    .
    .
    .
};
```

Only member functions that have been declared as const can be used with objects that are themselves declared const.

---

[1] It is actually legal in Java to use the final keyword in a parameter list to achieve this same effect, but Java programmers seldom use this feature.

When applied to a pointer value, the const keyword either indicates that the pointer itself is constant or that the value it references is constant, depending on the placement of the keyword:

```
int i = 7;

const int * p  = &i; // pointer to a constant
int * const q  = &i; // constant pointer

*p = 8; // not allowed, p points to a const
*q = 8; // allowed, q is pointing to non const
p = q;  // allowed, p itself is not constant
q = p; // not allowed q is constant

const int * const r = & i; // both aspects are constant
```

Casting away const is using a cast operator to remove the Const restriction

It is possible to remove the constant restriction by using an explicit cast operator. This is called *casting away const*:

```
const char * name = "Fred";
char * p = static_cast<char *>(name); // cast away the const part
p[0] = 'D'; // name is now Dred
```

The use of cast operations, such as static_cast, and dynamic_cast, is preferable to the traditional (now Java style) cast syntax.

12.5 Default Arguments

The use of default arguments can greatly reduce the amount of code in a class

Function headings, including constructor functions, are permitted to suggest default values to arguments. Should the corresponding parameter not be supplied, the default argument will be used. The type signatures of all functions must be such that a unique function can be determined once the argument values used by a call are known:

```
class box {
public:
    box (int v = 7) : val(v) { }
    void test (int v = 3, double d) { val = v + (int) d; }
private:
    int val;
};
```

```
box aBox(3); // explicit argument
box bBox; // uses default value of 7

aBox.text(2, 3.14); // both arguments specified
bBox.test(2.3); // uses implicit definition for first argument
```

Java programmers sometimes achieve the same effect by having one procedure simply invoke another of the same name:

```
class box {
    public box () { box(7); } // invoke myself
    public box (int v) { val = v; }

    public void test (int v, double d)
    {
        val = v  + (int) d;
    }

    public void test (double d)
    { // use more general method
        test(3, d);
    }

    private int val;
}
```

As this example illustrates, the use of default arguments can produce a more concise class description.

12.6   Friends

A friend is a function or class that is permitted to access the internal state of another class

It is often desirable to expose **private** and **protected** features to certain functions or classes, without making these features completely accessible. To do so, we can use a class to declare another class or a function as a *friend*. A friend is allowed to access all the features of a class, even if they are declared **private**:

```
class box {
public:
    box (int v) : value(v) { }
private:
    int value;
    // declare plus function as friend
    friend int plus(const box &, const box &);
};
```

```
int plus (const box & left, const box & right)
{
    // access to private data field value
    // is permitted, since plus is declare
    // as friend
    return left.value + right.value;
}

int minus (const box & left, const box & right)
{
    // error---will produce an error message
    // because access to private data field
    // is not permitted
    return left.value---right.value;
}

box a(3), b(4);

int i = plus(a, b);
```

Elsewhere we have pointed out that declaring all constructors private results in an object that cannot be created. Adding a friend makes such a class slightly more useful. For example, the following program fragment illustrates how to define a class that is guaranteed to have only a *single* instance:

```
class singletonBox {
public:
    int value;
private:
    singletonBox () : value(0) { }
    friend theBox();
};

const singletonBox & theBox()
{
    // declare the one and only one box
    static singletonBox actualBox;
    // return this singleton object
    return actualBox;
}
```

Here the unique box object is declared as **static** inside the function **theBox**. Because **theBox** is a friend, it is allowed to create an instance of the class. Because this instance is **static**, it will be created only once. Each call on **theBox** will return the unique object, which is the only object of its class that can be created.

Incidentally, a static object declared inside a function illustrates one of the fundamental C++ principles discussed in Chapter 1, namely, that a running program shouldn't pay in execution time for things that are not used. A static local variable will be initialized the first time the function in which it is declared is invoked. If the function is never used, the variable is never created.

12.7   Name Spaces

Large programs can encounter the problem of name collisions, that is, the same name being used by two different programmers or for two different purposes. This can also occur when components from different commercial vendors are combined into one program. To help alleviate this problem, the language C++ includes the concept of name spaces.

 The name space feature is a recent addition to the C++ language

A programmer can explicitly declare that all the functions and definitions in one part of a program are defined within a certain name space:

```
// declare everything in name space stack
namespace StackADT {
    int height;

    class Stack {
        .
        .
        .
    };
}
```

Names defined inside a name space can be used outside the name space description in one of two ways. The first way is to use a fully qualified name, similar to a fully qualified method name:

```
// read the value of the height variable
int max = StackADT::height;
```

Alternatively, all the names defined in a name space can be included in a program by using a single statement:

```
using StackADT; // include all the names defined in the namespace
```

12.8   Multiple Inheritance

In C++ a class can inherit from two or more parent classes. For example, suppose that we have an existing abstraction that represents a deck of cards and another abstraction that represents objects that know how to display their image on a graphical window. (In Java the latter would more commonly be represented by an interface, rather than a class. As C++ does not have interfaces, all abstractions are represented by classes.) We might define a visual deck of cards as follows:

```
class GraphicalDeck : public CardDeck, public GraphicalObject {
   .
   .
   .
};
```

The GraphicalDeck now inherits all the behavior from both classes and must implement the requirements of both.

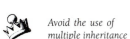
Avoid the use of multiple inheritance

Multiple inheritance has a reputation as a subtle and complex feature, to be avoided if at all possible because of the problems that can arise from its use. For example, there is the potential problem of ambiguous names. Suppose that draw is defined in class CardDeck as the method that removes a card from the deck but in class GraphicalObject as the method that instructs an object to display itself in the window. What should be the meaning in the class GraphicalDeck? In this case, the compiler will insist that the functions be overridden in the new class, if for no other reason than to pass control to the parent classes. If we are lucky, one method or the other method requires arguments, and thus the methods can be differentiated on the basis of argument types:

```
class GraphicalDeck : public CardDeck, public GraphicalObject {
public:
   void draw (Window * w) // draw image on window
   {
      GraphicalObject::draw(w);
   }

   Card & draw () // draw card from deck
   {
      return CardDeck::draw();
   }
   .
   .
   .
};
```

In the worst case, both names and argument type signatures match, and the only recourse is to rename one operation or the other. Of course, we can still reuse the behavior inherited from the parent class by using fully qualified names:

```cpp
class GraphicalDeck : public CardDeck, public GraphicalObject {
public:
    void draw () // draw image on window
    {
        GraphicalObject::draw();
    }

    Card & getCard () // draw card from deck
    {
        return CardDeck::draw();
    }
    .
    .
    .
};
```

A more serious problem arises if we try to combine two classes that inherit from a common ancestor. Suppose, for example, that classes B and C both inherit from class A:

```cpp
class A {
    .
    .
    .
private:
    int dataField;
};

class B : public A {
    .
    .
    .
};

class C : public A {
    .
    .
    .
};
```

```
class D : public B, public C {
    .
    .
    .

    // question: how many dataFields does this have?
};
```

If class D inherits from both B and C, should one copy or two copies of the data field be inherited from class A? Obviously, there is no "right" answer, as you can imagine situations in which either alternative might be appropriate. To resolve this dilemma, C++ allows inheritance to be described as virtual. If a class is inherited as virtual, only one copy will be included in the final object, regardless of how many times it is included as an ancestor:

```
class A {
    .
    .
    .

private:
    int dataField;
};

class B : virtual public A {
    .
    .
    .

};

class C : virtual public A {
    .
    .
    .

};

class D : public B, public C {
    .
    .
    .

};
```

Without the virtual keyword, D would have two copies of the A data field. With virtual, it has only one.

Virtual inheritance is one instance in which a class is permitted to invoke the constructor for a "grandparent"—that is, an ancestor that is not a direct parent. Let's assume, for example, that class A requires argument values and that B and C provide different argument values for this inheritance. Which one should be

used? There is seemingly no way to decide. The solution provided by C++ is that
D can supply the arguments in its initialization clause and that this value will be
used instead of any value supplied by B or C. The result can be unintuitive, since
it would appear that the invocations on the constructors in B and C are being
ignored:

```
class A {
public:
    // constructor
    A (int d) : dataField(d) { }
    .
    .
    .
private:
    int dataField;
};

class B : virtual public A {
public:
    B (int b) : A(7) { } // initialize A with 7
    .
    .
    .
};

class C : virtual public A {
public:
    C (int c) : A(11) { } // or initialize A with 11
    .
    .
    .
};

class D : public B, public C {
public:
    // No, neither; initialize A with 42
    D () : A(42), B(12), C(22) { }
    .
    .
    .
};
```

In Java, multiple inheritance is often replaced with the use of interfaces
(which can be combined in multiple ways) or with the use of inner classes.

12.9

Avoid using a goto statement, except to break out of nested loops

goto Statement

The C++ language includes a goto statement, which, along with the ability to label statements, allows control to be transferred to arbitrary locations inside a function:

```
int test (int i)
{
   i = i + 2;
   tst:
   if (i > 10)
      ret: return i + 2;
   i = i - 3;
   if (i < 1)
      goto ret;
   i = i + 5;
   goto tst;
}
```

One of the most common uses for the goto statement is to break out of multiple levels of looping, something that in Java is performed with a labeled break, as in the following code fragment:

```
static final int gold = 1;
static final int dross = 0;
int field[100][100];
   .
   .
   .
searchForGold: // a Java search of a doubly nested loop
for (int i = 0; i < 100; i++)
   for (int j = 0; j < 100; j++)
      if (field[i][j] == GOLD)
         break searchForGold;
   .   // execution comes here on break
   .
```

The same search could be written in C++ as follows:

```
for (int i = 0; i < 100; i++) // a C++ search of a doubly
                              // nested loop
```

```
    for (j = 0; j < 100; j++)
       if (field[i][j] == GOLD)
          goto FoundGold;
foundGold:
   .
   .   // execution comes here on found value
   .
```

Neither form is considered particularly good programming style. If you find yourself writing programs that use these features, you should reconsider your problem and perhaps use a different approach.

Test Your Understanding

1. What is a global variable?

2. In what way does a static global variable differ from one that has not been declared static?

3. Why should the use of global variables be avoided whenever possible?

4. At what stage during compilation are preprocessor directives analyzed?

5. How does the include directive of C++ differ from the import statement in Java?

6. What is the purpose of a typedef statement?

7. What are some of the ways the const keyword can be used? Indicate the meaning of the keyword in each situation.

8. What is a default argument? How can the use of default arguments reduce the number of functions a programmer may need to write?

9. What does the designation of a friend imply?

10. What does saying that a class is defined by using multiple inheritance mean?

11. Explain the problem of ambiguous names in multiple inheritance.

12. What is a virtual base class in a multiple inheritance hierarchy?

13. Explain the one situation in which a class can provide arguments to a "grand-parent" constructor as part of its initialization clauses, where a grandparent class is a class that is not an ancestor.

14. What is the effect of a goto statement?

13

Features Found Only in Java

In comparison to the number of features found in C++ that have no counterpart in Java, the number of features found in Java that have no C++ counterpart is relatively small. We have already discussed many of them in earlier chapters. In this chapter we mention only the most notable items that we have not discussed elsewhere.

13.1   Wrapper Classes

Template classes and functions eliminate most of the need for wrapper classes

The Java language defines a "wrapper" class for each of the primitive data types. Thus integer values can be held by an instance of Integer, character values by Character, and so on. The primary reason for the existence of these classes is that primitive data types are not objects, in the technical sense. Thus they cannot by themselves be assigned to a value of type Object and hence cannot be stored in any of the standard data structures.

    Data structures in C++ are handled differently (see Chapter 9). Template parameters are not restricted to holding object types, and thus there is no restriction to creating, for example, a list of integer values. The main purpose for wrapper classes simply does not arise in C++, and therefore the concept is not needed.

13.2   Interfaces

An interface describes the behavior associated with a class but does not provide
an implementation. Sometimes an interface is said to define a subtype but not
a subclass. The C++ language does not have any exact equivalent; the closest is
the notion of a pure virtual function. A pure virtual function is a virtual function
that does not have a body. Instead, following the prototype description of the
function, an assignment operator defines the body as null:

```
class GraphicalObject {
public:
   virtual draw() = 0; // every subclass must override
};
```

Any class that inherits from a class the includes a pure virtual function must
override these functions. The concept of a pure virtual function differs from an
interface in that the former can be applied method by method, allowing a class
to have some pure virtual methods and some ordinary methods. An interface, in
comparison, can be thought of as a class description in which every method has
been declared as pure virtual.

13.3   Inline Classes

The need frequently arises to create a class that will have only a single instance.
Giving a name to such a class introduces two new identifiers into the name scope:
the name of the class and the name of the single instance. Because the class name
is not needed, Java provides a way for creating instances of a class without naming
the class. Such a value is called an *inline class*.

Inline classes are formed by naming the parent class (since all classes must
ultimately descend from Object, all classes have a parent) and specifying whatever
new or overridden methods the class requires. For example, the Java event model
matches events with "listeners," or objects that sit and wait for an event to
occur and respond appropriately when required. Each graphical object, such
as a button, maintains its own collection of listeners. When a button is pressed,
the listener will execute a method to perform the button action. The following
structure is common in such cases:

```
class Example extends Frame {
   public Example ()
   {
      Button a = new Button("quit");
```

```
            .
            .
            .
      a.addActionListener(
         new ActionListener() { // create inline class
            public void actionPerformed(ActionEvent & e) {
               System.exit(1); // quit program
            }
         }
      );
   }
}
```

By carefully matching the braces, you will note that the argument to the function **addActionListener** extends over several lines. This argument creates a new instance of a subclass of **ActionListener**, redefining the inherited method **actionPerformed**. This object is the only instance of the unnamed class.

Inline classes cannot have constructors and cannot have more than one instance.

While C++ does not have an exact correspondence to the inline class feature, it is possible in C++ to create nested classes (see Section 5.7) that do not have names. As with Java, such classes cannot have either constructors nor destructors (self-evidently, as they do not have names). The following example class contains an unnamed nested class that defines two data fields. An instance of this class is held by the field named **data** in the outer class:

```
class Example { // C++ example of anonymous class
public:
private:
   class {
   public:
      int x;
      int y;
   } data;
};
```

13.4   Threads

Thread programming is both more difficult and less portable than in Java

The language Java includes extensive facilities for multiprocessing as part of the basic language. In C++ they are not part of the language but instead are provided as external libraries. There are several commercial and public domain thread libraries, each with slightly different functionality. Discussions of programming with threads in C++ can be found in several sources [see Lewis 96, Kleiman 96, Butenhof 97].

13.5   Reflection

The language Java permits the program to discover information about the currently running program. This is called *reflection* because it is analogous to a program discovering information about itself by looking in a mirror.

Reflection begins with the class **Class**. Every object can be asked its class and will respond with an instance of this class. Using the class object, we can discover the methods that an object implements. We can also use the class object to create new instances of a class. Finally, a class object can return the class object that represents its parent class.

The classes **Field** and **Method** provide similar information about data fields and members. We can even dynamically create, initialize, and load new classes into a running program.

Such facilities are not part of the standard language C++, although it is possible for objects to access their type as a string value (see Section 6.1.2). To a limited extent, reflection facilities can be implemented in a platform-specific manner by external libraries.

Test Your Understanding

1. Why does the C++ container class library not require the use of wrapper classes?

2. What is the C++ equivalent to an interface?

3. Why can't an unnamed nested class have a constructor?

Case Study—Fractions

In this case study, we illustrate the use of constructors, overloaded operators, conversion operators, assignment, and the motivation for the stream style of input and output. Our example data abstraction corresponds to the mathematical notion of an integer fraction, or rational number. We assume that you are familiar with fractions and operations on fractions (Figure 14.1), and thus there is little in the nature of algorithms that will be new in the material we present. Instead, we use this case study to introduce features of the language C++.

Our intent is to create a data abstraction that operates, as much as possible, like the primitive arithmetic types, such as integer or float. We can summarize some of our objectives as follows:

- We should be able to easily create new instances of the rational number abstraction.

- We should be able to manipulate rational numbers by using arithmetic operations, yielding new rational number results.

- We should be able to mix rationals and other arithmetic quantities (integers and floating point values) in the same expression.

- We should be able to assign a rational number value to a rational number variable.

- We should be able to support the modification forms of assignment (+= and the like).

Figure 14.1 Definitions of Operations on Rational Numbers

Operation	Calculation
$\frac{a}{b} + \frac{c}{d}$	$\frac{a \times d + b \times c}{b \times d}$
$\frac{a}{b} - \frac{c}{d}$	$\frac{a \times d - b \times c}{b \times d}$
$\frac{a}{b} \times \frac{c}{d}$	$\frac{a \times c}{b \times d}$
$\frac{a}{b} \div \frac{c}{d}$	$\frac{a \times d}{b \times c}$
$-\frac{a}{b}$	$\frac{-a}{b}$
$\frac{a}{b} == \frac{c}{d}$	$(a \times d) == (b \times c)$
$\frac{a}{b} < \frac{c}{d}$	$(a \times d) < (b \times c), \quad if\ b > 0, d > 0$

- We should be able to compare one rational number to another.

- We should be able to perform input and output operations with rational numbers.

The following is an example program showing the type of manipulations that we would like to be able to perform with rational numbers:

```
// probability one is 1 in 8
rational p1 (1,8);
// probability two is 2 in 3
rational p2 (2, 3);
// probability of both together is their product
rational p3 = p1 * p2;
// probability of either independent is their sum
rational p4 = p1 + p2;
// what is this probability?
cout << "combined probability is " << p3 << endl;
cout << "independent probability is " << p4 << endl;
```

14.1   Classes

Figure 14.2 shows the class description for our rational number abstraction. The majority of this chapter is devoted to a discussion of features of this class description.

Figure 14.2 The Rational Number Class Description

```
//
// class rational
// rational number data abstraction
//

class rational {
public:
    // constructors
    rational     () : top(0), bottom(1) { }
    rational     (int t) : top(t), bottom(1) { }
    rational     (int t, int b) : top(t), bottom(b) { normalize(); }
    rational     (const rational & r) : top(r.top), bottom(r.bottom) { }

    // accesser functions
    int          numerator   () const { return top; }
    int          denominator () const { return bottom; }

    // assignments
    void operator = (const rational & r)
          {top = r.top; bottom = r.bottom;}
    void operator += (const rational &);

    // other operations
    operator double () const { return top / (double) bottom; }
    const rational & operator++() { top += bottom; return this; }
    const rational operator++(int);

private:
    int          top;  // data areas
    int          bottom;

    void         normalize   (); // operation used internally
};
```

14.1.1   Interface and Implementation

Filenames in C++ do not necessarily have to match class names, as they do in Java

As we noted in Chapter 5, the language C++ makes a clear distinction between component interface and component implementation. In classes, this distinction is made on two levels. First, the code associated with a component is normally separated into two files. The interface file simply describes how to use the component—the name of the component, the names of operations, the argument types to be used with operations, and so on. A second file, the implementation file, contains the actual code to perform the actions. A class description, such as that shown in Figure 14.2, would be found in the interface file.

Second, the class description itself is divided into two parts. On the one hand, the fields following the public: keyword denote those behaviors and data fields that users of the data abstraction can access. The fields following the private: keyword, on the other hand, denote behavior and fields that are accessible only within the component, and are off-limits to other users.

14.2   Constructors

The logical place to start in our explanation of the behavior associated with the rational number component is with a discussion of how new rational numbers are created. As with all data types, the most common way to create a new rational number is through the use of a declaration statement. A simple declaration statement merely asserts that the programmer wants to allocate and manipulate a new variable. The following statement, for example, creates a new variable named x:

```
rational x;
```

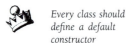

Every class should define a default constructor

We can observe from the class description shown in Figure 14.2 that a variable declared in this form is initialized with a 0 in the numerator field and a 1 in the denominator field. The constructor being executed in this case, the so-called *default constructor*, is implemented in the class declaration by using a pair of *initializers* that serve to set the data fields. In this situation, the effect of the initializers is exactly the same as an assignment. That is, the constructor written as

```
class rational {
    .
    .
    .
    rational () : top(0), bottom(1) { }
    .
    .
    .
};
```

has exactly the same effect as though it had been written by using assignments:

```
class rational {
    .
    .
    .
    rational () { top = 0; bottom = 1;}
    .
    .
    .
};
```

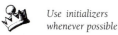

*Use initializers
whenever possible*

There are other situations, such as the initialization of constant fields, that can be performed only with using initializers. For data fields that are declared as instances of object types, using an assignment will result in unnecessary execution. The field will first be initialized with a default constructor and then assigned by using the assignment operator. Using an initializer has the effect of initializing the field only once (using the appropriate constructor). For these reasons, a C++ programmer should become conversant with the appearance and use of initializer fields.

You need to be aware of a common programming error. By analogy with declaration statements that provide arguments to constructors, at times you may want to use an empty pair of parentheses in a declaration statement in order to be sure that the default constructor is invoked:

```
rational x(); // error---not a variable declaration
```

*The declaration
that uses an empty
parentheses list is
not syntactically
incorrect; it is simply
not doing what the
programmer expects*

This statement is not correct. It is interpreted by the C++ compiler as a prototype that declares x to be a function that requires no arguments and returns a rational value. The proper declaration statement, as we showed earlier, uses no parentheses when no arguments are required. Nevertheless, the default constructor will still be invoked.

Other forms of constructor permit a rational number to be constructed with one or two integer values. A single integer argument creates a rational number with denominator 1, while two integer arguments specify both the numerator and denominator fields:

```
rational y(3);
rational z(2,3);
```

The two-argument form of the constructor calls the internal method normalize after it has initialized the data fields. We present the implementation of this method shortly.

*Every class should
define a copy
constructor*

Yet another form of the constructor, called a *copy constructor*, permits a rational number to be formed by using another rational object as a pattern:

```
rational q(z); // initialize q by copying the value from z
```

Copy constructors are used not only by declarations, but they are also invoked in several situations internally by the compiler. One invocation is to duplicate values that are passed by value. Thus almost all classes should define a copy constructor.

14.3   Behavior

14.3.1   Member Functions

Having created a rational number, what can we do with it? That is, what behavior is associated with the rational number abstraction?

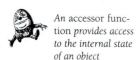

An accessor function *provides access to the internal state of an object*

Fundamental to all operations on the rational number data type is the ability to access the numerator and denominator fields. These data values are obtained via a pair of *accessor functions* that are named, appropriately, numerator and denominator. To illustrate, let's suppose that left and right are rational numbers. The following expression would perform the calculation, described in Figure 14.1, to determine the numerator in the sum of the two values:

```
left.numerator() * right.denominator() +
    right.numerator() * left.denominator()
```

A function defined as part of the behavior of a class is called a *member function*. The declarations of the member functions numerator and denominator are contained in the class description shown in Figure 14.2. (Occasionally, data fields are referred to as *data members* and member functions as *function members*.)

The const keyword following the argument list in both the class declaration and the function implementation specifies that the function is *constant*. This means that the function does not alter the value of the instance to which it is applied. Any value can be declared as constant in the language C++.

Note that the const keyword in C++ is not the same as the final keyword in Java. A variable defined with a final assignment in Java is not permitted to be reassigned. However, it *is* permitted to perform side-effect producing operations that may change its internal structure. In contrast, a const variable in C++ is constant: Once created, it cannot be changed by any means. Thus the only operations that are permitted on const values are those that are guaranteed not to alter the state of the value.

14.3.2   Operators

We would like to be able to treat instances of our rational data type as mathematical objects. For this reason, the main class of operations used to manipulate rational numbers comprises the normal arithmetic operations of addition, subtraction, multiplication, and division. In C++, these operations can be defined by declaring *operators* to be used with our rational numbers.

Although they are written in an infix (in the middle) format, operators are in fact treated in the language C++ much the same as functions. It is common in programming languages for the meaning of operators to be *overloaded*. This means that multiple function definitions are described by the same name, and ambiguity is eliminated by the type of arguments used with the operation. For example, in most languages the symbol + is used to indicate both integer and floating point addition, depending on the type of values used as arguments. In C++ all functions, including operators, can potentially have overloaded meanings (see Chapter 7). The only requirement is that a new definition of an existing name must not be ambiguous. This means that the definition must not require arguments that match any existing definition. This requirement is easily achieved if one or both arguments are a new data type, since no existing definition can be using these types.

To illustrate, the following code fragment shows how we might define the + operator when it is applied to two rational numbers. Recall the definition of addition from Figure 14.1. The body of the operator–function uses a declaration statement to create and initialize a new rational value. This value is then returned as the result of the function. Other operators can be similarly defined.

```
const rational operator + (const rational & left,
                                const rational & right)
{
   // return sum of two rational numbers
   rational result (
      left.numerator() * right.denominator() +
         right.numerator() * left.denominator(),
      left.denominator() * right.denominator());
   return result;
}
```

By declaring that the result is a constant value, we prohibit it from being used as the target of an assignment.

The ampersand (address operator) in the argument list indicates that the left and right values will be passed *by reference*. A reference parameter is merely an address—a pointer to the actual argument value. The alternative, pass *by value*, is the default if no ampersand is specified. Using pass by value creates a new copy of an argument for each function call. The copy constructor is used to form this temporary value. For large structures, this can incur a significant cost. Thus, for most types of values, pass by reference can be executed much more efficiently than pass by value.

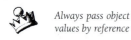

Always pass object values by reference

When pass by reference is used, the keyword const preceding a type designation indicates the parameter value is constant, and changes to the argument value are not permitted from within the procedure. The combination of these two features is called *pass by constant reference*. We have used this mechanism extensively in the declaration of the mathematical operations in the rational number abstraction. This combination has the advantage of efficient execution provided by pass by reference, with the guarantee that no changes will be made to the formal argument value as a result of invoking the procedure.

None of the parameter passing methods available in C++ correspond directly to the semantics found in Java. A Java parameter most closely resembles a pass-by-reference parameter. However, in C++ assignments to such a variable within a function will alter the argument value (unless the parameter is declared as const), whereas such an assignment in Java will simply change the local variable, not the original parameter.

Note that the addition operator as defined is not a member function; rather, it is merely a function that takes rational numbers as arguments. Having defined the arithmetic operators, we can then write expressions to manipulate rational quantities. For example, the following expression performs a calculation by using three rational variables, x, y, and z, and places the result in a new rational number called w:

```
w = x + y * z;
```

The definition of an operator would normally be found in an implementation file. The associated interface file would merely include an indication that such an operation is available. This information is provided by a function *prototype*. A prototype simply lists the function names and the types (and, optionally, names) of any arguments. A list of prototypes for the arithmetic operations might be given as follows:

```
// prototypes for arithmetic operations, including unary negation
const rational operator + (const rational &, const rational &);
const rational operator - (const rational &, const rational &);
```

```
const rational operator * (const rational &, const rational &);
const rational operator / (const rational &, const rational &);
const rational operator - (const rational &);
bool operator < (const rational &, const rational &);
bool operator == (const rational &, const rational &);
```

Binary operators require two arguments, but the unary negation operator requires only a single argument. It could be implemented as follows:

```
const rational operator - (const rational & val)
{
    // return negation of argument value
    return rational (- val.numerator(), val.denominator());
}
```

This example also illustrates the creation of a nameless temporary, or anonymous, value. Rather than declare a new variable, as we did with the addition operator, in this case we simply invoke the constructor directly as a function. The function creates a new value and initializes it, as though we were creating a variable. Such expressions are frequently useful as arguments to another function or, as here, as values being returned from a function.

Another set of operators that should be defined for our rational number data abstraction are the comparison operators. The following illustrates how one of them, the < operator, might be defined. Note that the return type is declared as boolean, whereas the return type of the arithmetic operations given earlier was declared as rational:

```
bool operator < (const rational & left, const rational & right)
{
    // less than comparison of two rational numbers
    return left.numerator() * right.denominator() <
        right.numerator() * left.denominator();
}
```

The equality comparison operator could be written as follows:

```
bool operator == (const rational & left, const rational & right)
{
    return left.numerator() * right.denominator() ==
        right.numerator() * left.denominator();
}
```

The STL includes template definitions for the remaining relational operators (inequality, less than or equal to, greater than, and greater than or equal to) that are defined in terms of these two. Thus defining just these two makes it possible to use all six operations.

14.3.3   Increment and Decrement

The increment and decrement operators are unique in two regards. First, as a side effect they modify the value they are applied to. Second, there are two versions of each: a prefix version that produces a change before the result is determined and a postfix version that yields the original value prior to the modification.

To distinguish these two cases, the language C++ introduces an extra argument to the postfix version of the operator. The class description in Figure 14.2 illustrates these two cases. The prefix operator is simple enough to be coded inline:

```
class rational {
    .
    .
    .
    const rational & operator ++ ()
                              { top += bottom; return *this; }
    .
    .
    .
};
```

The result can here be defined as a rational number *reference*, not a value. This is because the result is a rational that is guaranteed to exist once the method returns, namely, the receiver. Returning a reference is slightly more efficient than returning a value. (Also, a reference value can be used as the target for an assignment, although that is unlikely in this case.) Because the method returns a reference, the pseudovariable this, which is a pointer to the receiver, must be *dereferenced* in the return statement.

The variable this *is a value in Java but is a pointer in C++*

The postfix version is too complex to be coded inline and hence is found in the implementation file. Performing the postfix operation is a three-step process. First, a clone of the current value is produced, using the copy constructor. Next, the current value is incremented, as in the prefix form. Finally, the clone is returned, yielding the original value. Since the clone is a local variable that will disappear once this operation has been completed, the result here must be declared as a value, not as a reference. The integer argument is not used within the operator and hence need not even be provided with a name. Thus:

```
const rational rational::operator++ (int)
{
    // increment fraction, but return original value
    // make clone
    rational clone(*this);
    // make change
    top += bottom;
    // return clone
    return clone;
}
```

Once again, the pseudovariable this is being dereferenced, in order to access the value to which it points rather than the pointer itself. By declaring the result as constant, we prohibit it from being used as the basis for a further increment or as the target of an assignment.

14.3.4   Functions

Ordinary functions can be defined with arguments that are new user-defined data types. Unlike member functions, ordinary functions do not have a receiver and are invoked by a simple function call. They cannot access the internal (private) structure of any class, unless they have been declared as a *friend*. However, the names of ordinary functions can be overloaded, just as we overloaded the names of operators.

To illustrate, we provide a definition of the absolute value function when used with a rational number argument. The function definition could be given as follows:

```
const rational abs (const rational & num)
{
    // return the absolute value of a rational number
    int newtop;
    int newbottom = num.denominator();

    // get nonnegative numerator part
    if (num.numerator() < 0)
        newtop = - num.numerator();
```

```
    else
        newtop = num.numerator();

    // create and return result
    return rational(newtop, newbottom);
}
```

14.3.5   Member Function Operators

Some operators are defined, not as simple functions, but as member functions. The most common situation in which this occurs is the definition of assignment and the various forms of assignment permitted by the language C++. Defining these operators as member functions gives them access to the internal fields of the left argument, something that is not permitted ordinary functions.

Figure 14.2 illustrates both the declaration and the implementation for simple assignment as well as the declaration, but not the implementation, for the addition increment form of assignment as a member function. When a binary operator is declared in this way, the left argument is the instance and is thus not declared; the declaration is needed only for the right argument. Note, also, that in C++ an assignment is an operator, not a statement. To indicate that no "result" is produced by the assignment operator the result type is declared as void.

The addition assignment operator is similar. One problem is that, as a consequence of an addition, the result may no longer be in lowest denominator form. This would occur, for example, in the addition of 3/8 and 1/8, since the result should be 1/2, not 4/8. This type of problem is common to all the arithmetic operations, so we provide a single function to give the result in lowest denominator form:

```
void rational::operator += (const rational & right)
{
    // modify by adding right-hand side
    top = top * right.denominator() + bottom *
                                    right.numerator();
    bottom *= right.denominator();

    // normalize the result, ensuring lowest denominator form
    normalize();
}
```

Figure 14.3 Normalizing a Rational Number

```
void rational::normalize()
{
   // normalize rational by:
   // a) moving sign to numerator
   // b) making sure numerator and denominator have no common divisors
   int sign = 1; // sign is 1 if non-negative, -1 if negative
   if (top < 0) {
      sign = -1;
      top = - top;
      }
   if (bottom < 0) {
      sign = - sign;
      bottom = - bottom;
      }

   // make sure we are not dividing by zero
   if (bottom == 0)
      throw range_error("fraction with zero numerator");

   // find greatest common divisor
   int d = gcd(top, bottom);

   // move sign to top and divide by gcd
   top = sign * (top / d);
   bottom = bottom / d;
}
```

The normalize function is simply a member function, or part of the behavior of the rational number abstraction. Figure 14.2 shows that the normalize function is declared as private. This means that it can be invoked only from within other member functions in the rational number component. Another feature to note is that, when one member function is invoked from within another member function, the receiver does not need to be named; it is assumed to be the same as the current instance. We see this in both the call on normalize in the addition assignment operator and the two-argument constructor function.

A qualified name specifies both the class and member name

Since the implementation of the normalize function (Figure 14.3) is separated from the class, the *qualified name* must be used in the function header. The qualified name indicates that this is the function normalize defined in the class rational. You can think of qualified names as being similar to the use of both a first (given) and second (family) name. We indicated another use of the qualified name earlier in the definition of the increment operator.

The normalize function first checks the sign of the proposed top and bottom values, ensuring that both nonnegative and storing the sign of the result in the variable sign. The proposed values are then converted to lowest denominator form by dividing by their greatest common divisor. The function gcd, which is not shown, is used to compute the greatest common divisor of two integer values.

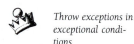
Throw exceptions in exceptional conditions

One other feature of the normalize routine is the use of an *exception*, which is thrown when a fraction with zero numerator is created. Such a value has no mathematical validity and can only be a sign of error. Functions that use the fraction data abstraction can test for this condition, using a try block:

```
try {
    .
    .     // computation involving rationals
    .
} catch (range_error & e) {
    printf("got exception %s", e.what());
    }
```

The data type range_error is one of several exception types provided by the standard library (see Section A.2 in Appendix A.)

14.3.6   Conversion Operations

In addition to their use with declaration statements, constructors are also used implicitly by the language C++ to define conversions. Let's consider the following sequence of statements:

```
rational x, y;
    .
    .
    .
x = y * 3;
```

In order to give this expression meaning, the integer constant 3 must be converted into a rational number, as a rational number can be multiplied only by another rational number. The fact that such a conversion is possible is indicated by the constructor that takes a single integer argument. The actions performed by that constructor are used to implicitly create a new temporary rational number, which is then be used as the right argument in the multiplication. Following the execution of the statement, the temporary value will be discarded.

Temporary values can also be created directly by the programmer, by invoking the constructor as though it were an ordinary function. The following statement illustrates creation of a temporary value to hold the rational number 3/4:

```
x = y * rational(3, 4);
```

Conversions in the other direction—from one object type to another type—are defined by using a *conversion operator*. A conversion operator is an operator whose name is a type. An example is shown in Figure 14.2, which gives the function that converts a rational number into a double precision value:

```
class rational {
    .
    .
    .
    operator double () const { return top / (double) bottom; }
};
```

As with constructors, no return type is given for a conversion operator. The conversion operator specifies the semantics for converting a rational number into a double precision float. This would occur, for example, as a consequence of using a cast:

```
rational x(3, 4);
cout << "3/4 of pi is " << (3.14 * double(x)) << '\n';
```

Avoid casts if possible, but if unavoidable use a static or dynamic cast

Note the use of the **type(value)** syntax for cast, instead of the earlier (now Java style) **(type) value** syntax. Even better is the use of cast operations, such as **static_cast** or **dynamic_cast** (see Section 6.3).

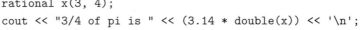

14.4   Input and Output Streams

In Chapter 10 we described the Stream I/O Library and suggested the use of overloaded operators for output operations. As we noted there, output is easily accommodated by redefining the left shift operator **<<**. Generally, this is simply a matter of outputting component elements from the new data type. For example, to output rational numbers, the programmer need only define the following operator:

```
ostream & operator << (ostream & out, const rational & value)
{
    // print representation of rational number on an output stream
    out << value.numerator() << '/' << value.denominator();
    return out;
}
```

Remember that the output function should return the value of the first argument.

An obvious question is, Why did the designer of C++ decide to use the left-shift symbol << for output? The answer actually is simple—and illustrates some of the features (and problems) of using operator overloading in C++. To start with, it is not possible to invent a new binary token to represent output. The language C++ has a fixed set of operators and no more. (The list of operators is shown in Figure 7.1.) Thus the possibilities are somewhat limited.

The assignment operator was one possibility. Input could be specified by using cin on the right-hand side of an assignment, as in:

```
intvar = cin;
```

and output could be indicated by an "assignment" to cout:

```
cout = intvar;
```

However, this would mean that the same symbol would be used for both input and output, potentially causing confusion. Furthermore, the equals sign associates the wrong way: The expression cout = x = y means cout = (x = y), not cout = x; cout = y. Worse, assignment can only be described by member functions. Thus the creation of a new data type would require adding a new member function to the user-defined class in order to perform input and to the stream abstraction in order to perform output.

Early versions of C++ involved use of the operators < and >, but most users then confused input and output with the more conventional comparison meanings of these operators.

The operators << and >> do not appear to cause the same type of confusion. Their use as shift operators is relatively rare in programming, and thus most people readily accept a new interpretation. They are asymmetrical and so suggest data flowing "to" and "from." They associate left to right, allowing sequences of operations to be performed end to end. Finally, their predefined precedence is low enough to allow arithmetic expressions to appear in output without using parentheses, as in:

```
cout << "a + b * c is " << a + b * c << '\n';
```

The left shift operator with its conventional meaning can be used in an output statement by surrounding it with parentheses:

```
cout << " a left shift by 3 is " << (a << 3) << '\n';
```

14.4.1   Stream Input

There is a corresponding data type istream for input streams. Just as the global variable cout represents the standard output, on many systems the global variable cin represents a standard input device. A characteristic of stream input is that "white space" characters (spaces, tabs, and newlines) are ignored during input. If intval is declared as an integer variable, the expression:

```
cin >> intval;
```

reads an integer value into the variable. As with the << operator, the >> operator returns the value of the left argument. When used in situations where a boolean value is expected, such as an if or a while statement, the boolean result generated is used to indicate end of file. Thus a loop that would read values repeatedly from the input until reaching end of file could be written as:

```
while (cin >> intval) {
   // process intval
   .
   .
   .
}
// reach this point on end of input
.
.
.
```

Input for user-defined types is usually built from input for the component parts. Figure 14.4 shows a function to read rational numbers. The input is expected to be an integer, which can optionally be followed by a division sign and a second integer. The function putback returns an unwanted character to the input stream. The next input operation subsequently performed will yield this character.

An easy way to remember the stream I/O operations is to visualize them as arrows. The input operator, >> x, points data into x, while the output operator, << x, copies data out of x.

Figure 14.4   A Function to Read Rational Numbers

```
istream & operator >> (istream & in, rational & r)
{
   // read a rational number from an input stream
   int t, b;

   // read the top
   in >> t;

   // if there is a slash, read the next number
   char c;
   in >> c;
   if (c == '/')
      in >> b; // read bottom part
   else {
      in.putback(c);
      b = 1;
      }

   // do the assignment
   rational newValue(t, b);
   r = newValue;

   // return the stream
   return in;
}
```

Test Your Understanding

1. What type of statements would typically be found in an interface file? What type would be found in an implementation file?

2. Explain the meaning of the statement

   ```
   rational limit();
   ```

3. What is the purpose of a copy constructor?

4. What information is provided by a function prototype?

5. What are the parts of a qualified name?

6. Verify that the correct outcome will be produced by the addition of a fraction to itself, using the compound assignment statement:

```
a += a;
```

What error would occur if the two assignment statements were interchanged in the definition of this operator? Explain.

15

Case Study—Containers

In this case study we illustrate the use of several of the container classes provided as part of the STL (see Chapter 9). To do so, we examine two example problems. The first is an algorithm for computing the shortest path between pairs of points in a graph. The second involves scanning a text document and developing a concordance.

15.1 Shortest Path Graph Problem

Imagine that we have a weighted graph that represents the cost of travel between pairs of cities. The graph is directed, meaning that travel can be made in one direction but not the other. Such a graph is shown in Figure 15.1. The task is to determine not only the minimum cost of travel from one city to each of the others, but also the path to follow in making the journey.

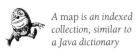
A map is an indexed collection, similar to a Java dictionary

To see how we could represent a graph internally, let's consider first the information we need to maintain for a single city in isolation. If we consider just one city—Phoenix, for example—we need to know the names of the cities that can be reached starting from Phoenix and the cost of each journey. This information could be maintained by a *map*, which is an indexed dictionary structure. The keys in the map will be the destination cities, and the value fields will be the costs:

    Phoenix: [Peoria, 4]
                 [Pittsburgh, 10]
                 [Pueblo, 3]

Figure 15.1 A Weighted Graph

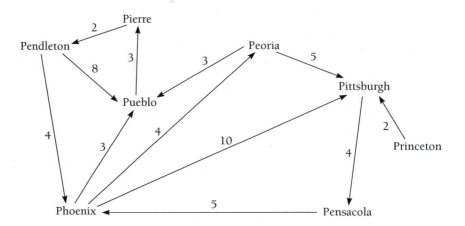

Let's call this information a cityInfo. In terms of the STL data structures, this could be represented by a map in which the keys are represented by constant character pointers (the common representation for strings in C++) and the value fields by integers. To use the map data type, we need a *function object* that defines the ordering on keys. Since the default ordering on pointer values (ordering by location in memory) is not appropriate, we must create a new data type:

```
class charCompare {
public:
    bool operator () (const char * left, const char * right) const
    {
       return strcmp(left, right) < 0;
    }
};
```

An instance of charCompare is a function object, an object that can be used like a function. The behavior we desire is a simulation of the < operator applied to our key values. When invoked as a function, it takes two arguments, which are pointers to character arrays. Using the STL routine strcmp, it compares the two string texts. A negative value indicates that the first is lexicographically smaller than the second and hence that the < operator should return a true value.

Using charCompare, we could define the cityInfo data type as:

```
typedef map <const char *, unsigned int, charCompare> cityInfo;
```

That is, we declare the name cityInfo to be a synonym for a type of map in which the key field is a character pointer and the value field is an unsigned integer. The third argument represents the comparison algorithm that will be used to determine the ordering of the keys. We have chosen to use a typedef (see Section 12.3) to declare the new name, rather than defining a new class. This is because all the behavior we need is provided by the map data type when properly parameterized. The typedef creates a *synonym* name for the new structure, but does not create a new class structure. We can use this synonym name in our later programs to help simplify the code and make it more readable.

To represent the entire graph, we need only maintain the city information for each city. We can again use a map for this purpose. The key field in the map will once again be a city, and the value field will be a cityInfo that encodes the information associated with the city. Let's use the name graph to represent the entire data structure:

```
typedef map <const char *, cityInfo, charCompare> graph;
```

Once more, we have used a typedef because all the functionality we desire is provided by the map data abstraction. Next, we create an instance of graph and initialize it with the information described in the graph shown in Figure 15.1:

```
graph cityMap;

cityMap["Pendleton"]["Phoenix"] = 4;
cityMap["Pendleton"]["Pueblo"] = 8;
cityMap["Pensacola"]["Phoenix"] = 5;
cityMap["Peoria"]["Pittsburgh"] = 5;
cityMap["Peoria"]["Pueblo"] = 3;
cityMap["Phoenix"]["Peoria"] = 4;
cityMap["Phoenix"]["Pittsburgh"] = 10;
cityMap["Phoenix"]["Pueblo"] = 3;
cityMap["Pierre"]["Pendleton"] = 2;
cityMap["Pittsburgh"]["Pensacola"] = 4;
cityMap["Princeton"]["Pittsburgh"] = 2;
cityMap["Pueblo"]["Pierre"] = 3;
```

The first subscript indexes the graph and returns a cityInfo, creating a new cityInfo if no such value exists. The second subscript is then applied to the cityInfo, creating a new position for an unsigned integer value. The assignment then changes the association in the cityInfo map. The type graph is, in effect, a two-dimensional sparse array, indexed by strings and holding integer values.

15.1.1   Shortest Path Algorithm

We now turn our attention to the problem of finding the shortest path to each reachable city, starting from a given initial location. The algorithm that we use is a well-known technique, named *Dijkstra's algorithm* in honor of the computer scientist credited with its discovery.

The idea of Dijkstra's algorithm is to start with a city of origin and make a list of the cities that can be reached in one step. Then order this list by cost, with the least costly city listed first.

Remove the first element from this list. This cannot help but be the least costly way to reach this first city. Any other path to the city would have to originate in another reachable city, and we know that all other reachable cities are more costly.

Now comes the key insight. Determine the cities that are reachable from this first destination and add the costs of travel for each to the cost of the first leg. Using these combined cost figures, add these new destinations to the list of reachable locations, again keeping the list ordered by the total cost.

To complete the algorithm, we need only put a loop around this operation and note that we need not consider a city when it reaches the top of the list if we have already discovered a less costly way to reach the city.

15.1.2   Developing the Data Structures

The final result we desire is a list of cities and the cost of travel to each. We can use the cityInfo data type defined earlier to hold this information and the name travelCosts for this data structure.

The list discussed in the informal description consists of entries that hold two values: a name and a cost. There is no ready-made data type for this structure, so we are forced to define a new class. The constructor for the class will take a city name and a cost. Because some of the data structures in the STL require elements to have a default constructor, we provide one, although it will never be used in our algorithm. Because we want to be able to compare two such values, we override the comparison operator:

```
class Destination {
public:
    Destination () : distance(0) { }
    Destination (const char * dt, unsigned int ds)
       : distance(ds), destination(dt)  { }

    bool operator < (const Destination & right) const
       { return distance < right.distance; }
```

```
    unsigned int distance;
    const char * destination;
};
```

We have here overloaded the comparison operator as a member function. In the rational number case study described in Chapter 14, we illustrated overloading the comparison operator as an ordinary (that is, nonmember) function.

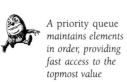

A priority queue maintains elements in order, providing fast access to the topmost value

Recall that we want the list ordered by cost, least to first. This action will be performed for us automatically if we use a *priority queue*. The priority_queue data type in the STL requires two template arguments, the first indicating an underlying container to use for holding the actual values and the second indicating the operation used in comparing values. We can use a vector for the first, and a library-provided function object lesser for the second (lesser is a function object that invokes the comparison operator for our data type and eliminates the need to define a special function object.) The queue is initialized with a single entry, corresponding to a "trip" with no cost to the initial city:

```
priority_queue< vector<Destination>, lesser<Destination> > que;
// put starting city in queue
que.push (Destination(startingCity, 0));
```

At each step of the algorithm, we pull an entry from the priority queue and ask whether we have yet visited this city. There is no direct way to determine whether a map has an entry under a given key, but the information can be indirectly inferred. We do so by counting the number of entries in the cost map that have the new city as a key. If this count is zero, we have not yet visited the city:

```
// remove top entry from queue
char * newCity = que.top().destination;
int cost = que.top().distance;
que.pop();
if (travelCosts.count(newCity) == 0) {
    .
    :    // have not seen it yet
    .
}
```

If we have not been to the city, an entry is made in the travelCosts map:

```
travelCosts[newCity] = cost;
```

Next, we want to add to the priority queue the cities that are reachable from the new city. To do that, we create iterators that cycle over the city information map associated with the new city. Recall that iterators for a map data type yield values of type Pair. The key field in such a value is obtained as the field named first, while the value portion is found in a field named second. At each step of the iteration, we add the cost to date to the new cost and create a new destination entry:

```
cityInfo::iterator start = cityMap[newCity].begin();
cityInfo::iterator stop = cityMap[newCity].end();
for (; start != stop; ++start) {
   const char * destCity = (*start).first;
   // make the new routine
   unsigned int destDistance = (*start).second;
   que.push(Destination(destCity, cost + destDistance));
}
```

We can put everything together in the algorithm shown in Figure 15.2. Note how, in this one algorithm, we have made use of the STL collections map, vector, and priority_queue and the function object lesser.

To complete the program, we need a main procedure. The following double-nested loop will print the cost of travel from each city to every other reachable city:

```
int main()
{

   graph cityMap;
   .
   :   // initialization of the map
   .

   graph::iterator start = cityMap.begin();
   graph::iterator stop = cityMap.end();
   for ( ; start != stop; ++start) {
   const char * city = (*start).first;
      cout << "\nStarting from " << city << "\n";
      cityInfo costs;
      dijkstra(cityMap, city, costs);
      cityInfo::iterator cstart = costs.begin();
      cityInfo::iterator cstop = costs.end();
      for ( ; cstart != cstop; ++cstart) {
         cout << "to " << (*cstart).first <<
            " costs " << (*cstart).second << '\n';
      }
   }
   return 0;
}
```

Figure 15.2 Dijkstra's Shortest Path Algorithm

```
void dijkstra(graph cityMap, const char * start, cityInfo & travelCosts)
// Dijkstra's single source shortest path algorithm
{
    // keep a priority queue of distances to cities
    priority_queue < vector<Destination>, lesser<Destination> > que;
    que.push (Destination(start, 0));

    // while queue not empty
    while (! que.empty() ) {
        // remove top entry from queue
        const char * newCity = que.top().destination;
        int cost = que.top().distance;
        que.pop();
        // if so far unvisited,
        if (travelCosts.count(newCity) == 0) {
            // visit it now
            travelCosts[newCity] = cost;
            // add reachable cities to list
            cityInfo::iterator start = cityMap[newCity].begin();
            cityInfo::iterator stop = cityMap[newCity].end();
            for (; start != stop; ++start) {
                const char * destCity = (*start).first;
                unsigned int destDistance = (*start).second;
                que.push(Destination(destCity, cost + destDistance));
            }
        }
    }
}
```

15.2   A Concordance

Our second example program to illustrate the use of the STL collection data abstractions is a concordance. A *concordance* is an alphabetical listing of words in a text that indicates the line numbers on which each word occurs. Data values are maintained in the concordance by a map, indexed by strings (the words) and holding sets of integers (the line numbers). A set is employed for the value stored under each key because the same word often appears on multiple different lines; indeed, discovering such connections is one of the primary purposes of a concordance.

```
class concordance {
    typedef set<int, less<int> > lineList;
    typedef map<string, lineList, less<string> > wordDictType;
public:
    void readText (istream &);
    void printConcordance (ostream &);

protected:
    wordDictType wordMap;
};
```

Note that the class definition does not include a constructor function. In such situations, a default constructor is automatically created, which in turn invokes the default constructor for the wordMap data field. The default constructor for a map creates a collection with no entries.

Creation of the concordance involves two steps: First, the program generates the concordance (by reading lines from an input stream); then the program prints the result on the output stream. This is reflected in the two member functions readText() and printConcordance(). The first, readText(), is written as:

```
void concordance::readText (istream & in)
// read all words from input stream, entering into concordance
{
    string line;
    for (int i = 1; getline(in, line); i++) {
    // translate into lowercase, split into words
        allLower(line);
        list<string> words;
        split(line, " ,.;:", words);
        // enter each word on line into concordance
        list<string>::iterator wptr;
        for (wptr = words.begin(); wptr != words.end(); ++wptr)
            wordMap[*wptr].insert(i);
    }
}
```

Lines are read from the input stream one by one. The text of the line is first converted to lowercase; then the line is split into words, using the function split() described in Chapter 8. Each word is then entered into the concordance. Subscripting the map creates an entry for the line list if one does not already exist. Using the insert method for sets, the word is then entered into the container.

The second step is to print the concordance, which is performed as follows:

```
void concordance::printConcordance (ostream & out)
// print concordance on the given output stream
{
    string lastword = "";
    wordDictType::iterator pairPtr;
    wordDictType::iterator stop = wordMap.end();
    for (pairPtr = wordMap.begin(); pairPtr != stop; ++pairPtr) {
        out << (*pairPtr).first << " ";
        lineList & lines = (*pairPtr).second;
        lineList::iterator wstart = lines.begin();
        lineList::iterator wstop = lines.end();
        for ( ; wstart != wstop; ++wstart)
            out << *wstart << " ";
        cout << endl;
    }
}
```

An iterator loop is used to cycle over the elements being maintained by the word list. Each new word generates a new line of output; thereafter, line numbers appear separated by spaces. For each word, a nested iterator loop cycles over the line numbers. If, for example, the input was the text:

It was the best of times,

it was the worst of times.

The output, from best to worst, would be:

best: 1

it: 1 2

of: 1 2

the: 1 2

times: 1 2

was: 1 2

worst: 2

Test Your Understanding

1. Explain the purpose of the function object required as the third argument in the map data type.

2. How does the priority_queue data abstraction differ from the queue data type?

1|6

Case Study—A Card Game

In this third case study, we examine a simple card game, a version of solitaire. A slightly different version of this program was presented in C++ in the first edition of our introductory OOP book. It was translated into Java in the second edition [Budd 97] and revised, once again in Java, in a later book [Budd 98b]. The program presented here is yet another revision, this time translating back into C++ and making use of the Microsoft Foundation Classes (MFC) for the graphical interface.

16.1   The Class **Card**

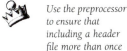

Use the preprocessor to ensure that including a header file more than once will not cause error

Whenever possible, software development should strive for the creation of general-purpose reusable classes—classes that make minimal demands on their environment and hence can be carried from one application to another. This idea is illustrated by the first class, representing a playing card and defining the playing card abstraction. This class is shown in Figure 16.1.

    Preprocessor directives (see Section 12.2) are placed at the beginning and the end of the file containing the class definition. These directives ensure that, if the file is included more than once, the compiler will nevertheless see only one definition for the class **Card**. This is accomplished by testing to determine whether a name—one that should occur only in this context—has been defined. If not, the name is given a definition (here a null definition), and the text is included. On subsequent inclusions the name will be known, and the text between the **ifndef** and the corresponding **endif** statement will be ignored.

Figure 16.1   Definition of the Class Card

```
# ifndef CARDH // ensure that card is included only once
# define CARDH

//
// Playing Card Abstraction
//

class Card {
public:
    enum Suits {Heart, Spade, Diamond, Club};
    enum Colors {Red, Black};

    // constructors
    Card (Suits sv, int rv) : s(sv), r(rv) { fup = false; }

    // return attributes
    int rank () { return r; }
    Suits suit() { return s; }
    bool faceup () { return fup; }
    Colors color ();

    // change attributes
    void flip () { fup = ! fup; }

private:
    const Suits s;
    const int r;
    bool fup;
};

# endif
```

Within the class definition for Card, two enumerated data types are defined for the discrete classes of suits and colors. The enumerated type declaration not only creates names for these values, but it also defines the range of elements that they can hold.

The definition of the playing card abstraction is divided between an interface file, which defines the structure of the class, and an implementation file. In this particular case, all but one method is defined in the class body in the interface file. The one remaining method is found in the file Card.cpp:

```
# include "card.h"

Card::Colors Card::color ()
{
    if (suit() == Heart || suit() == Diamond)
        return Red;
    return Black;
}
```

Names defined within a class declaration must always be qualified when they are used outside the class

The implementation file must include the interface file. Also, a qualified name must be used to indicate the return type, as the return type is generally processed before the method name is read, and at that point the compiler does not yet know that the method is to be considered part of class Card. By the time the compiler starts to consider the method body, however, it has determined that the function is part of a method for class Card, and hence names such as Red and Black do not need to be qualified.

Note that the class Card has no information about the application in which it is developed. Thus it can easily be moved from this program to another program that uses the playing card abstraction.

16.2   Data and View Classes

Techniques used in the creation of visual interfaces have undergone frequent revisions, and this trend will likely continue for the foreseeable future. For this reason it is useful to separate classes that contain data values, such as the card abstraction, from classes that are used to provide a graphical display of those values. By doing so, we can modify or replace the display classes as necessary, leaving the original data classes untouched.

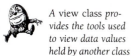

A view class provides the tools used to view data values held by another class

The display of the card abstraction is provided by the class CardView. CardView is a *view class,* a class used only to provide the graphical representation of the data held by another class. To isolate the library-specific aspects of the card view, the actual display methods are declared as *pure virtual* methods (see Section 6.2). Later, these methods will be subclassed and replaced with functions that, in the case of the present application, use the MFC to generate the graphical interface:

```
# ifndef CardViewH
# define CardViewH

# include "card.h"

//
// CardView---display a graphical representation of a card
//

class CardView {
public:
    static const int Width = 40;
    static const int Height = 70;

    virtual void display (Card * aCard, int, int) = 0;
    virtual void halfDisplay (Card * aCard, int, int) = 0;
};

# endif
```

The CardView class contains a pair of static constants that represent the height and width of a card on the display. The Card class itself knows nothing about how it is displayed. Two static methods are prototyped: The first displays the entire face of a card at a given position on the display; the second displays only the upper half of a card.

It can be argued that even including the height and width as values in this class is introducing some platform dependencies. However, the height and width are less likely to change than are the libraries used to perform the actual graphical display.

16.3   The Game

The version of solitaire we will describe is known as klondike. The countless variations on this game make it probably the most common version of solitaire—so much so that when we say "solitaire," most people think of klondike. The version used here is the one described by Morehead [Morehead 49].

The layout of the game is shown in Figure 16.2. A single standard deck of 52 cards is used. The *tableau*, or playing table, consists of 28 cards in 7 piles. The

Figure 16.2 Layout for the Solitaire Game

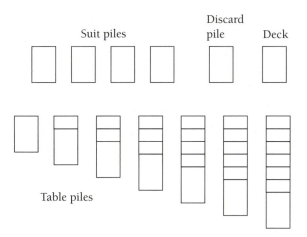

first pile has 1 card, the second 2, and so on up to 7. The top card of each pile is initially face up; all other cards are face down.

The suit piles (sometimes called *foundations*) are built up from aces to kings in the respective suits. They are constructed above the tableau as the cards become available. The object of the game is to build all 52 cards into the suit piles.

The cards that are not part of the tableau are initially all in the *deck*. Cards in the deck are face down and are drawn one by one from the deck and placed, face up, on the *discard pile*. From there, they can be moved onto either a tableau pile or a foundation. Cards are drawn from the deck until the pile is empty; at this point, the game is over if no further moves can be made.

Cards can be placed on a table pile only on a card of next higher rank and opposite color. They can be placed on a suit pile only if they are the same suit and next-higher card or if the suit pile is empty and the card is an ace. Spaces in the tableau that arise during play can be filled only by kings.

The topmost card of each table pile and the topmost card of the discard pile are always available for play. The only time that more than one card is moved is when an entire collection of face-up cards from one table pile (called a *build*) is moved to another table pile. This can be done if the bottommost card of the build can be legally played on the topmost card of the destination table pile. Our initial game will not support the transfer of a build, but we do discuss it as a possible extension of the game. The topmost card of a table pile is always face up. If a card is moved from a table pile, leaving a face-down card on top, the latter card can be turned face up.

Clearly, the game of solitaire mostly involves manipulating piles of cards. Each type of pile has many features in common with the others and a few aspects unique to the particular type. In Section 16.4, we investigate in detail how inheritance can be used in such circumstances to simplify implementation of the various card piles by providing a common base for the generic actions and permitting this base to be redefined when necessary.

16.4   Card Piles—Inheritance in Action

Use inheritance to factor out common behavior from similar classes

Much of the behavior that we associate with a card pile is common to each type of pile in the game. For example, each pile maintains a linked list of the cards in the pile, and the operations of inserting and deleting elements from this linked list are common. Other operations are given default behavior in the class CardPile, but they are sometimes overridden in the various subclasses. The class CardPile is shown in Figure 16.3.

Each card pile maintains the coordinate location for the upper-left corner of the pile and a linked list containing the cards in the pile. The list abstraction from the STL (see Chapter 9) is used for the latter. All these values are set by the constructor for the class—the first two explicitly by means of initializer classes and the last implicitly—since no other initialization instruction is provided to the compiler. The data fields are declared as **protected** and thus accessible to member functions associated with this class and to member functions associated with subclasses.

The class PopError is a nested class (see Section 5.7) and declares no data fields and no methods. The sole purpose of the class is to provide a unique identifier for the exceptions thrown by an attempt to read from an empty list.

The three functions top(), pop(), and empty() manipulate the list of cards, using functions provided by the list class. Two are provided with inline definitions, while the top method is found in the implementation file:

```
Card * CardPile::top() throw (CardPile::PopError)
{
    if (cards.empty())
        throw new PopError();
    return cards.front();
}
```

As would be expected—given the C++ philosophy of valuing efficiency over run-time checks—the list abstraction in the standard library is not obligated to report an error if an attempt is made to access the first element of an empty

Figure 16.3   Description of the Class CardPile

```
# ifndef CardPileH
# define CardPileH

# include "card.h"
# include <list>

//
// CardPile---representation of a pile of cards
//

class CardPile {
public:
    CardPile (int xl, int yl) : x(xl), y(yl) { }

    // exception on pop from empty stack
    class PopError { };

    // drawing cards from pile
    bool empty () { return cards.empty(); }
    Card * top () throw (PopError);
    Card * pop () throw (PopError)
       { Card * result = top(); cards.pop_front(); return result; }

    // virtual methods that can be overridden
    virtual bool includes (int, int);
    virtual void addCard (Card *);
    virtual void display (CardView &);
    virtual bool canTake (Card *);
    virtual void select ();

protected:
    list<Card *> cards;
    const int x; // location of display
    const int y;
};

   // definitions of subclasses

# endif
```

container. Thus, if we desire to make the program more robust, we must explicitly test for this condition. Doing so makes the program more reliable, at the expense of slowing down executions of the top and pop operations.

To catch the potential stack underflow, the main program will at some point be surrounded by a try clause:

```
try {
    .
    .   // execute the program
    .
} catch (CardPile::PopError & e) {
    .
    .   // handle the exception
    .
}
```

The remaining five operations defined in class CardPile are common to the abstract notion of our card piles, but they differ in detail in each case. For example, the function canTake(Card) asks whether it is legal to place a card on the given pile. A card can be added to a suit pile, for instance, only if it is an ace and the foundation space is empty, or if the card is of the same suit as the current topmost card in the pile and has the next higher value. A card can be added to a table pile only if the tableau space is empty and the card is a king, or if its color is opposite that of the current topmost card on the pile and has the next lower value.

The actions of the five virtual functions defined in CardPile can be characterized as follows:

includes Determines whether the coordinates given as arguments are contained within the boundaries of the pile. The default action simply tests the topmost card; this action is overridden in the table piles to test all card values.

canTake Indicates whether a pile can take a specific card. Only the table and suit piles can take cards, so the default action is simply to return no; this action is overridden in the two classes mentioned.

addCard Adds a card to the card list. It is redefined in the discard pile class to ensure that the card is face up.

display Displays the card deck. The default method merely displays the topmost card of the pile but is overridden in the tableau class to display a column of cards. Only the top half of each card except the topmost is displayed. So that the playing surface area is conserved, only the topmost and bottommost face-up cards are displayed (this permits giving definite bounds to the playing surface).

select   Performs an action in response to a mouse click. It is invoked when the user selects a pile by clicking the mouse in the portion of the playing field covered by the pile. The default action does nothing but is overridden by the table, deck, and discard piles to play the topmost card, if possible.

The following table illustrates the important benefits of inheritance. With five operations and five classes, there are 25 potential methods we might have had to define. By making use of inheritance, we need to implement only 13. Furthermore, we are guaranteed that each pile will respond in the same way to similar requests.

	CardPile	SuitPile	DeckPile	DiscardPile	TableauPile
includes	×				×
canTake	×	×			×
addCard	×			×	
display	×				×
select	×		×	×	×

16.4.1   The Default Card Pile

Let's now examine each of the subclasses of CardPile in detail. We point out various uses of object-oriented features and differences between the C++ definitions and similar Java procedures as they are encountered. Each of the five virtual methods is first defined in the class CardPile. These implementations represent the default behavior, if they are not overridden:

```
bool CardPile::includes (int tx, int ty)
{
    // default behavior: is point within bounds of card?
    return x <= tx && tx <= x + CardView::Width &&
        y <= ty && ty <= y + CardView::Height;

}


void CardPile::addCard (Card * aCard)
{
    // default behavior: push card on front of stack
    cards.push_front(aCard);

}
```

```
void CardPile::display (CardView & cv)
{
    // default behavior: print topmost card
    if (empty())
        cv.display(0, x, y);
    else
        cv.display(top(), x, y);
}

bool CardPile::canTake (Card *)
{
    // default behavior: just say no
    return false;
}

void CardPile::select ()
{
// default behavior: do nothing
}
```

16.4.2   The Suit Piles

The simplest subclass is the class SuitPile, which represents the pile of cards at the top of the playing surface, the pile being built up in suit from ace to king. The interface for this class is as follows:[1]

```
class SuitPile : public CardPile {
public:
    SuitPile (int xl, int yl) : CardPile(xl, yl) { }
    bool canTake (Card *);
};
```

The class SuitPile defines only two methods. The constructor for the class takes two integer arguments and does nothing more than invoke the constructor for the parent class CardPile. Because this action is simple, the method is defined inline as part of the class description. The method canTake determines whether a

---

[1] In the code distributed with this case study, the interfaces for the various types of card piles have been combined into a single file, so as to reduce the number of files needed to create the program.

card can be placed on the pile. A card is legal if the pile is empty and the card is an ace (i.e., has rank zero) or if the card is the same suit as the topmost card in the pile and of the next higher rank (e.g., a three of spades can be played only on a two of spades). The code that provides this behavior is more complex and is therefore defined in the implementation file rather than in the class definition itself:

```
bool SuitPile::canTake (Card * aCard)
{
    // can take ace if empty
    if (empty())
        return aCard->rank() == 1;
    // otherwise must be next card in suit
    Card * topCard = top();
    return (aCard->suit() == topCard->suit()) &&
        (aCard->rank() == 1 + topCard->rank());
}
```

All other behavior of the suit pile is the same as that of our generic card pile. When selected, a suit pile does nothing. When a card is added, it is simply inserted into the linked list. To display the pile, only the topmost card is drawn.

16.4.3   The Deck Pile

The DeckPile maintains the deck from which new cards are drawn. It differs from the generic card pile in two ways. When constructed, rather than creating an empty pile of cards, it initializes itself, using an array of card values passed as argument to the constructor. The method select is invoked when the mouse button is used to select the card deck. If the deck is empty, it does nothing. Otherwise, the topmost card is removed from the deck and added to the discard pile. Thus:

```
class DeckPile : public CardPile {
public:
    DeckPile (int, int, Card * []);
    void select ();
};
```

The implementation of the constructor shows how initialization clauses are written when code is not being defined inline:

```
DeckPile::DeckPile (int xl, int yl, Card * orig[ ])
   : CardPile(xl, yl)
{
   for (int i = 0; i < 52; i++) {
      Card * theCard = orig[i];
      if (theCard->faceup())
         theCard->flip();
      addCard(theCard);
   }
}
```

Implementation of the **select** method presents us with a new problem. When the mouse is pressed on the deck pile, the desired action is to move a card from the deck pile onto the discard pile, turning it face up in the process. The problem is that we now need to refer to a single unique card pile, namely, the pile that represents the discard pile.

One approach would be to define the various card piles as global variables, which then could be universally accessed. In fact, this approach is used in the program described in our earlier version of the game [Budd 97]. In Java the equivalent of global variables is a series of **static** values, as in the program described later in Budd [Budd 98b].

In this version of the program we reduce the number of global variables to one, which represents a "game manager." The class definition for the game manager is shown in Figure 16.4. We postpone a discussion of some of the details of this class until after we describe the various card piles.

The global variable **gameManager** is defined as an instance of this class. This variable is declared as **external** to the class deck implementation file:

```
# include "Game.h" // include description of game manager
extern Game gameManager;

void DeckPile::select ()
{
   // move topmost card to discard stack
   if (empty())
      return;
   gameManager.discardPile()->addCard (top());
   pop();
}
```

Figure 16.4 Definition of Application Class

```
# include "CardPile.h"

//
// Game---Game Manager
//

class Game {
public:
    // constructor, initialization, and destructor
    void init ();
    ~Game ();

    // access to the piles
    CardPile * deckPile () { return piles[0]; }
    CardPile * discardPile () { return piles[1]; }
    CardPile * suitPile (int i) { return piles[2+i]; }
    CardPile * tableau (int i) { return piles[6+i]; }

    // handling actions
    void repaint(CardView &);
    void mouseDown (int, int);

private:
    CardPile * piles[13];
};
```

An important point must be made here concerning circularities. It is not legal for interface files to have a circular structure. Such a structure would put the preprocessor into an infinite loop, since preprocessing is performed before the analysis of the source program. However, circularity seems inevitable here. The application class, SolitaireApplication, must of necessity know about the various types of card piles, and the card piles must know about the application class.

What saves us in this case is the separation between interface and implementation. Only the *implementation* of class DeckPile must know about the game application; the *interface* says nothing about it. Thus the interface file for CardDeck need not include the interface file for the application; however, this file is needed by the implementation file for the abstraction.

As circularities of this sort are common in programs, you should study this situation until it is clear to you where the various different files, both interface and implementation, are being used.

16.4.4   The Discard Pile

The class DiscardPile redefines the addCard and select methods. The interface is described as follows:

```
class DiscardPile : public CardPile {
public:
    DiscardPile (int xl, int yl) : CardPile(xl, yl) { }
    void addCard (Card *);
    void select ();
};
```

Implementation of these methods is interesting in that they exhibit two very different forms of inheritance. The select method *overrides* or *replaces* the default behavior provided by class CardPile, replacing it with code that when invoked (when the mouse is pressed over the card pile) checks to determine whether the topmost card can be played on any suit pile or, alternatively, on any table pile. If the card cannot be played, it is kept in the discard pile:

```
void DiscardPile::select ()
{
    if (empty())
        return;
    Card * topCard = top();
    for (int i = 0; i < 4; i++)
        if (gameManager.suitPile(i)->canTake(topCard)) {
            gameManager.suitPile(i)->addCard(topCard);
            pop();
            return;
        }
    for (int i = 0; i < 7; i++)
        if (gameManager.tableau(i)->canTake(topCard)) {
            gameManager.tableau(i)->addCard(topCard);
            pop();
            return;
        }
}
```

The method addCard is a different sort of overriding. Here the behavior is a *refinement* of the default behavior in the parent class. That is, the behavior of the parent class is completely executed, and, in addition, new behavior is added. In this case, the new behavior ensures that when a card is placed on the discard pile it is always face up. After satisfying this condition, the code in the parent class is invoked to add the card to the pile. A fully qualified name is necessary to avoid the confusion with the addCard method being defined:

```
void DiscardPile::addCard (Card * aCard)
{
    if (! aCard->faceup())
        aCard->flip();
    CardPile::addCard(aCard);
}
```

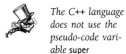

The C++ language does not use the pseudo-code variable super

In Java the same problem would be addressed by sending a message to super (as in super.addCard(aCard)).

Another form of refinement occurs in the constructors for the various subclasses. Each must invoke the constructor for the parent class to guarantee that the parent is properly initialized before the constructor performs its own actions. The parent constructor is invoked by an initializer clause inside the constructor for the child class.

16.4.5   The Table Piles

The most complex of the subclasses of CardPile is that used to hold a tableau, or the table pile. The interface for this class redefines nearly all the virtual methods defined in ClassPile:

```
class TablePile : public CardPile {
public:
    TablePile (int xl, int yl, int p);

    bool canTake (Card * aCard);
    bool includes (int tx, int ty);
    void display (CardView & cv);
    void select ();
};
```

When initialized, by the constructor, the table pile removes a certain number of cards from the deck, placing them in its own pile. The number of cards so removed is determined by an additional argument to the constructor. The topmost card of this pile is then displayed face up:

```
TablePile::TablePile(int xv, int yv, int p) : CardPile(xv, yv)
{
    // copy correct number of cards into deck
    for (int i = 0; i < p; i++) {
        Card * aCard = gameManager.deckPile()->top();
        if (aCard->faceup())
            aCard->flip();
        addCard(aCard);
        gameManager.deckPile()->pop();
    }
    // flip topmost card
    top()->flip();
}
```

A card can be added to the pile (method canTake) only if the pile is empty and the card is a king, or if the card is the opposite color from that of the current topmost card and one smaller in rank:

```
bool TablePile::canTake (Card * aCard)
{
    if (empty())
        return aCard->rank() == 12;
    Card * topCard = top();
    return (aCard->color() != topCard->color()) &&
        (aCard->rank() == topCard->rank() - 1);
}
```

When a mouse press is tested to determine whether it covers the pile (method includes), the bottom bound is not tested because piles may vary in length:

```
bool TablePile::includes (int tx, int ty)
{
    return x <= tx && tx <= x + CardView::Width && y <= ty;
}
```

When the pile is selected, the topmost card is flipped if it is face down. If it is face up, an attempt is made to move the card first to any available suit pile and then to any available table pile. Only if no pile can take the card is it left in place:

```
void TablePile::select ()
{
```

```
// if empty, do nothing
if (empty()) return;

// if face down, then flip
Card * topCard = top();
if (! topCard->faceup()) {
    topCard->flip();
    return;
}

// else see if any pile can take card
for (int i = 0; i < 4; i++)
    if (gameManager.suitPile(i)->canTake(topCard)) {
        gameManager.suitPile(i)->addCard(pop());
        return;
    }
for (int i = 0; i < 7; i++)
    if (gameManager.tableau(i)->canTake(topCard)) {
        gameManager.tableau(i)->addCard(pop());
        return;
    }
}
```

Finally, to display a pile all the underlying cards are displayed in half form, and the topmost card is displayed in full:

```
void TablePile::display (CardView & cv)
{
    if (empty())
        CardPile::display(cv);
    else {
        int lx = x;
        int ly = y;
        list<Card *>::iterator cptr = cards.end();
        list<Card *>::iterator front = cards.begin();
        for (--cptr; cptr != front; --cptr) {
            cv.halfDisplay(*cptr, lx, ly);
            ly += CardView::Height/2;
        }
        cv.display(*front, lx, ly);
    }
}
```

16.5   Playing the Polymorphic Game

A polymorphic variable is declared as one type, but holds a value of a different type

The game manager class described in Figure 16.4 stores the various card piles in an array. The array is declared as pointers to CardPile, although in fact the values are polymorphic and hold various types of card piles. These values are initialized in the method init:

```
void Game::init ()
{
    // first, create a deck and randomize it
    int j = 0;
    for (int i = 1; i <= 13; i++) {
        originalDeck[j++] = new Card(Card::Diamond, i);
        originalDeck[j++] = new Card(Card::Spade, i);
        originalDeck[j++] = new Card(Card::Heart, i);
        originalDeck[j++] = new Card(Card::Club, i);
    }

    randomInteger swapper; // declare the random function object
    random_shuffle(originalDeck, originalDeck+52, swapper);

    // then initialize each of the deck piles
    piles[0] = new DeckPile(335, 5, originalDeck);
    piles[1] = new DiscardPile(268, 5);
    j = 2;
    for (int i = 0; i < 4; i++) {
        piles[j++] = new SuitPile(15 + 60 * i, 5);
    }
    for (int i = 0; i < 7; i++) {
        piles[j++] = new TablePile(5 + 55 * i, 80, i+1);
    }
}
```

There is a subtle reason why initialization must be performed by a method and not by the constructor for this class: The constructor for TablePile, described in Section 16.4, uses the global variable gameManager, which is an instance of this class. The C++ language does not consider an object initialized until the constructor has completely finished. Thus the value of gameManager used by the TablePile constructor may not be available at the point it is needed. However, a careful reading of the init method shows that the deck pile is the first pile initialized, and therefore if executed as part of a function will be available for use by the initialization routine for TablePile.

The method random_shuffle, used to shuffle the deck, is one of the generic algorithms provided by the standard library. This particular function requires a function object that will generate random integer values from a given range. Such an object can be produced by the following class declaration:

```
class randomInteger {
public:
   unsigned int operator () (unsigned int max)
   {
      unsigned int rval = rand();
      return rval % max;
   }
};
```

Space for the card values is created in the method init. This space is freed by the destructor:

```
Game::~Game()
{
   // free up all the old card values
   for (int i = 0; i < 52; i++)
      delete originalDeck[i];
}
```

Memory management techniques, such as reference counting (see Chapter 4) are not necessary in this case because the cards are neither created nor destroyed while the application is in execution.

By storing the card values in a polymorphic array, the game manager need not distinguish the characteristics of the individual piles. For example, to repaint the display it is necessary only to tell each pile to repaint itself:

```
void Game::repaint(CardView & cv)
{
   // simply repaint each of the card decks
   for (int i = 0; i < 13; i++)
      piles[i]->display(cv);
}
```

The method display will be different, depending on the actual type of card pile. Similarly, to repond to a mouse down move, the manager simply cycles through the list of card piles:

```
void Game::mouseDown(int x, int y)
{
    for (int i = 0; i < 13; i++)
        if (piles[i]->includes(x, y)) {
            piles[i]->select();
            return;
        }
}
```

16.6   The Graphical User Interface

Isolate the graphical interface from the rest of a program

We have taken pains in the development of this program to isolate the details of the graphical interface. This is because, of all the elements of a program, the user interface is the most likely to require change as new graphical libraries are introduced or existing libraries are changed. In this application, all the graphical aware routines can be isolated in one file.

Recall that the display of a card was provided by a method CardView that was described as abstract. To produce actual output, we must create a subclass that implements the pure virtual methods. We call this class MFCardView:

```
class MFCardView : public CardView {
public:
    // constructor saves drawing context
    MFCardView (CPaintDC & idc) : dc(idc) { }

    // implement the interface
    void display (Card * aCard, int, int);
    void halfDisplay (Card * aCard, int, int);

private:
    CPaintDC & dc; // drawing context
    void paintCard(Card * aCard, int, int);
};
```

This is not a text on fancy graphics, so the actual display will be rather simple. Basically, a card draws itself as a rectangle with a textual description. Empty piles are drawn in green, the backsides of cards in yellow, the faces in the appropriate color:

```
void MFCardView::paintCard (Card * aCard, int x, int y)
{
    char buffer[80];
    if (aCard == 0) {
        strcpy(buffer,"mt"); // mt = empty
        dc.SetTextColor(RGB(0,255, 0)); // green
        dc.TextOut(x+5, y+5, buffer, strlen(buffer));
    }
    else {
        if (aCard->faceup()) {
            char suitCard;
            switch (aCard->suit()) {
                case Card::Heart: suitCard = 'H'; break;
                case Card::Spade: suitCard = 'S'; break;
                case Card::Diamond: suitCard = 'D'; break;
                case Card::Club: suitCard = 'C'; break;
            }
            switch (aCard->rank()) {
                case 1: sprintf(buffer,"A %c", suitCard); break;
                case 11: sprintf(buffer, "J %c", suitCard); break;
                case 12: sprintf(buffer, "Q %c", suitCard); break;
                case 13: sprintf(buffer, "K %c", suitCard); break;
                default: sprintf(buffer, "%d %c", aCard->rank(),
                                    suitCard);
                    break;
            }
            if (aCard->color() == Card::Red)
                dc.SetTextColor(RGB(255, 0, 0)); // red
            else
                    dc.SetTextColor(RGB(0, 0, 0)); // black
            dc.TextOut(x+5, y+5, buffer, strlen(buffer));
        }
        else {
            strcpy(buffer, "back");
            dc.SetTextColor(RGB(255, 255, 0)); // yellow
            dc.TextOut(x+5, y+5, buffer, strlen(buffer));
        }
    }
}
```

```
void MFCardView::display (Card * aCard, int x, int y)
{
   dc.Rectangle (x, y, x + Width, y + Height);
   paintCard(aCard, x, y);
}

void MFCardView::halfDisplay (Card * aCard, int x, int y)
{
   dc.Rectangle (x, y, x + Width, y + Height/ 2);
   paintCard (aCard, x, y);
}
```

Graphics in the MFC is based around a *display context*, here stored in the variable **dc**. We do not discuss details of the graphical output routines provided by the MFC, although many of the names are self-explanatory. The display for our game is rather primitive, consisting simply of line rectangles and the textual display of card information.

Applications in the MFC framework are created by means of two classes: a window class and an application class. The two are linked, and the creation of the latter involves initialization of the game manager. The main window is an instance of an MFC-provided window, called **CFrameWnd**:

```
class SolitaireMainWindow : public CFrameWnd  {
public:
   SolitaireMainWindow() {  Create(NULL, "Solitaire Game"); }
   afx_msg void OnPaint();
   afx_msg void OnLButtonDown (UINT flag, CPoint loc);
   DECLARE_MESSAGE_MAP()
};
```

The window class is responsible for trapping the actual mouse presses and repainting the window. In our application, these activities are simply passed on to the game manager:

```
void SolitaireMainWindow::OnPaint()
{
   CPaintDC dc(this);
   MFCardView cv(dc);

   gameManager.repaint(cv);
}
```

```
void SolitaireMainWindow::OnLButtonDown(UINT flag, CPoint loc)
{
    try {
        gameManager.mouseDown(loc.x, loc.y);
    }
    catch (CardPile::PopError & e) { } // do nothing on error

    InvalidateRect(NULL);
}
```

The application class is again subclassed from an MFC provided parent called CWinApp. The child class must redefine a virtual method named InitInstance. In this method the application class is linked to the window class, and the window class is told to display. Other application-specific initialization, such as the initialization of our game manager, can be placed here. Creating an instance of the application class begins the application:

```
class SolitaireApplication : public CWinApp  {
public:
    BOOL InitInstance();
};


SolitaireApplication theApp;

BOOL SolitaireApplication::InitInstance()
{
    gameManager.init();
    m_pMainWnd = new SolitaireMainWindow();
    m_pMainWnd->ShowWindow (m_nCmdShow);
    m_pMainWnd->UpdateWindow();
}
```

In this simple application, we have only scratched the surface of the functionality provided by the MFC system. However, the details of how MFC programs are created are complicated and are beyond the issues being discussed here. A good introduction to the MFC system is provided by Schildt [Schildt 96].

Test Your Understanding

1. Explain the purpose of the ifndef/endif pair that surrounds the interface file for class Card (Figure 16.1).

2. Why is the color method of class Card defined in the implementation file while all other methods are defined in the interface file?

3. Why should data view classes be separated from data value classes?

4. Explain why the containers provided by the STL, such as list or vector, do not detect an attempt to access an element in an empty container.

5. Explain why the Game class cannot be initialized in a constructor.

Case Study—Combining Separate Classes

A common problem encountered by programmers is how to combine elements from two or more classes when they are not permitted to make changes to the original classes. For example, the original classes may be distributed in binary form by two separate vendors. Nevertheless, the programmer would like to maintain these values in a common representation and perform common tasks on them. Solving this problem is an excellent illustration of the different uses of inheritance, templates, overloaded functions, and the interactions among these mechanisms.

Suppose, for example, that you have Apples and Oranges, which are products of different vendors. Apples (Figure 17.1) can print themselves on an output stream, using the method printOn(ostream), whereas Oranges (Figure 17.2) perform a similar operation, using the method writeTo(ostream). You want to keep both apples and oranges on the same list and write them out to an output stream, using a single polymorphic function.

We can address this problem in a sequence of small steps. Since the class descriptions for apples and oranges are distributed only in binary form, we cannot add a new member function to these classes. However, nothing prevents us from writing new ordinary functions that take their respective types as arguments. By doing so, we can use a single name, print, for the operation of printing to a stream:

```
void print (const Apple & a, ostream & out)
{
    a.printOn(out);
}
```

Figure 17.1   Class Description for Apple

```
// class Apple
// created 1987 by Standard Apple of Ohio
class Apple {
public:
    // constructors
    Apple () : variety("generic") { }
    Apple (string & v) : variety (v) { }
    Apple (const Apple & r) : variety (r.variety) { }

    // apple operations
    ostream & printOn (ostream & out)
        { return out << "Apple: " << variety; }
private:
    string variety;
};
```

Figure 17.2   Class Description for Orange

```
// Orange code
// written by Chris (Granny) Smith, 1992
// House of Orange
class Orange : public Produce {
public:
    // constructor
    Orange ();
    void writeTo (ostream & aStream)
        { aStream << "Orange"; }
};
```

```
void print (const Orange & a, ostream & out)
{
    a.writeTo(out);
}
```

This is a small step toward combining apples and oranges. We now have a single common function name, print, that can be used for both data types:

```
Apple anApple("Rome");
Orange anOrange;
```

```
// can print both apples and oranges
print (anApple, cout);
print (anOrange, cout);
```

Unlike Java containers, containers in C++ are homogeneous and can hold only one type of value. Thus, to combine apples and oranges in the same container, we need an adaptor that will convert the type into a more suitable data value. We get one first by defining a common parent class that will describe the behavior that we want all fruit to possess:

```
class Fruit {
public:
    virtual void print (ostream &) = 0;
};
```

Because the specific implementation of the behavior will be different for each fruit, we make the description of this function a pure virtual method.

Using a template method, we can create a fruit adaptor that will take either an apple or an orange and satisfy the fruit interface:

```
template <class T>
class FruitAdaptor : public Fruit {
public:
    FruitAdaptor (T & f) : theFruit(f) { }

    T & value () { return theFruit; }

    virtual void print (ostream & out) { print(theFruit, out); }

public:
    T & theFruit;
};
```

The template argument allows us to use the adaptor with both apples and oranges, but it always yields a new value that is a subclass of Fruit:

```
Fruit * fruitOne = new FruitAdaptor<Apple> (anApple);
Fruit * fruitTwo = new FruitAdaptor<Orange> (anOrange);
```

We now have a common representation for apples and oranges, so creating containers that will hold fruit values is easy:

```
list<Fruit *> fruitList; // make a list of fruits
fruitList.insert(fruitOne); // add an apple
fruitList.insert(fruitTwo); // add an orange
```

A template function can simplify the creation of the adaptor. The template argument types are inferred from the parameter values and need not be specified when a template function is invoked:

```
template <class T>
Fruit * newFruit (T & f)
{
    return new FruitAdaptor<T>(f);
}
```

When we use the newFruit function, the fruit types will be inferred from the function arguments and need not be specified explicitly:

```
Fruit * fruitThree = newFruit (anApple);
Fruit * fruitFour = newFruit (anOrange)
```

Now we have all the elements necessary to maintain both apples and oranges in the same collection (for example, in a list) and to perform polymorphic operations on these values:

```
Apple anApple("Rome");
Orange anOrange;

list<Fruit *> fruitList; // declare list of pointers to fruits

fruitList.insert(newFruit(anApple));
fruitList.insert(newFruit(anOrange));

list<Fruit *>::iterator start = fruitList.begin();
list<Fruit *>::iterator stop = fruitList.end();

// loop over and print out all fruits in container
for ( ; start != stop; ++start) {
    Fruit  & aFruit = *start; // get current fruit
    aFruit.print(cout);
}
```

Note how this solution has made use of all the polymorphic mechanisms that we have discussed: overloaded functions, template classes, template functions, inheritance, and overriding.

Test Your Understanding

1. Why is it necessary to introduce the class Fruit?

2. What is the advantage of using the function newFruit instead of creating instances of FruitAdaptor directly?

3. Explain what problem is being solved by each of the following object-oriented mechanisms used in this case study: overloaded functions, template classes, template functions, inheritance, and overriding.

Include Files

In this appendix we describe the include header files that are provided as part of the C++ standard. The discussion is divided into the primary categories of services provided. Note that many of the header files are part of the C++ legacy from C and are (or should be) rather infrequently used in C++ programs.

A.1   Input and Output

\<cstdio\>	C-style standard I/O operations
\<iostream\>	Stream I/O operations
\<ios\>	Iostream base classes
\<streambuf\>	Stream buffers
\<iomanip\>	Manipulators
\<istream\>	Input stream operations
\<ostream\>	Output stream operations
\<sstream\>	String stream operations
\<fstream\>	File stream operations

The cstdio library contains the definitions for the older C-style standard I/O operations (see Chapter 10). This file was formerly known as stdio.h, and most compiler vendors still support it under that name. The remaining files support the newer stream I/O system.

The header files iostream, ios, streambuf, and iomanip are largely for internal use and seldom need be explicitly included in programs.

A.2   Diagnostics

\<stdexcept\>	Standard exceptions
\<cassert\>	Assertion facility
\<cerrno\>	C-style error handling

The standard exception categories are found in stdexcept. The file cassert was formerly known as assert.h and the file cerrno as errno.h. The assert macro was used in an example in Section 7.8. This macro tests a boolean condition, and, if false, will immediately halt the program.

The integer global variable errno is set by various operations—for example, the mathematical routines (see Section A.6). The file cerrno (forerly errorno.h) provides symbolic names for some of the more common values.

A.3   Strings

\<string\>	The string data type
\<cctype\>	Character classification functions
\<cwtype\>	Wide character classification functions
\<cstring\>	C-style string functions
\<cwchar\>	C-style wide string functions

The cctype header file was formerly known as ctype.h. This file contains functions such as isdigit, used for classifying individual character values (see Section 8.1.1).

The cstring header file was formerly known as string.h. This file contains the traditional C style character manipulation functions strlen, strcpy, and the like (see Section 8.1.3).

For historical reasons, a few string operations are also defined in the header cstdlib (see Section A.8).

A.4   STL Containers

\<vector\>	Extendable one-dimensional array
\<list\>	Linked list
\<deque\>	Double-ended queue
\<queue\>	Queue
\<stack\>	Stack

`<map>`	Associative array, or dictionary
`<set>`	Set
`<bitset>`	Set of integer values

The STL containers were discussed in Chapter 9. Each class has template arguments indicating the element type. The map data type takes a second argument that indicates the value type. The ordered containers (set, map) also take a template argument that represents the function to be used in comparing elements.

The multimap data type (a map that allows multiple occurrences of the same key value) is described in the map header file. Similarly, the multiset data type (a set that allows multiple occurrences of the same value) is found in set. The priority_queue data type is found in queue.

A.5   STL Utility Routines

`<utility>`	Various utility functions
`<functional>`	Functional objects
`<memory>`	Memory allocators
`<iterator>`	Iterator support
`<algorithm>`	Generic algorithms
`<numeric>`	Numerical operations

Generic algorithms (see Section 9.3.3) are described in the algorithm header file. The numeric header file provides a few generic algorithms for computing common array operations, such as inner product. The memory header contains the auto_ptr facility for managing pointer values (see Section 4.3.1). The others are used infrequently.

A.6   Numeric Support

`<limits>`	Numeric limits
`<climits>`	C-style numeric limits
`<cfloat>`	C-style numeric floating point routines
`<complex>`	Complex numbers
`<valarray>`	Numeric vectors and operations
`<cmath>`	C-style mathematical library

The limits header defines the limits for floating point values in the current environment and is different on different platforms. These limits are described by using a template class. Older preprocessor macros with similar information are found in climits and cfloat, a pair of files formerly known as limits.h and float.h.

The valarray library is a set of routines for the manipulation of vector and matrix elements.

The cmath header file, formerly known as math.h, provides definitions for the usual mathematical operations, such as square roots and trigonometric functions. Errors are generally reported by setting the global variable errno from library cerrno (see Section 2.2).

A.7   Run-Time Support

<new>	Dynamic memory allocation
<typeinfo>	Run-time type identification
<cstddef>	C-language support
<cstdarg>	Variable-length argument support
<csetjmp>	C-style stack unwinding
<csignal>	C-style signal handling

The typeinfo library defines the RTTI system (see Section 6.3). These other libraries are used rather infrequently. The header csignal was formerly known as signal.h. The C-style signal facility has been largely replaced by exception handling in C++ programs.

A.8   Miscellaneous

<ctime>	C-style date and time
<cstdlib>	C-style date and time
<locale>	Local platform information
<clocale>	C-style local platform information

The ctime header file was formerly known as time.h. It provides facilities for accessing the current date and time.

The cstdlib header file was formerly known as stdlib.h. It contains a number of routines that possibly could have been better placed elsewhere, but for historical reasons are lumped together. They include:

bsearch	Binary search
qsort	Quick sort
rand	Pseudo-random integer
atoi	Convert C-style string to integer
atof	Convert C-style string to float
exit	Exit program immediately

References

Appel 97   Andrew W. Appel, *Modern Compiler Implementation in Java*, Cambridge University Press, Cambridge, England, 1997.

Arnold 98   Ken Arnold and James Gosling, *The Java Programming Language*, 2nd ed., Addison-Wesley, Reading, Mass., 1998.

Boone 96   Barry Boone, *Java Essentials for C and C++ Programmers*, Addison-Wesley, Reading, Mass., 1996.

Budd 94   Timothy A. Budd, *Classic Data Structures in C++*, Addison-Wesley, Reading, Mass., 1994.

Budd 97   Timothy A. Budd, *An Introduction to Object-Oriented Programming*, 2nd ed., Addison-Wesley, Reading, Mass., 1997.

Budd 98a   Timothy A. Budd, *Data Structures in C++ Using the Standard Template Library*, Addison-Wesley, Reading, Mass., 1998.

Budd 98b   Timothy A. Budd, *Understanding Object-Oriented Programming with Java*, Addison-Wesley, Reading, Mass., 1998.

Butenhof 97   David R. Butenhof, *Programming with POSIX Threads*, Addison-Wesley, Reading, Mass., 1997.

Cargill 92   Tom Cargill, *C++ Programming Style*, Addison-Wesley, Reading, Mass., 1992.

Chew 98   Frederick F. Chew, *The Java/C++ Cross-Reference Handbook,* Prentice-Hall, Englewood Cliffs, N.J., 1998.

Cline 95   Marshall Cline and Greg Lomow, *The C++ FAQs*, Addison-Wesley, Reading, Mass., 1995.

Coplien 92   James O. Coplien, *Advanced C++*, Addison-Wesley, Reading, Mass., 1992.

Daconta 98   Michael C. Daconta, Al Saganich, Eric Monk, and Martin Snyder, *Java 1.2 and JavaScript for C and C++ Programmers*, John Wiley & Sons, New York, 1998.

Eckel 89   Bruce Eckel, *Using C++*, McGraw-Hill, New York, 1989.

Ellis 90   Margaret A. Ellis and Bjarne Stroustrup, *The Annotated C++ Reference Manual*, Addison-Wesley, Reading, Mass., 1990.

Glass 96   Graham Glass and Brett Schuchert, *The STL Primer*, Prentice-Hall, Englewood Cliffs, N.J., 1996.

Hanson 97   David R. Hanson, *C Interfaces and Implementations*. Addison-Wesley, Reading, Mass., 1997.

Horstmann 95   Cay S. Horstmann, *Mastering Object-Oriented Design in C++*, John Wiley & Sons, New York, 1995.

Kanerva 97   Jonni Kanerva, *The Java FAQ*, Addison-Wesley, Reading, Mass., 1997.

Kleiman 96   Steve Kleiman, Devang Shah, and Bart Smaalders, *Programming with Threads*, Prentice-Hall, Englewood Cliffs, N.J., 1996.

Lewis 96   Bil Lewis and Daniel J. Berg, *Threads Primer*, Addison-Wesley, Reading, Mass., 1996.

Lippman 91   Stanley B. Lippman, *C++ Primer*, 2nd ed., Addison-Wesley, Reading, Mass., 1991.

Lippman 96   Stanley B. Lippman, *Inside the C++ Object Model*, Addison-Wesley, Reading, Mass., 1996.

Lippman 98   Stanley B. Lippman, *C++ Primer*, 3rd ed., Addison-Wesley, Reading, Mass., 1998.

Meyers 96   Scott Meyers, *More Effective C++*, Addison-Wesley, Reading, Mass., 1996.

Meyers 98   Scott Meyers, *Effective C++*, 2nd ed., Addison-Wesley, Reading, Mass., 1998.

Morehead 49   Albert H. Morehead and Geoffrey Mott-Smith, *The Complete Book of Solitaire and Patience Games*, Grosset & Dunlap, New York, 1949.

Musser 96   David R. Musser and Atul Saini, *STL Tutorial and Reference Guide*, Addison-Wesley, Reading, Mass., 1996.

Pappas 96   Chris H. Pappas and William H. Murray, *Java with Borland C++*, Academic Press, New York, 1996.

Schildt 96   Herbert Schildt, *MFC Programming from the Ground Up*, McGraw-Hill, New York, 1996.

Stroustrup 94   Bjarne Stroustrup, *The Design and Evolution of C++*, Addison-Wesley, Reading, Mass., 1994.

Stroustrup 97   Bjarne Stroustrup, *The C++ Programming Language*, 3rd ed., Addison-Wesley, Reading, Mass., 1997.

Stroustrup 98   Bjarne Stroustrup, "The *Real* Stroustrup Interview," *IEEE Software*, 31(6):110–114, June 1998.

Summit 96   Steve Summit, *C Programming FAQs*, Addison-Wesley, Reading, Mass., 1996.

Tyma 98   Paul Tyma, "Why Are We Using Java Again?" *Communications of the ACM*, 41(6):38–42, June 1998.

Waldo 93   Jim Waldo, *The Evolution of C++: Language Design in the Marketplace of Ideas*, MIT Press, Cambridge, Mass., 1993.

Wigglesworth 99   Joe Wigglesworth and Paula Lumby, *Java Programming, Making the Move from C++*, International Thomson Publishing Company, New York, 1999.

Index

!!, 123
%, 12
&, 30, 122, 222
&&, 123
++, 113, 159
+=, 118, 226
<<, 115, 229
=, 2
=, 116
->, 35
>>, 12
>>>, 12, 116

abort, 185
abstract class, 94
adaptor, 271
address operator, 30, 122, 169
  implicit, 130
  use with functions, 34
ambiguous names, 205, 221
ampersand operator, 30, 222
anonymous class, 213
anonymous value, 122, 162, 190, 223
appearance of programs, 1
Appel, Andrew, 5
argument
  constant, 200
  default, 77, 201

evaluation order, 22
  template, 150
arithmetic on pointers, 36
array
  allocation, 47
  bounds check, 47
  declaration, 18
  initialization, 18
  and pointer, 35
arrow operator, 125
ASCII order, 140
assembly language, 2, 16
assert, 120, 181
assignment
  exception values, 189
  and inheritance, 119
  Java semantics, 37
  nested, 117
  operator, 2, 116, 226
    implicit, 130
  semantics, 20
  slicing, 47
auto_ptr, 57, 189

backward compatibility, 3, 15, 166, 191
Bell Labs, 1
binary operator, 110, 223
bit field, 15

exception *(cont.)*
  handling, 179
  mathematical, 16
  rethrow, 187
  standard, 186
  user-defined, 186
  values, 186
Exception, 186
execution speed, 8, 65
exit, 185
explicit, 134
extern, 68, 196

ferror, 180
Field, 214
field access, 35
file
  header, 275
  implementation, 65, 218
  interface, 65, 218
  names, 66
  pointer, 179
  stream, 174
final
  versus **const**, 200
final class, 86, 95
finalize
  versus destructor, 55
finally clause, 188
flag, 179
floating point, 16
fopen, 167, 179
for statement, 124
formatted output, 167
forward reference, 68
fputc, 180
friend, 202
function
  definition, 225
  friend, 202
  invocation
    implicit, 131
  members, 220
  object, 121, 161, 236
  pointer, 34

  prototype, 67, 222
  signature, 67
fundamental data types, 11
fwrite, 180

garbage collection, 8
generic algorithm, 109, 159, 160
  find, 159
  find_if, 122
  random_shuffle, 263
  sort, 35
getchar, 166
getClass, 93
global variable, 46, 195
goals, design, 1
Gosling, James, 6
goto statement, 209
graph data type, 235
graphical user interface, 264

Hanson, David, 184
hardware dependency, 12
hash table, 155
header file, 275
  cassert, 181
  cctype, 138
  csetjmp, 182
  cstdio, 166
  fstream, 174
  iostream, 170
  signal.h, 185
  stdexcept, 186
  stdio.h, 166
  string.h, 139
heap-resident memory, 4, 29, 44, 190
hexadecimal constant, 13
history of C++, 1

immutable value, 141
implementation file, 218, 246
implicit conversion, 112
implicit function invocation, 131
implicit functions, 128
import statement, 197
include files, 197